THE STORY

AC/DC

LET THERE BE ROCK

SUSAN MASINO

OMNIBUS PRESS
Part of **The Music Sales Group**
New York/London/Paris/Sydney/Copenhagen/Berlin/Tokyo/Madrid

Omnibus Press
A Division of Music Sales Corporation, New York

Exclusive Distributors:
Music Sales Corporation
257 Park Avenue South, New York, NY 10010 USA

Music Sales Limited
14-15 Berners Street, London W1T 3LJ England

Music Sales Pty. Limited
120 Rothschild Street, Rosebery, Sydney, NSW 2018, Australia

Order No. OP52921
ISBN: 978-0-8256-3701-8

Jacket Design by Fresh Lemon
Front cover photo by Michael Putland/Retna
Back cover photo by London Features International
Printed in the United States of America

Visit Omnibus Press on the web at www.omnibuspress.com

Library of Congress Cataloging-in-Publication Data

Masino, Susan, 1955-
  Let there be rock : the story of AC/DC / by Susan Masino.
      p. cm.
  Includes bibliographical references (p.   ), discography (p.   ), and index.
  ISBN 0-8256-3469-5 (hardcover : alk. paper)
1. AC/DC (Musical group) 2. Rock musicians—Australia—Biography. I.
Title.
  ML421.A28M37 2006
  782.42166092'2—dc22
  [B]

                                                              2006019845

TABLE OF CONTENTS

*This book is dedicated to Angus, Malcolm, Phil, Cliff, Brian,
and especially to Bon—who was and always will be—the lightnin' flash
in the middle.*

*And to Perry Cooper and Cody Jessup,
who both truly loved AC/DC.*

INTRODUCTION

As I sit here on the twenty-eighth anniversary of the day I first met AC/DC, I am still in awe of what an incredible twist of fate it was. I've been a rock journalist since 1977 and have met hundreds of bands along the way. But one band in particular would become the inspiration for me to follow my rock 'n' roll heart. And almost three decades later, that same band would help make my ultimate dreams come true: to become an internationally published author.

Over the past year, whenever I told someone that I was writing a biography of AC/DC, their most common response was, "Why did you decide to do that?" Well, I guess the answer to that question goes back to a hot August afternoon in 1977, actually it was the same day that Elvis Presley died. AC/DC was scheduled to perform at the Stone Hearth, a little rock club in the downtown area of Madison, Wisconsin—right in the middle of my hometown.

At the time, I was a 21-year-old single mother going through a bitter break-up, desperately trying to find my own way in the world. A girlfriend of mine introduced me to a local band, who in turn introduced me to the publishers of a rock newspaper. At first I started out reviewing bar bands for them for free. It was something I loved doing and eventually I worked my way up from free-lance writer—put the emphasis on free—to a salaried associate editor. Pure nirvana. Just think, getting paid to hang out and interview rock 'n' roll bands. And some people think I'm just a ditzy blonde!

On this particular Tuesday afternoon while listening to all the radio stations lament the passing of the King, I was driving by the newspaper and something told me to pull over and check for new assignments. Clearly divine inter-vention. The only person in the office was Gary Sohmers, the editor, who had just gotten off the phone with a representative from Stardate. The pro-moter had booked a band into the Stone Hearth that night. They had just called the paper to see if someone would be willing to come down and help out. My compensation would be free admission to the show, plus a friend on the guest list. Almost as good as money. I didn't have anything else planned for that evening, so I jumped at it. As I was running out the door to go home and change, I asked Gary who the band was. He shook his head and said, "I don't know, some band from Australia called AC/DC." No words spoken to me since would have such an impact on my life.

I went home and freshened up, putting on a clean pair of jeans, a white T-shirt, and my Frye cowboy boots. A little concealer, blush, clear lip-gloss, and mascara: all I needed for my creaseless 21-year-old face. Ah, those were the days…My outfit was standard gear for running around bars, audi-toriums, and backstage areas. Plus, it helped distinguish me from the groupies that were always dressed in satin, spandex, cleavage, and stiletto heels. Although many times that combat gear didn't help me from being grouped—or at times, groped—along with the rest.

I arrived at the club by four o'clock that afternoon, and spent my time running to the liquor store to buy Blue Nun wine for the lead singer and arranging the deli trays in the dressing room. I won't go into details here, because that would spoil part of the story. What I can tell you, is that it changed my life for the better, and nothing has been the same since.

Twenty-four years later, I wrote a book about my escapades during this time of my life called *Rock 'N' Roll Fantasy: My Life and Times with AC/DC, Van Halen, Kiss*…which I published as an eBook in May of 2001. Thanks to glowing reviews on some of the best AC/DC fan websites, it sold well in 14 countries. That eBook snagged me a publishing deal with Badger Books to write *Famous Wisconsin Musicians*. Once the publisher, Marv Balousek, saw the reviews for my eBook, he offered to print it on demand without a signed contract. That way, I could still look for an international publishing deal for *Rock 'N' Roll Fantasy*. I know this sounds confusing, but stick with me, it gets better.

Once you have a couple of books out, everyone asks you what your next book will be. My next book? I wasn't even thinking about my next book! That is, until I went to the Gulf coast of Florida on my annual summer vaca-tion. It was July of 2003, and for some reason, I was inspired by the idea of writing a biography of AC/DC. I know, I know, my husband John even laughed at me!

A few months later, Badger Books invited me to Chicago for Book Expo America, the publishing industry's version of the SuperBowl, to do a book signing for *Rock 'N' Roll Fantasy.* Initially I looked at it as an excuse to party in Chicago for the weekend. I never imagined that this seemingly innocent trip to Illinois would be another major opportunity to change my life…again. And AC/DC would have something to do with it.

When we arrived at McCormick Place on Saturday, June 5, 2004, I was delighted with the fact that all the major hitters were there in the flesh, flaunting their big, bad publishing companies. You know the ones; they list their credentials, and then state that they do not accept unsolicited materials. Now for an unknown writer, that is the ultimate Catch-22. It's very hard to get an agent without being published, and it's impossible to send your materials to a publisher without an agent. How the hell did people like Stephen King get started anyway?

So there I was with 500 booths, 600 authors, hundreds of publishers, and about 30,000 people who loved books, all under one roof. It was like dying and going to literary heaven, or literally heaven, whichever you prefer. Instead of finding my own booth and settling in to get ready for my book signing, I had the urge to roam around with a vengeance. I was on a mission looking for something. What…I didn't know.

After about an hour of wandering around, getting hopelessly lost (and no, those numeric markers hanging from the ceiling do not help), I walked around a corner and to my left was a massive black and red, well-lit wall of rock 'n' roll books on about every musician you can imagine. I stopped cold. I remember seeing the lights and all the books with a fuzzy haze around everything. Just like when Wayne spots Cassandra, the chick bass player in the movie *Wayne's World,* while the song "Dream Weaver," plays in the background. I had the same experience, minus Gary Wright's soundtrack.

I discovered that I was standing in the booth of the Music Sales Group, which includes the Omnibus Press imprint. Music Sales is a prestigious publishing company whose specialty is music tablature books and biographies. They have offices in eight countries and were established in the 1930s. Not only are they one of the most-respected companies in the industry, but they also publish AC/DC's music tablature books. Hello?!! When I figured out who they were, I started laughing and carrying on to my husband saying, 'I'm home! This is it! They're going to sign me and that's all there is to it!' As I was laughing and kidding around, a very nice young woman came over and said, "I'm sorry, you are…?" She was polite, but I knew she thought I was nuts. When I told her who I was and that I had a book they might be interested in, Alison Wofford, Omnibus publicist said, "Editors don't usually come along to these things, but our managing editor happens to be with us this weekend. You should talk to her." Could she have said anything better? Standing a few feet away from me, their managing editor, the angelic Andrea Rotondo, was just finishing a conversation with someone else, then she turned to me. You can imagine after several rejections and experiencing the Catch-22 agent/publisher quagmire, my introduction and sales pitch to her was on the level of grabbing for a lifeboat on the Titanic. Luckily, I didn't scare her away!

Andrea is an accomplished writer herself, having published several books, and editing *Pro Sound News* and *Musician* magazines before becoming managing editor at Music Sales. She's a rock 'n' roll sister, who loves the music, the musicians, and all the history surrounding it. Many of their biographies are just that, the historical documentation of our love affair with rock 'n' roll and the musicians who created it. Thankfully, she listened to me and was genuinely interested in my book, and my desire to see it published on an international level. When I told her my name and the title of my book, she looked at me and said, "Oh, I was going to come find you." And I laughed and said, "Ah, yeah, sure you were." She looked at me seriously, and repeated, "No, I was going to come find you." And then she showed me my name and the time of my book signing written into her day planner. Out of the thousands of people at that Book Expo, I walked up and introduced myself to the one person who was going to come find me? The magnitude of this synchronicity only gets more fantastic from here.

Soon I had to leave for my signing, so we agreed to talk more at the end of the day. When my husband, who had been chatting up sales rep Phil Smith, walked away, he turned to me and said, "Did she tell you what they were looking for?" As we kept walking, I said, 'No, are they looking for something? What are they looking for?' He stopped and said, with a completely straight face, "They're looking for someone to write the biography of AC/DC."

Did you feel it? I did, just as I typed the words. I stopped walking, got goose bumps all over my arms, turned and looked at him in front of all those people and said, or screamed, actually, "What did you say? Say it again, slowly from the top!" And as he repeated it to me several times, I knew why I had met this band and why I had been in love with them for the last 27 years of my life. It was my destiny to write this book. I was lucky enough to meet them, to stay in touch with them for almost three decades, to have had a drink (or two) with Bon, and now, lucky enough to write the biography of AC/DC for Omnibus Press. No privilege will ever mean more to me.

When *Rock 'N' Roll Fantasy* came out, it was easy for me to say, 'I'm a professional acquaintance of the band. I see them when they're out on tour, but I'm no expert.' Once the book was reviewed and scrutinized by some of AC/DC's most dedicated fans, it passed muster and actually entertained people. I was truly relieved. When I was signed to write this book, it was time for me to become an AC/DC expert, or at least try to get the facts straight. The responsibility of this sank in over the weeks ahead, and at times paralyzed me with pure panic. Will the band like it? Will the fans enjoy it? Will we ever know if it was a vacuum cleaner or a sewing machine that had the letters AC/DC written on the back of it, thus sparking the idea for the band's name? Lots of details, much more pressure.

After almost nine weeks of waiting to see if I was going to be offered the contract, I dwelled in the deepest depression I've been in since disco took over the airwaves in the mid-seventies. The thought of getting that close to my dream, and having it disappear right before my eyes was almost too much to bear. Luckily, God didn't deem me strong enough for that tragedy, so things went in my favor. They probably heard my rebel yell all the way to Australia, when I found out that Omnibus Press decided to go with the girl up in Wisconsin!

One lucky girl, who walked into a nightclub on August 16, 1977 and met one of the greatest rock 'n' roll bands to ever grace this planet. One who got to meet them before they were known here in the States, when they were driving around in a used station wagon, wearing the same clothes they would wear onstage that night. Before I give away any more details about what else I got to do with them, I am just going to say that the pleasure was all mine.

With the help of Andrea Rotondo, everyone at Music Sales Group, my family and friends, and the best fans a band could ask for, I've tried to create an interesting and accurate account of who and what made AC/DC one of the most influential bands in rock 'n' roll history.

I pray that the band, their families, friends, and fans old and new, will enjoy reading *Let There Be Rock,* the *amazing* story of AC/DC. Which actually began way back in the Fifties...

AC 1 DC

SHOW BUSINESS

In the beginning, back in 1955, man didn't know 'bout a rock 'n' roll show, 'n' all that jive. The white man had the schmaltz, the black man had the blues, no one knew what they was gonna do, but Tchaikovsky had the news. He said, "Let there be sound, and there was sound, let there be light, and there was light, let there be drums, 'n' there was drums. Let there be guitar, there was guitar, let there be rock, and there was rock...And it came to pass, that rock 'n' roll was born. —Let There Be Rock

That's not all that was born in 1955. That same year the future schoolboy gone bad, Angus McKinnon Young, was born on March 31 in Glasgow, Scotland. He was the seventh son and youngest of eight children born to William and Margaret Young. Malcolm Mitchell Young, older brother and riff maniac-to-be, made his debut two years earlier on January 6, 1953.

The Young household was a musical one; there was always an instrument of some kind lying around. They had a piano, guitar, banjo, saxophone, and clarinet...anything to make noise with, as Angus has fondly recalled. He claims the first thing he tried to strum on was a banjo that was missing some strings.

Eldest sibling and only sister, Margaret, introduced the family to Chuck Berry, Fats Domino, and Little Richard: the literal blueprints of rock 'n' roll in its purest form. Angus once said that "Rock Around The Clock" by Bill Haley was one of the first songs that really did it for him. Even as a toddler, he already had good taste in music!

Once, Margaret took the kids to see the great Louis Armstrong perform. Angus remembered in an August 1996 issue of *Guitar World,* "My sister took me to see him when I was a kid, and I still think he was one of the greatest musicians of all time. Especially when you listen to his old records, like these ["Basin St. Blues" and "St. James Infirmary"], and hear the incredible musicianship and emotion coming out of his horn. And the technology in those days was almost nonexistent, all the tracks had to be done in one take. I can picture him in that big football stadium where I saw him. He wasn't a big man, but when he played, he seemed bigger than the stadium itself!"

All the Young boys were encouraged to play the guitar on their weekend family camping trips. Oldest brother Alex was first to become a professional musician as George Alexander, playing saxophone in Emile Ford's Checkmates. By the time the family immigrated to Australia in 1963, he was playing with the Big Six. Their claim to fame was backing Tony Sheridan after The Beatles had left him. Alex would go on to form the band, Grapefruit, that was the first group signed to Apple Records, The Beatle's label.

When their father couldn't find work in their hometown of Glasgow, the Youngs—like many Scottish families—took advantage of the Assisted Passage Scheme, that was implemented in 1947. It allowed immigrants to sail to Australia for the economical price of 10 pounds each, which is about $25. The Youngs arrived in Sydney and first moved to Villawood Migrant Hostel before settling in a bunkerstyle neighborhood in the suburb of Burwood. Many English, Scottish, and Dutch families chose Burwood...some with sons who owned musical gear. It soon became a breeding ground for garage bands. That's where older brother George met Dutchman, Johannes Jacob Hendricks Vandenberg. Better pronounced as Harry Vanda, who had been in the band, Starfighter. George and Harry recruited fellow Brit vocalist Stevie Wright, bassist Dick Diamonde, and drummer Gordon "Snowy" Fleet. Playing their first gig at the Beatle Village in Sydney in late 1964, they called themselves The Easybeats.

Soon after The Easybeats formed, they signed Mike Vaughan as their manager. Mike introduced them to Ted Albert, a third-generation publishing mogul of J. Albert and Son. The company was Australia's oldest and most-respected music publishing house. The first order of business for the Alberts was to sign The Easybeats. This would be the one key factor that would benefit all of their futures.

They quickly went into the studio to record and their second single, "She's So Fine," made them the top recording act in Australia. Glenn A.

Baker wrote in *Billboard* magazine, "From the first single, "For My Woman," in March of 1965, The Easybeats became astronomical superstars. While England reeled under the onslaught of Beatlemania, Australia was shaken by "Easyfever." Airports, television stations, theaters, and hire cars were reduced to rubble, fans were hospitalized, and general mayhem reigned wherever they set foot. Like The Beatles, the group was public property, with their private lives spread across the front pages of the daily newspapers."

The Easybeats had broken into the international music scene with their single, "Friday On My Mind." That song made it to Number 16 on the U.S. charts and Number Six in Britain, which prompted the band to relocate to London. This would also become an advantage to Malcolm and Angus, who would ask George to send them all the best music from the U.K., since many of these albums weren't available in Australia.

Following in their big brother's footsteps, Malcolm started playing guitar around the age of four, strumming to Elvis or whatever he was listening to. By the time he was 11, he was playing along to Beatles songs. Angus played whatever he could get his hands on, also starting around the age of four or five. Their mother finally went out and bought them each a 10-dollar acoustic guitar, saying, "Here's one for you and Mal. Now behave yourselves." She could only hope.

When Malcolm was 14, Harry Vanda gave him his Gretsch guitar, which Malcolm had always admired. [It is widely reported that George gave him the guitar, but Malcolm was quoted in *Guitar Player* magazine saying it was a gift from Harry.] When Malcolm graduated to a Gretsch, Angus got a Hofner guitar. But when he saw a Gibson SG in a friend's guitar catalog, he decided to switch and has played one ever since. Angus was known to play the guitar constantly around the house, even taking to sleeping with the instrument. Don't ask.

Both brothers attended the Sydney Ashfield Boys High School. Well, sort of. It seems Malcolm attended school and learned how to fight well, especially when he had to defend his little brother. Angus on the other hand, didn't seem to attend much school at all. When he did attend, his favorite subject was art because it was the only class that would let him do what he wanted. He once recalled scaring everyone on the school bus with a six-foot papier-maché housefly. Although it's hard to believe Angus would ever be big enough to carry home a six-foot fly, even today.

Brother George's rise to fame was not lost on Angus or Malcolm, who once recalled coming home from school to find dozens of girls trying to do anything they could to get a look at him. Angus once joked to me that when he saw that, both he and Malcolm knew that rock 'n' roll was going to be the life for them. He was quoted as saying, "One day George was a 16-year-old sitting on his bed playing guitar, the next day he was worshipped by the whole country."

In the February 1984 issue of *Guitar Player* magazine, Angus affirmed, "It was definitely an inspiration. There was a hell of a lot that came from that band; they were the forerunners of a lot of things. They were at the time of the early stages, when people didn't know how to react. Mal and me were kept away from them. In school, you got frowned upon because obviously your brother or your family was an influence to rebel. At that time, it was better for us not to be sort of pushed at it. My parents thought we'd be better off doing something else." Even though The Easybeats were quite successful, their father kept asking George when he was going to get a proper job!

This didn't deter Malcolm who loved to listen to The Beatles, The Rolling Stones, The Yardbirds, and The Who. He also got into Eric Clapton with John Mayall's Blues Breakers and the Paul Butterfield Blues Band...all the while perfecting his own unique playing style.

Angus had two bands—Kentuckee and later, Tantrum—before joining up with Malcolm. He often ran home from school and would leave again for rehearsal without changing out of his school uniform. When a headmaster gave Angus grief over brother George being a pop star and declaring that his older brother was now in "a profession for perverts," his parents defended him. They didn't care for Angus being pushed around, so they didn't protest when he stopped going to school all together. His father encouraged him to keep learning and suggested he spend some time in the library. This is where Angus discovered the American rock 'n' roll magazine, *Down Beat*. These were magazines you couldn't buy on newsstands in Australia and he loved reading about his favorite blues artists.

At 14 and nine months, he was officially asked to leave school. Obviously they didn't want to wait until he turned 15. Angus once said, "If you weren't there for so many days a year, they figured you weren't worth teaching, so they got rid of you." Malcolm had already dropped out two years earlier, taking work as an apprentice fitter, then later as a sewing machine maintenance mechanic for Berlei, a brassiere factory. Angus ended up working as a typesetter at the soft porn magazine, *Ribald*. Both jobs are quite ironic, considering much of AC/DC's future lyrical content.

In 1971 at the age of 18 while working at Berlei, Malcolm met and joined The Velvet Underground—not to be confused with the band of the same name that was fronted by Lou Reed. This band formed in Newcastle, England in 1967 and had become a top dance band playing covers by The Doors and Jefferson Airplane. After they lost their lead singer, they moved to Sydney. The band included drummer Herm Kovac, guitarist Les Hall, bassist Michael Szchefswick, and singer Andy Imlah (who joined after they relocated to Australia).

When the band met Malcolm, they needed another guitar player. And they all needed to get out of the brassiere factory! Once Malcolm joined the band, he added songs by his idol, T. Rex's Marc Bolan. Supposedly, "Bang A Gong" Bolan was the only rock star to ever have graced the walls of Malcolm's bedroom.

Drummer Herm Kovac remembered in Clinton Walker's book, *Highway To Hell,* "We used to go round and pick Malcolm up. The first time, this little punk skinhead answered the door. It was Angus. I hid behind Les (the guitarist); in those days you'd hear about the skinheads down at Burwood Station, Strathfield Station. Shaved head he had, big boots. He said, 'Eh, come in 'ere.' So we follow him into his room, he straps on his SG, jumps on the bed, and goes off on this exhibition, running over the dressing table, showing off, couldn't play any chords, just lead, and when he finishes he says, 'Whaddya reckon?' You had to say, 'Pretty good, Angus.' Every time you'd go there, you'd have to go through this same ritual." It sounds like nothing much has changed.

Angus was allowed to come out and see his big brother play in The Velvet Underground, where he would stand in front of the stage, transfixed. Only receiving a few formal lessons around the age of 11, Angus became a self-taught musician. Once he was out of school, he would hang out with older musicians and jam with any band that would let him. He quickly started catching on and was later billed as the "baby guitar star." Since he was underage and very small in stature, they often told club owners who would question his age that [Angus] was a dwarf, which usually got him in.

Even though George and Harry had written their biggest hit, "Friday On My Mind," The Easybeats would never repeat the success of that song, constantly chasing their true sound. George believed that a band should stay loyal to their roots, a philosophy he would wholeheartedly teach his younger brothers. The Easybeats did have two more minor hits in 1968, "Good Time" and "St. Louis." In 1969, they would leave England one last time to tour Australia, where they were supported by The Valentines before officially breaking up.

From 1970 to 1973, George and Harry would hone their expertise, practically living in their London recording studio. Since J. Albert and Son hadn't yet found a hit band in England, Ted Albert persuaded them to move back to Australia. They immediately went to work with an Albert's prodigy, John Paul Young (no relation). They wrote the song "Pasadena" for him, which almost made it into the Top 10. This success inspired Ted Albert to finance their recording studio and Albert Productions was born.

The next project for Albert Productions was recording the Marcus Hook Roll Band, which started out as a casual project. When EMI's American division expressed interest in a full-length album, as producer, George brought Angus and Malcolm into the studio as supporting players. This would be their first time in a studio where they recorded tracks for the album, *Tales Of Old Grandaddy*. George later told Australian rock journalist, Glenn A. Baker, "We didn't take it very seriously, so we thought we'd include them to give them an idea of what recording was all about."

Malcolm had been working steadily in The Velvet Underground and by 1972, they were playing their own sets and providing backup for one of Albert Production's artists, Ted Mulry. By this time, Malcolm had become disenchanted with The Velvet Underground's musical direction and was looking to do something on his own.

When he got his first taste of recording, he decided he didn't believe rock 'n' roll was meant to be overdubbed and recorded to perfection. Malcolm wanted to record rock 'n' roll like it was played, live without any studio trickery. Now he just had to find the right people to record it with. Although his future band would go through several incarnations, the fact that he eventually did find the right people could be one of rock's biggest understatements!

AC 2 DC

HIGH VOLTAGE

Malcolm placed an ad in Sydney's *Sunday Morning Herald* and recruited bassist Larry Van Kriedt and former Masters Apprentices drummer, Colin Burgess. Ironically, vocalist Dave Evans had just left the same band Malcolm had been in, when he saw the ad and called the number listed. He was more than surprised to hear Malcolm pick up the phone.

Dave Evans had grown up in a musical household, as well. Born in Carmarthen, Wales, his family had also immigrated to Australia. Dave sang at school concerts and in the school choir. As a young teenager, he listened to The Rolling Stones, The Kinks, and The Beatles. By the time he started playing in bands, he was into Led Zeppelin, Free, and Deep Purple. It has been said that Dave was hired more for his image than anything else. The look of the day was glam rock and Dave definitely had that nailed down.

Malcolm's new band started rehearsing in an office complex in Newtown, at the corner of Wilson Street and Erskineville Road. Once Angus's band fell apart, Malcolm asked the rest of the guys if his brother could audition for them. Even though they were brothers, Dave remembers Malcolm being very considerate to ask first, instead of just telling them Angus was joining. Originally Malcolm had planned on adding keyboards, but changed his mind and decided a second guitar was what he was looking for. Once Angus joined the band, he and Malcolm would—for a while—alternate between playing rhythm and lead guitars.

They had tossed around ideas for a band name and came up with Third World War. Their sister Margaret had a better idea when she noticed the phrase

AC/DC written on the back of her sewing machine. Some sources say it was a vacuum cleaner, but I'm sticking with the sewing machine since Margaret would eventually make some of Angus's first schoolboy uniforms. Although in an interview with Dave Evans, writer Peter Hoysted noted in an article for *Axs Magazine,* "Malcolm claims it was a vacuum cleaner, and it was his sister-in-law Sandra, George's wife, who came up with it."

Regardless of who came up with it, they agreed on the name AC/DC because it suggested power and electricity. Although for years the band would have to fend off the theory that it referred to their sexual preferences. Malcolm once told me the first time he realized the sexual connotation was when a cab driver asked him about it. He quickly shot back, "What, are you trying to start a fight or something?" If you consider how much this band loves the ladies, the very idea is completely comical.

AC/DC's first professional appearance was at a small club called Chequers at 79 Goulburn Street in Sydney on New Years Eve, 1973. Much of their set included covers of songs by Chuck Berry, the Stones, Free, and The Beatles. Dave Evans remembers how well they were received: "From the very first gig at Chequers, the crowd just reacted to the energy of the band which did not let up from the word go and actually intensified as we neared the end of our set. Our attitude was to absolutely KILL the audience, and that is still AC/DC's attitude today."

Angus's stage antics were encouraged by George. One night when he was still playing in Tantrum, he tripped over his own guitar cord and fell down. Instead of getting up, he used it for effect and rolled around on the stage screaming in pain through his guitar. It was the only applause they received all night. When George heard about that, he suggested Angus make it part of his act.

His inability to stand still goes back to the way he feels about music. He simply can't stay in one place while he's playing. Angus claims he's a rotten guitar player when he can't move around. He once told Jim Miller of *Newsweek,* "An Australian audience likes to drink a lot...So I used to jump on tables, anything to get them to stop drinking for 10 seconds. They would be throwing beer cans and I thought, 'Just keep moving,' and that's how it all started."

Their sister Margaret suggested he wear his schoolboy uniform, remembering how he looked after school, sitting in his room for hours playing his guitar. Angus explained the original plan in 1982 in *Circus* magazine: "The uniform was originally a one-off thing. The drummer in my previous band talked me into doing something outrageous, so I dressed up like a school kid. The idea was to become a nine-year-old guitar virtuoso who would play one gig, knock everyone out, and disappear into obscurity. I'd have been a legend. But then I kept doing it. Now...well, I'm stuck with it."

Wearing the schoolboy uniform started out as a gimmick and ended up being an international trademark. Try thinking of another everyday inanimate object that is so universally connected to a rock 'n' roll band. Obviously, instruments and elaborate Kiss costumes don't count!

Playing around the clubs in Sydney, Larry Van Kriedt also played saxophone while Malcolm covered the bass. In February, they went into EMI Studios to cut their first single, "Can I Sit Next To You Girl" and B-side "Rockin' In The Parlour." George and Harry produced it, with George recording the bass parts and Malcolm playing lead guitar on "Can I Sit Next To You Girl." A week later, when drummer Colin Burgess collapsed onstage at Chequers, presumably from too much drink, he was immediately fired. Big brother George once again saved the day and played drums for their second set. Soon after, Larry Van Kriedt was let go as well.

When Malcolm was asked to fill in on guitar for the band Jasper, he quickly asked their drummer Noel Taylor and bassist Neil Smith to join AC/DC. In March they all moved into the Hampton Court Hotel in Sydney where they were booked four nights a week. They continued to play as many dates as possible, including opening for Sherbet in Newcastle. After only six weeks in the band, Noel Taylor and Neil Smith just weren't cutting it and were fired. One can imagine that playing in the rhythm section of AC/DC is a tough job. When the band played a Victory Park concert with the band Flake, Malcolm immediately hired their drummer Peter Clack and bassist Rob Bailey.

Somewhere between Colin Burgess and Peter Clack, there were drummers Ron Carpenter and Russell Coleman. Obviously, both didn't play in the band very long because Dave Evans remembers Ron Carpenter, but not Russell Coleman and he was there! Luckily, any time AC/DC was minus a bass player, George was always there to fill in. That is, when he wasn't in the studio with Harry Vanda revolutionizing the Australian music scene.

George and Harry had been busy working with their ex-vocalist, Stevie Wright, who was battling a nasty heroin addiction at the same time he was starring in a production of *Jesus Christ Superstar.* (Now there's a thought that should send most of the Bible belt reeling: Jesus played by a junkie.) Stevie was recording his album, *Hard Road,* at EMI Studios and Malcolm was asked to contribute some guitar tracks. The record featured the 11minute hit single, "Evie." Later, when Wright's band played a free show at the

Sydney Opera House on May 26, 1974 in front of 2,500 people, AC/DC got to open for them. A reported 10,000 fans had to be turned away. Wright's band that night included Malcolm on guitar, as well as Harry Vanda and George Young. After the show, AC/DC was approached by Sherbet's ex-frontman, Dennis Laughlin. He loved the band and immediately signed on as their first manager.

AC/DC's performance got the attention of the local press, *GoSet,* who wrote that, "AC/DC opened the show and showed they're a force to be reckoned with. They play rock 'n' roll intelligently adding their own ideas to sure crowdpleasers like "Heartbreak Hotel" and "Shake, Rattle, And Roll." They also cited Malcolm and Angus's double guitar attack and compared Dave to the teen idol, David Cassidy.

In June, AC/DC officially signed a deal with Albert Productions with distribution through EMI. On July 22, "Can I Sit Next To You Girl" and "Rockin' In The Parlour" were released in Australia. The single was also released on the Polydor label in New Zealand. It soon became a regional hit in Perth and Adelaide and eventually reached the Top Five. The record received rave reviews: "It starts off like rubber bullets, builds right into a power chord structure just bristling with energy and includes some incredible dynamic effects—like pure fuzz noise echoing from channel to channel, then fading out as a machine gun rhythm guitar fades in, rising to a powerful blast as they scream out the title over and over. Overall, a stunning record."

The country got its first look at AC/DC live on film when a clip of the band playing at the Last Picture Show Theater in Cronulla aired on *GTK* (at the time, Australia's only national rock television show). Even though Peter Clack and Rob Bailey didn't play on the recordings of "Can I Sit Next To You Girl," they appear in the film.

Dave reminisced about seeing "Can I Sit Next To You Girl" racing up the charts and hearing it on the radio every couple of hours each day. The adoration from the fans was "all very new and exciting." Luckily, George had lots of experience with the pitfalls of rock stardom. He had his dream come true and then watched it fall apart. He urged AC/DC to stay true to their roots, a sentiment they took to heart and have never forgotten.

For a while, AC/DC auditioned several wardrobe options. Aside from Angus's schoolboy uniform, he tried dressing as Spiderman, Zorro, and as Super A(ngus), complete with a fake telephone booth. After he got stuck in it during one of their shows, that idea was scrapped. For a while, the drummer dressed as a harlequin clown, Malcolm was a pilot, and the bass player was a motorcycle cop. Dave stuck with what he knew best and remained a rock god. Now we know where The Village People got their ideas from. Remembering George's advice, they eventually dumped the costumes, except, of course, for Angus's schoolboy outfit.

Along with playing the clubs in Sydney, Melbourne, Adelaide, and Perth, their manager Laughlin got them an opening spot on Lou Reed's Australian tour in August. They spent much of their time—when they weren't on stage—riding in the back of a truck. Dave fondly recalled, "In Australia the bands had to endure long hours on the road driving between towns and cities. It would take about 12 to 14 hours to get from Sydney to Melbourne, depending on the weather. When we drove from Adelaide to Perth, it took two days to get there. Most times, band members would try to doze off. There weren't many humorous moments really. We got to see the countryside as it passed by and, of course, there are some really beautiful parts of Australia, but we were on a schedule and had to keep driving."

The most humorous thing that did happen to Dave while performing with the band was revealed to Brian Coles in *Electric Basement* in September 2000. "I remember falling off the stage at the Sydney Opera House," he reminisced. "It was a free gig and it was packed with thousands outside who couldn't get in. I overbalanced at the front of the stage and made it look as if I had jumped off. You wouldn't believe it but right in the middle of the front row was an empty chair that I spun around and sat in, and watched the show along with the audience during Angus's lead break. Then I jumped up onto the stage in time for my cue for the vocals to begin again. People complimented me on a great stage act, but now I can reveal the truth."

The most bizarre gig that AC/DC played was a friend's wedding. The brother of the bride was a good friend of the band's and had lent them PA equipment when they needed it. The band got quite a laugh when they realized they were playing in a backyard with no stage. Dave told Hoysted of *Axs Magazine* in October 1998, "We did a set—a bit of Chuck Berry, a bit of The Rolling Stones—the stuff we were doing. The father of the bride came up to me and asked us if we could play 'Zorba The Greek.' I said, 'Mate, we're a rock 'n' roll band. There's no way.' Then Malcolm said, 'Give me a minute.' He went away and practiced for a while, all from ear. That's how good the guy was. Then Malcolm said, 'Tell him, yeah. We'll do it.' The band went back and played following Malcolm's lead. It was an instrumental piece, so I was in the clear. It sounded good. We killed 'em. The people at the wedding danced and cheered when it was over. I hope they all remember that day. The one and only time AC/DC ever played 'Zorba The Greek.'" Boy, wouldn't you just love to have a bootleg of that?

By the fall of 1974, AC/DC was looking for a new singer. Tensions had been building with Evans, who was often booted off the stage so the band could jam on blues boogies. Malcolm and Angus both thought the band sounded better without him. At times when they played two to four shows a day, Dave's voice would give out and Dennis Laughlin, their manager, would fill in for him. Plus, they felt his "glam" image contrasted too much with the rest of the band. An eventual punch up between Dave and Dennis sealed his fate.

Vince Lovegrove first met George Young when his band opened for The Easybeats. Lovegrove had stayed in touch with George and when he heard AC/DC was looking for a new singer, he recommended Bon Scott. Vince and Bon had shared lead vocals in the band The Valentines and Vince was helping Bon by giving him odd jobs while he recovered from a near-fatal motorcycle accident. When George passed along the information to Malcolm and Angus, they deemed Bon too old for the job, considering he was the ancient age of 28. He was nine years older than Angus.

When Bon saw them live for the first time in Adelaide, he knew he was right for the band. Much has been written about him being their driver and/or roadie, probably because he hung out with them and drove Angus and Malcolm around in his 90-dollar Holden. Bon himself explained how he was hired in the documentary movie, *Let There Be Rock*. "I knew their manager. I'd never seen the band before. I'd never even heard of AC/DC and their manager said, 'just stand there,' and the band comes in two minutes, and there's this little guy, in a school uniform, going crazy, and I laughed. I'm still laughing. I took the opportunity to explain to them how much better I was than the drongo they had singing with them. So they gave me a chance to prove it, and there I was."

Lovegrove told *No Nonsense* in May, 1999, "One day Malcolm told me they were going to sack their singer and he asked me if I knew anyone. I told him I did, that it was Bon, and that I'd introduce him that night as they were playing at my venue. They said to me that Bon was too old, that they wanted someone young. I told Malcolm that Bon could rock them 'til they dropped, that he could out-rock them anytime. When I told Bon, he told me they were too young, that they couldn't rock if their lives depended on it.

"After the show we all went back to Bruce Howe's place for a jam session. He was the bass player for Fraternity and they rocked on until dawn doing Chuck Berry songs. It worked a treat. Next day, Bon came around to the house, packed his bags, and said he was going to Sydney to join AC/DC. He was in the back seat of their hire car. They were in the front. We waved goodbye and that was that. A legend began."

Luckily for Bon, he waited to officially join the band until after they completed a six-week stint supporting transvestite, Carlotta, at Perth's Beethoven Disco. Bon's first appearance with the band was actually more of a jam session at the Pooraka Hotel. AC/DC asked Dave to leave after his last concert in Melbourne, and Bon's real debut with the band was at Brighton-LeSands Masonic Hall in Sydney on October 5, 1974. There were no hard feelings between Dave and Bon. After that, Dave ran into Bon on several occasions. "We shook hands, wished each other luck, and had no animosity towards each other."

Dave told *Rock-E-Zine* in September 2000, "At first I was shocked and so was the Sydney audience who were my fans, but Bon made his own character work brilliantly with the band and he endeared himself with his cheekiness and he always seemed to have a twinkle in his eyes. Also his voice was unique and had an unusual quality. Some of my favorite rock songs are ones that Bon sings." Dave went on to find his own success with the band Rabbit, who scored a hit with their song, "Too Much Rock 'N' Roll."

On Bon's first performance with the band, Angus recalled, "For the first gig the only rehearsal we had was just sitting around an hour before the gig, pulling out every rock 'n' roll song we knew. When we finally got there, Bon downed about two bottles of Bourbon with dope, coke, speed, and says, 'Right, I'm ready,' and he was too. He was fighting fit. There was this immediate transformation and he was running around yelling at the audience. It was a magic moment." The brothers affectionately nicknamed Bon "the old man."

Right after Bon joined the band, AC/DC went on a two-month tour of Australia. They also switched managers, leaving Dennis Laughlin and signing on with Michael Browning. They were dissatisfied with the way Laughlin had been handling the band and their finances. When money was tight, he would try to pay the band in booze, smokes, or other illicit materials. That tender worked for most of the band at times, but not at all for Angus, who neither drank nor indulged in anything stronger than a cigarette.

Browning was the manager of the Hard Rock Cafe in Melbourne, not to be confused with the now-famous restaurant chain. He had previously managed the Australian rock star Billy Thorpe and his band, The Aztecs. He gave up though, after five years of trying to break Billy overseas. George went to Melbourne to check Michael out and was impressed with his vision for the band. His leadership abilities were going to catapult AC/DC out of Australia and into the international music scene.

Chris Gilby, the promotions man for Alberts from 1973 to 1977, said in an interview with *No Nonsense* in August 2001, "Michael was a really visionary guy who saw the promise of the band and the way to break them. He was really the brains behind the band in the early days. I think that he was quite instrumental in bringing Bon into the band...Frankly it was when Bon joined the band and started writing lyrics that sounded like graffiti that I started thinking that this was a band that was going to go somewhere. Bon was a great guy who had a tremendous attitude and great stage presence — a fantastic communicator." With rock giants like Led Zeppelin and Black Sabbath dominating the rock world, AC/DC's shoot-from-the-hip approach to rock 'n' roll in the mid-Seventies was a breath of fresh air — or cigarette smoke — depending on where you were standing.

One of their regular stops for the band was the Hard Rock Cafe where they played the weekly gay nights. This probably didn't help the fact that their sexuality was always being questioned, thanks to their name. As long as the band was playing in front of an audience, they really didn't care. Malcolm remembers the gay nights, "Upfront, bisexual women would come in and hold up vibrators. They had T-shirts on with holes cut out in front, and their boobs would poke through. It was great." So appropriate for an ex-brassiere factory worker, don't you think?

In November, they went into the studio for 10 days to cut their first album. The tracks included "Baby, Please Don't Go" (a Muddy Waters cover), "She's Got Balls," "Little Lover," "Stick Around," "Love Song," and with Malcolm on lead, "Soul Stripper," "You Ain't Got A Hold On Me," and "Show Business." "She's Got Balls" was apparently a tribute to Bon's ex-wife, Irene, who wasn't too happy with it. *My guess is the line,* "Likes to crawl my lady, hands and knees all around the floor. No one has to tell her what a fella is for" *is what ticked her off.*

When Angus's amplifier blew up and started smoking during one of their recording sessions, George madly waved at him from the control room to keep on playing. When you listen to the raw energy immortalized on their first album, you can almost smell the smoke! The Australian cover featured a cartoon of a power generator behind barbed wire, littered with empty beer cans. For added disrespect, included in the picture was a dog relieving himself. They most appropriately called it, *High Voltage.*

In a 1992 edition of *Metal CD,* Malcolm states, "Back then we never went into the studio with anything more than a riff. In fact, we thought a riff was a song. Fortunately, we had the producers there to turn them into songs and it's been pretty much the same ever since. Back then we really didn't know any better."

George ended up playing the bass and session drummer, Tony Kerrante, cut most of the drum tracks. Drummers Peter Clack and John Proud, who played on the Marcus Hook Roll Band album, appear on one track each.

AC/DC rang in the New Year by playing at Festival Hall in Melbourne. There is a great picture of Bon onstage wearing a pair of red satin-bibbed overalls with no shirt on. *God, I miss the Seventies!* At Michael Browning's suggestion, AC/DC had relocated to Melbourne and moved into a house at 6 Lansdowne Road in the East St. Kilda district. Five musicians: hot, single, and ready to take the world by storm. Everyone was in their twenties, except Angus who was just nineteen. Years later, Malcolm would say that living together in that house was some of the happiest times of their lives...also some of the craziest.

It seems there were two distinct types of female AC/DC fans or, some would say, groupies. There were friends, like Trudy Worme, whose mom used to drop her off at their house on Sunday afternoons so she could cook dinner for them. Being out of the house for the first time, Angus and Malcolm both missed home cooking. She also baked Angus his favorite chocolate cakes.

Then there were the other girls who wanted to do more than cook for them. Evidently, many lovely creatures of the female persuasion came and went. So much so that this is where Bon got the personal inspiration for the song, "The Jack." Bon once said, "The story is, we all had a house together in Melbourne. And we had about 20 chicks who would come around and service the band, the whole thing. So the whole band got the jack. And so Malcolm said one day: 'Why don't we do a song about it?' So we wrote it ["The Jack"] that afternoon and played it that night and during the quiet part in the middle I went around and pointed out all the girls, you know...'She's got the jack' and 'She's got the jack' and so on. And all these chicks are makin' a mad dash for the door. It was quite funny actually."

Due to the band's promiscuity, there was even one horrifying outbreak of crabs that traveled all the way from the house into the band car! Of course, in future interviews the band blamed all this on the roadies. There must be some unwritten cardinal rule in rock 'n' roll: "If questioned, blame the roadies." This medical or sexual dilemma, if you will, inspired Bon to write the song, "Crabsody In Blue." His take on the classic number, "Rhapsody In Blue." *And Bon was a classic guy, let me tell you.* The boys were kept so busy keeping their slates clean that some say they once had a group rate at the local clinic. If the phrase "sex, drugs, and rock 'n' roll" didn't originate here, it at least was carried on for future generations to come, and come again...*I know. I couldn't help it.*

Once they hired Bon Scott, the Young brothers had met their match. Bon's love of life, and everything else for that matter, would come through in his stage persona. He loved to sing, laugh, drink, play, and live rock 'n' roll. His sexual escapades would inspire much of his lyrics, that is when he wasn't writing about the rough and winding road to becoming a rock star. Bon's use of double entendres were at times genius, and his personal magnetism and charisma are now legendary. "The old man" lived a couple of lifetimes before he joined AC/DC. And he barely stuck around long enough to tell us about them.

AC 3 DC

ROCK 'N' ROLL SINGER

Ronald Belford Scott was nicknamed "Bonny Scotland" when he first immigrated to Australia in 1952. Just like the Youngs, Bon was a Scotsman. 'Bonny' is what the kids called him until he got older, and then they shortened it to Bon. He once explained, "My new schoolmates threatened to kick the shit out of me when they heard my Scottish accent. I had one week to learn to speak like them if I wanted to remain intact. 'Course, I didn't take any notice. No one railroads me, and it made me all the more determined to speak my own way. That's how I got my name, you know. The Bonny Scot, see?"

He was born to Charles (Chick) Belford Scott and Isabella (Isa) Cunningham Mitchell at 11:30 pm on July 9, 1946 at the Fyfe Jamieson Maternity Home in Forfar Kirriemuir, which lies in the foothills of Cairngorms in the county of Angus. The same birthplace as J.M. Barrie, the author of *Peter Pan*.

Bon's grandfather, Alec, had established a bakery there on Bank Street in 1920. Two years later, Bon's father, Charles, was born. Chick, as he was known, originally wanted to go to sea but was encouraged to apprentice at the bakery with his brother, George. He later joined the local Citizen Military Forces (CMF). When World War II broke out, Chick at 22 was one of the first to go, serving in the army as a baker.

Stationed in Kirkcaldy, a seaport just across from Edinburgh, Chick found his future wife, Isa. They were both music lovers and met at a dance. They were married in 1941. Two years later, Isa would give birth to their first son Sandy,

17

who Chick would never see. He died at nine months old while Chick was still away at war.

The first day of 1945, Chick was discharged from the army and he and Isa moved to Roods, Kirriemuir. Chick's father bought them their first house and became a member of the local amateur light opera company and the Kirriemuir Pipe Band.

As a young boy, Bon—or Ronnie—as his mother called him, learned to walk on his own and once in school would never come directly home at the end of the day. Isa always had to chase after him. Once he got interested in music, there was no stopping him. He loved the drums and used to practice on biscuit tins and the breadboard. Every Saturday night, when his father's pipe band would march through town, Bon marched along with them.

Bon loved the pipe band, although he eventually turned his back on the kilt. As his mother said, "Once he turned 17, he refused to wear a skirt." Except for the one time years later, when he appeared singing with AC/DC on the British television show *Countdown,* wearing braids and a school-girl's dress. Even though he looked quite cute in it, his choice of wardrobe caused a complete uproar.

In 1949, the family welcomed their third son, Derek. By now, hordes of Scots looking for a better life had immigrated to Australia. In 1951, Isa's sister and her family left for Melbourne. A year later, Chick, Isa, and the boys followed. Bon was six years old. They immediately moved in with Isa's sister and eventually got their own home down the street in Sunshine, a suburb of Melbourne. They enrolled Bon in the Sunshine Primary School and he immediately accompanied the class on drums as they marched to school every morning.

Bon first learned how to play a recorder and then tried the piano. But learning piano required lessons and Bon wasn't interested in that. He even tried the accordion but went back to his first love—and something he had a natural talent for—the drums.

In 1956, their fourth son, three-year-old Graeme, was diagnosed with asthma so the family moved 1,700 miles away to Perth. Chick went ahead of the family, securing a house on Harvest Road in north Fremantle, just 12 miles from Perth. He secured a position with the firm he worked for in Melbourne and immediately became a member of the Fremantle Caledonian Scots pipe band.

Bon was enrolled in secondary school at John Curtin High. His first performance in his new town was a duet on recorder with a schoolmate at the age of 12 at the North Fremantle Town Hall. Bon also followed his father's pipe band around, eventually joining as a side drummer where he remained the under-17 champion for five years. Father and son appeared together in the opening ceremony of the Empire Games in Perth at Perry Lakes in 1962. [The British Empire and Commonwealth Games, which take place every four years, are similar to the Olympics.]

His brother Graeme was quoted in Clinton Walker's book, *Highway To Hell,* "Before TV, we used to sit around and listen to the radio. My dad and Ron used to go out to practice for the pipe band, drumming. It was a big occasion when the bands played, the whole family used to go out, put on their kilts, strap the drums on. Me and Derek would follow behind. Those were the big occasions, Scottish things."

The three brothers enjoyed the run of the house, but were respectful of their parents. They loved playing by the Swan River, which was just minutes from their home. Once in high school, Bon would hang out on the river smoking and chasing girls around. By the time he was 15, he had dropped out of school.

At first he became a farmhand, driving a tractor. He later switched to working on a crayfish boat. Fishing was back-breaking work, so Bon quickly left the water to work as an apprentice weighing machine mechanic for Avery Scales.

Bon loved listening to Elvis Presley, Chuck Berry, Little Richard, and Jerry Lee Lewis: rock 'n' roll outlaws, with a take-no-prisoners attitude. His main interest was being a rocker, not a "bodgie." Bodgies could be identified by their Tony Curtis-hairstyles and cardigan sweaters. Rockers slicked their hair back and wore skin-tight jeans and leather jackets. They also got lots of inspiration from American movies at the time, like *The Girl Can't Help It, King Creole,* and *Jailhouse Rock.*

Now able to travel around in cars, Bon and his friends drove up to east Perth to get tattoos. His friend Terry Henderson got one that said, "Death Before Dishonour" and Bon got his first tattoo on his lower stomach, right above his hairline. Terry and his sister Maureen sat on either side of him, as tears rolled down his face. He wore his jeans so tight that he couldn't button them up due to the pain and had to stay home for weeks!

Fremantle was a tough place to grow up, full of bodgies and rockers. If you weren't in a gang, you were most likely beaten up by someone in one. Bon had become a street fighter, regardless of his size. He and his friends hung out at the local pub, Cafe de Wheels. This is quite coincidental since their other pastime was drag racing, or pinching (stealing) cars for a joy ride. They also pinched gas when someone was on the lookout while somebody else siphoned it. Bon and Terry became two of Fremantle's toughest rockers. They also became well known by the local police.

All this and Bon still received an Avery Best First Apprentice Award for being such a diligent worker. You see, Bon was a rocker with a conscience. At least he learned to perfect the image of a bad boy, while hiding a heart of gold.

Bon and his friends had started going to dances, or "stomps" as they were called, at Perth's Port Beach. They often saw the band, The Nomads, which was fronted by Johnny Young, a future Australian pop star. [Young is a very common surname and no relation to the Young brothers.] Following their set, some of the local boys would get up and sing. Bon was often requested by the girls, who went wild when he did a cover of "Blue Suede Shoes" or "Long Tall Sally." Supposedly, Johnny Young wasn't all that thrilled.

One night after Bon had gone outside with a local girl, upon their return, he had to fight off some other boys who wanted to "take a walk" with her, as well. When the local police arrived, Bon fled in a car. He was later arrested for trying to pinch some gasoline. An item ran in the local West Australian newspaper on March 13, 1963: *A 16-year-old youth pleaded guilty in Fremantle Children's Court yesterday to charges of having given a false name and address to the police, having escaped legal custody, having unlawful carnal knowledge, and having stolen 12 gallons of petrol. He was committed to the care of the Child Welfare Department until he was 18 with a recommendation that he be kept in an institution of maximum security. He was put on a five-pound bond to come up for sentence if called on in the next two years on the unlawful carnal knowledge charge.*

I can understand the petrol part, but the unlawful carnal knowledge was a little severe considering the girl went outside with Bon willingly. Plus, how many 16-year-olds haven't had unlawful carnal knowledge? *I'll bet you can think of a few. I know I can.* Instead of being turned over to his parents, Bon was so ashamed that he pleaded guilty and was sent to serve nine months at the Riverbank boy's home.

Even though his parents tried to visit, he refused to see them. During this time he also missed a visit from his grandparents who came over from Kirriemuir. They would go back to Scotland and Bon would never again see them alive. He suffered behind bars, always freezing, scrubbing floors on his hands and knees, and trying to stay out of trouble. Bon spent nine months in Riverbank, but those closest to him said he spent the rest of his life trying to make up for it. He was released to his family by Christmas of

1963 and the unlawful carnal knowledge charges were dropped. Bon's parole officer suggested he enlist in the Citizens Military Forces (CMF), but he was refused. Bon was quoted as saying, "I was rejected by the army, because they said I was socially maladjusted." One thing his incarceration taught him was that rock 'n' roll was his only true escape. He quickly set up his drums in his mother's living room and got a job as a storeman with the egg board.

Bon formed his first band, The Spektors, in 1965. Wyn Milson played guitar, Brian Gannon played bass, and—on occasional numbers—Bon switched places with vocalist, John Collins. For about a year, The Spektors performed every weekend in Perth playing covers by Them, The Beatles, and the Stones. In *Highway To Hell,* Wyn remembered, "The whole problem with being a band in Perth back then was the search for material. It was a consuming process because you just couldn't get anything, no blues, or anything like that. You used to have to dig for it."

During one of their many weekend road trips while Bon was driving his father's borrowed Falcon station wagon to carry his drums, he fell asleep at the wheel and crashed into a light post in Claremont, which is in a section of Perth. Bon was treated at the local hospital for facial cuts and his only passenger, bassist Brian Gannon, suffered cuts and a concussion. Eerily, nine years later, Bon would almost lose his life on this same stretch of highway.

The Spektors became one of the top five bands and once they went as far as they could go in the local scene, they joined forces with another Perth band, The Winztons, to form the group, The Valentines. Bon later said, "I was a drummer in those days, and I used to play half the night on drums and spend the other half singing. The singer also played the drums—but not as good as me! Then I got an offer from The Valentines as a drummer. But I wanted to be a singer, so I joined as a singer. It wasn't because I wanted to be up front—it was because the singer used to get more chicks." Bon was always thinking.

By now Bon had left the egg company to become a postman. Can you imagine having Bon Scott deliver your mail? Now that would be something to tell the grandkids!

While in The Valentines, Bon shared the vocals with Vince Lovegrove. Lovegrove was quoted in the local newspaper, *RAM,* "Bon was the cute little drummer with cute little eyes, pixie-like ears, a cute turned-up nose, a cute little Scottish accent, and about four very obvious cute little tattoos. In rock 'n' roll in those days, you could go a long way being cute. We became friends."

Once the bands merged, they inherited both followings and that made The Valentines the biggest band in the country. Lovegrove and Bon, along with The Spektors guitarist Wyn Milson, guitarist Ted Ward, bassist Brian Abbott, and drummer Warwick Findlay would play their first big show in front of 3,000 fans at a concert for the Torchbearers for Legacy in Perth's Supreme Court Gardens. Findlay was quickly replaced on drums by Doug Lavery and John Cooksey would take over the bass from Abbott.

Their repertoire were covers of American hits, drawn from the music library of Allan Robertson, the group's manager, who was also a DJ at radio station 6KY in Perth. They quickly signed a contract with independent label, Clarion Records, and went into the studio to record two songs, "Everyday I Have To Cry" and "I Can't Dance With You," a Small Faces cover. The B-side made it to the Top Five on the charts in Western Australia. The Vallies, as their fans called them, were on their way. Things were going so well, they all quit their day jobs.

When The Easybeats came back to Sydney for two shows at His Majesty's, after the worldwide success of "Friday On My Mind," The Valentines opened for them. This was possibly the first time George Young met Bon Scott. Bon in turn idolized The Easybeat's lead singer, "Little" Stevie Wright. The two bands would get along so well that The Easybeats came up with the first of three songs they would write for them, called "She Said." This first single didn't do all that well, but after almost winning a battle of the bands in Melbourne, they decided to leave Perth, agreeing not to return until they were all big stars. In those days, Melbourne competed with Sydney as the music capitol of Australia. They arrived in Australia's newly crowned rock Mecca on the thirteenth day of October 1967.

After the band moved into a group house, they were literally starving when they hooked up with Ivan Dayman, an agent who booked them all over Australia. Through the spring of 1968, they traveled around in a van...all living on a salary of $300 dollars a week.

In April they scored an eight-week stay in Sydney and in May went into the studio to cut their second Easybeats song, "Peculiar Hole In The Sky." which wasn't as successful as they had hoped. They found a new house to move into and Lovegrove secured them a deal with an agency who had just added Michael Browning to their staff. Browning was running two discos and managing Doug Parkinson in Focus, which was the hottest new act in Sydney.

While the rest of the world was becoming "experienced" by Jimi Hendrix, Australia was more interested in bubblegum pop at the time, like The Monkees and the 1910 Fruitgum Company. This would prompt The Valentines to declare themselves as a pop group "unafraid of commercialism." Their image changed to flashier clothes and trimmed hair and Bon started using makeup to cover his tattoos.

Their official greeting card for the 1968 holidays read, "Be My Valentine In '69." Some of the highlights from Bon's band profile which listed his favorite things as: The Beatles, Moody Blues, John Lee Hooker, Otis Redding, The Supremes, "soul, worried jazz," and Scottish pipe band music. His also liked painting his room red, long blonde hair, showers, swimming, and sex. His dislikes were people who hate Crater Critters (whatever they are), and being disturbed whilst thinking, washing, and ironing…Bon ironed?!

The band finished up the year by recording their third Easybeats tune, "My Old Man's A Groovy Old Man," backed by "Ebeneezer." It was officially released on Valentines Day 1969 and was very successful. When they appeared at the disco, That's Life, a reporter from *GoSet* wrote, "The audience screamed in unison, 'We love The Valentines.' As soon as they appeared, the audience went completely berserk and started to storm the stage. The two lead singers, Vince and Bon, were dragged to the floor and Bon's pants and jacket were completely ripped off him." See, Bon was right. It's good to be the singer.

This reaction from the audience was a constant at all their concerts, and on March 10 they played in front of 7,000 at the Alexandra Gardens, at which a riot broke out. Lovegrove was arrested for booting a policeman from the stage. He was released after being put on a 12-month good behavior bond, and fined $50. Shortly thereafter, drummer Lavery left to join the band, Axiom, and with new drummer, Paddy Beach, they continued to gain support playing gigs around Melbourne. Eventually "My Old Man" made it up the charts to Number 23.

Their next, and perhaps strangest release, was "Nick Nack Paddy Whack" with the B-side being Bon's first writing credit, "Getting Better," which he shared with Wyn. Bands like Led Zeppelin and the like were finally making an impact on the Australian music scene, and it was the beginning of the end for The Valentines…especially when they became the first Australian rock band to get busted for possession of marijuana. Unbeknownst to the band, the local police had been watching them and one Saturday night showed up at their rehearsal place with a search warrant. The band protested by telling *GoSet,* "We believe it should be legalized."

As they declared before they left, The Valentines returned to Perth rock stars, being met at the airport by 4,000 screaming fans to play a New Years

Eve show at the Supreme Court Gardens for radio station 6KY. That February, they pleaded guilty in court to possession and each received a $150 fine. Their final release was "Juliette," which sounded suspiciously like The Beatle's "Dear Prudence." It barely made it into the Top 30. After playing one more gig, the band decided to go their separate ways.

Within months of The Valentines disbanding, Bon was invited to move to Sydney by Fraternity leader, Bruce Howe. Fraternity was the hottest band in Australia and included Howe, Mick Jurd, John Freeman, Sam See, John Bisset, and "Uncle" John Ayers. Bon jumped at the chance to become their singer. The Australian radio ban was lifted in 1970 and Woodstock's effects were being felt throughout the music world, even down under. [The radio ban had been a standoff between major record labels and the Australian radio stations. When the record companies demanded payment for playing their artists, the radio stations retaliated and only played music from independent labels.]

Bon moved into the band house on Jersey Road in Sydney and immediately painted his bedroom fire engine red...a ritual he would do every time he moved into a new place. So anyone in Australia who finds a bedroom or an attic painted fire engine red, Bon Scott used to sleep there. Put up a plaque, for God's sake!

Bon spent his spare time listening to King Crimson, Deep Purple, Rod Stewart, and Procol Harum. The band worked on their originals, playing regularly at the local disco, Jonathan's. Eventually they went into the studio and recorded Livestock, which was released on Sweet Peach Records [a small Australian label]. Much of the album features Bon playing the recorder. Even though the album wasn't that impressive, Fraternity still appeared on the new television show, GTK. Bon was also featured on the cover of the new national magazine, Sound Blast, with his face done up with war paint. Billed as the "Wild Man of Fraternity," he looked more like an aborigine than a rock star.

Fraternity played a few shows opening for the 1910 Fruitgum Company, and then supported Jerry Lee Lewis in Adelaide at Apollo Stadium. While in Adelaide, they played at the club, Headquarters. There they ran into Bon's ex-bandmate, Vince Lovegrove. Lovegrove was writing his column "Move" for the Australian newspaper, the News. He also launched a television show that was named after his column. Lovegrove had a lot to do with hyping Fraternity in Adelaide, writing a review for GoSet stating, "They came, they played, they conquered!"

Local entrepreneur Hamish Henry saw them at Headquarters and offered them a deal they couldn't refuse: he wanted to house them, manage them, buy equipment for them, and pay a weekly wage. What musician would turn down an offer like that?

By 1971, Australia was finally catching up to the rest of the world, hosting their own outdoor rock festivals. Australian acts like Daddy Cool, Blackfeather, Chain, and Billy Thorpe's Aztecs were ruling the national charts. Henry financed Myponga, a rock festival featuring an exclusive appearance by Black Sabbath. After their appearance at Myponga, Fraternity finally went into the studio to record "Seasons Of Change," featuring Bon on vocals.

In April, they supported Deep Purple and Free when they came through Adelaide. Afterwards, Fraternity moved up into the hills to live on a farm 17 miles from Adelaide, à la The Band. This would further isolate them from what was really going on in the world of music.

Their new single, "Seasons of Change," was disregarded when Blackfeather released their own version of it. After all, the song was written by Blackfeather's John Robertson. Bon actually appeared on their new album, playing recorder on several tracks. Fraternity's record wasn't doing so well, but they continued to play at the Largs Pier Hotel as the house band. Frequent brawls broke out, many caused by Bon flirting with the wrong girls. Or more accurately, Bon flirting with girls who had really jealous boyfriends!

By the end of the summer, Fraternity confirmed their hold as kings of the mountain when they won the Battle of the Sounds. The only other band that came close was Sherbet. Adelaide's Channel Nine produced a special about the band, which featured them on their farm with Bon doing stunts on his trail bike.

Bon's riding skills were legendary, supposedly riding around nude and driving his bike up a staircase to one of his gigs. Once he even rode from Adelaide to Melbourne, with no protection other than a T-shirt. He got badly sunburned and froze at night while sleeping in a ditch on the side of the road. His escapades courageously earned him the nickname "Ronnie Roadtest."

Bon had a way with motorbikes and with women. In September of 1971, he would meet his future wife, Irene Thornton. Irene was a tall blonde, who laughed at his dirty jokes and appreciated Bon's sense of humor. She also enjoyed smoking and drinking; and Bon was crazy about her.

Early in 1972, with Hamish Henry having connections in England, the band decided to relocate to London. Before they took off, they went into the studio and recorded, *Flaming Galah*. The record included three new songs, "Getting Off," "Welfare Boogie," and "Hemming's Farm." The rest of the material was older music, rewritten or re-recorded.

When Hamish offered to pay for wives to move as well, only knowing each other a few months, Bon and Irene tied the knot on January 24, 1972. Before they left for England, Fraternity took a big black bus on tour through South Australia. Bruce Howe remembers Bon going for a swim one hot day, among a pack of huge jellyfish with long stingers. Bon grabbed everyone's attention when he dove right in, swam underneath the jellyfish, and then jumped right back out, much to everyone's horror! Bon loved an audience and diving underneath deadly jellyfish couldn't have been any more dangerous than swimming with the sharks in the music business.

Hamish secured a deal with RCA Records, who released their single, "Welfare Boogie," in March. The entire album was released a month later when the band left for England. The move to England was a wakeup call with the British music charts dominated by glam rock like T. Rex, Gary Glitter, and David Bowie's "Ziggy Stardust." Fraternity's grass roots rock couldn't have been more out of place. They were unable to get many bookings and soon the band members and wives all had to take day jobs. Bon found work knitting wigs in a factory.

It took them until November to get their first gig at the Speakeasy in London. By 1973, they got to open some shows for a band in Newcastle, called Geordie. Their lead singer was a working-class bloke named Brian Johnson. Bon's brother Graeme remembers visiting Bon in *Highway To Hell,* "They had the bus and the thing was if they'd support a band, they'd use the other band's equipment too, and they were booked to go with Geordie. I think we went to Torquay first, and then we packed up that night and went on to Plymouth. Brian used to carry his guitar player on his shoulders too. I think that's where Ron got the idea, because when he joined AC/DC there was no one around doing that sort of thing. Angus was the perfect guy to carry around. He was so small."

Bon remembered seeing Brian perform and being quite impressed with him. Brian later recalled in an interview that Bon actually saw Brian on a night that he was suffering from an appendicitis attack. Apparently Bon took this as one incredible performance!

When Hamish couldn't recoup any of his investment in Fraternity, or Fang, as they later called the band, he pulled the plug and bailed. He explained, "I think the real reason Fraternity failed in England was because they were too loud!" Umm, that didn't hurt The Who any. As they saw the band fall apart, crushing their dreams of stardom in England, Bon took a job bartending in a pub. By Christmas, they all returned to Australia with band and personal relationships in ruins.

Bon got busy with a day job loading fertilizer at a plant in Wallaroo. He also bought a Triumph motorbike to get around. To stay involved in the music business, he jammed with Peter Head's Mount Lofty Rangers. As he tried to pick up the pieces of his life, his marriage to Irene fell apart.

One night, after a drunken fight with Irene, Bon went to a Lofty Rangers rehearsal. After telling the band to fuck off, he climbed on his motorbike and took off down Stirling Highway in Claremont...The same highway where he had crashed his dad's station wagon into a light pole nine years earlier. After driving his motorcycle directly into an oncoming car, Bon laid in a coma in serious condition in the intensive care unit of Queens Elizabeth Hospital for three days. He suffered a broken arm, collarbone, leg, and nose. He had severe cuts to his face, a concussion, and had lost several teeth.

Some later believed that the extensive injuries to his mouth and throat gave him that unique raspy quality to his voice. After the doctors had to restart his heart, he spent four weeks in traction, with his mouth wired shut. Being the trouper that he was, Bon quickly learned how to drink liquor through a straw, while still smoking an endless stream of joints. It *is* medicinal, you know.

Irene never left his side and his mother, Isa, moved in with Bon and cared for him after Irene went back to work. No matter how much he suffered, he never lost his sense of humor. Bon once sent a picture of himself right after the accident to a friend, writing on it, "I left my teeth behind on the road."

As he slowly recovered, Bon went into the studio to record two songs with Pete Head. They recorded "Carey Gully" and "Round And Round And Round" which wouldn't be heard by the public until 1996. To help him out, Vince Lovegrove gave Bon odd jobs to do, like putting up posters, driving bands around, and painting. Things finally started looking up when Lovegrove told him about this exciting new band from Sydney who needed a lead singer. He persuaded Bon to check them out at the Pooraka Hotel. The band was called AC/DC.

AC 4 DC

IT'S A LONG WAY TO THE TOP
(IF YOU WANNA ROCK 'N' ROLL)

After Bon joined the band, things started looking up for everybody. AC/DC gave Bon the freedom to finally be himself. "When I sang, I always felt that there was a certain amount of urgency to what I was doing. There was no vocal training in my background, just a lot of good whiskey...I went through a period where I copied a lot of guys and found when I was singing that I was starting to sound just like them. But when I met up with [AC/DC], they told me to sound like myself, and I really had a free hand doing what I always wanted to do."

When Michael Browning took over as their manager, he formed a company called TransPacific Artists that he ran with Bill Joseph. The company would pay off the band's debts, set them up in their house in Melbourne, provide them with transportation and a crew, cover their expenses, and pay them a wage. George, in particular, was very agreeable to this arrangement. The next order of business was to keep them playing as much as possible. This constant performing is what made AC/DC into the band it is today.

They played wherever they could, to whomever they could, including pub-crawlers, teenyboppers, and the gay crowd. Melbourne had a healthy gay circuit—and Bon dressed in his leather pants—was always welcome. Although he was still recovering from his injuries, you couldn't tell that when he was performing on stage. The majority of their audience was male, working class, and looking to raise hell. AC/DC's music became known as pub rock: songs to drink by.

The new rock magazine, *Juke,* which took the place of *GoSet* wrote, "[AC/DC were] new faces refusing to be restricted by an established music scene…brash and tough, unashamed to be working at a music style that many describe as the lowest common denominator of rock music, gut-level rock, punk rock."

The band was now traveling around in an old Clipper bus, which continually broke down. Julius Grafton, who heads his own companies, *CX* magazine, and Juliusmedia College in Melbourne, recalls his brief brush with the band. "I did lights for AC/DC at some shows in my home state of New South Wales. Bon Scott was the new singer and the band was uncompromising. They had an old Flexible Clipper tour bus that broke down regularly. The band was forced to sit in the front, smoking and drinking Scotch, while the crew loaded the gear in the back. At the time, AC/DC had an edge that no other band could match. Nothing has changed!"

Bon had written home to Irene complaining of the bus breaking down and being without booze, dope, or a woman to play with…even though they were the hottest band in the country, which wasn't bad, as he said, for a "29-year-old third time around has-been."

Playing consistently, Malcolm and Angus had agreed that the rhythm section wasn't what they wanted it to be. Peter Clack didn't cut it and bassist Rob Bailey insisted on bringing his wife along with him everywhere. The kiss of death for any band member, famous or not! Their search for someone to keep the beat with the unrelenting passion that they played their instruments with, brought them to the only Australian-born member of the band. His name was Phil Rudd.

Phillip Hugh Norman Witschke Rudd, nee Rudzevecuis, was born in Melbourne, Australia on May 19, 1954. He told Steven Scott Fyfe for *Cyber Drum* in August of 2000, "My first inspiration to play drums and to be excited about music was probably a song called "Tin Soldier" by Small Faces, where you have a breakdown in the middle section, then the guitar comes blaring in."

Phil first made his living washing cars and started out playing drums in the band Charlemagne, before joining Colored Balls, a skinhead outfit formed by guitarist Lobby Lloyd. Their singer was Gary "Angry" Anderson, who went on to form the popular Australian group, Rose Tattoo. Colored Balls conquered the local club circuit during the early Seventies. They recorded two singles: "Liberate Rock" and "Mess Of Blues." In 1974, they changed the name of the band to Buster Brown and recorded one album, *Something To Say,* for Mushroom Records. By the beginning of 1975, Phil was ready for something new and jumped at the chance to audition for AC/DC. Once they heard him play, they looked no further. Former member Larry Van Kriedt was asked to come back until they could find a more suitable replacement on bass.

At the end of January, AC/DC was scheduled to perform at the Sunbury Festival in Melbourne featuring Deep Purple. The event had been booked by Michael Browning. When Deep Purple found out that they had to go on before AC/DC, a fight broke out between the band and the roadies…in front of 20,000 people. AC/DC left the venue without playing a note. Perhaps this is what prompted Deep Purple's hot-headed guitarist, Ritchie Blackmore, to later accuse the band of "circus tricks." The fact that the roadies sided with Deep Purple and not the local boys, convinced Browning more than anything, that it was time for AC/DC to get out of the country.

High Voltage was released in Australia in February 1975, with the first single being "Love Song (Oh Jene)" and "Baby, Please Don't Go." The B-side started getting airplay, which pushed the song to Number 10. It stayed on the national charts for an unprecedented 25 weeks.

Local musician Mark Evans had heard they were looking for a new bass player and passed the audition just in time to celebrate the album's release. They played a special performance at the Hard Rock Cafe, where admission was only one dollar. Evans moved into the house on Lansdowne Road and happily noted that there were women everywhere! Malcolm soon nick-named him the "Sand Man," because whenever they climbed into a car to go anywhere, Mark would fall asleep within five minutes. *I'm not sure if it was all the performing or, um, all the performing, that was tiring him out so much.*

Before they hired Mark, they had also tried a bass player by the name of Paul Matters. I couldn't really determine how long he played with them, but he did last long enough to be included in a band picture that appears on the back of Clinton Walker's book, Highway To Hell. *Anyone can easily see that he was clearly too tall for the job.*

In March, the band made their first appearance on the ABC television show, *Countdown,* which was hosted by Ian "Molly" Meldrum. Meldrum, known as Australia's "oldest teenager," was a disc jockey and had created *Countdown.* They played "Baby, Please Don't Go" with Bon singing live and Angus wearing his Super A(ngus) outfit. *Countdown* became an impor-tant tool for the band, which was watched by most Australian households every Sunday evening.

The band ended the month with a concert at the Myer Music Bowl where over 2,500 people showed up. A local newspaper noted that AC/DC got the best response and, when they were finished, half the audience decided to leave as well. As a reward that night, the band was gifted with super groupie, Ruby Lips, who Bon immortalized in the song, "Go Down." [The song is on their fourth album, *Let There Be Rock*.]

They made their second appearance on *Countdown* in April, this time with Angus in his schoolboy uniform and Bon in blond braids and a schoolgirl's dress...complete with make-up, earrings, and fake breasts. At the time, men in drag were not all that popular on television and his cross-dressing caused a flurry of complaints. *I'm not sure what was most upsetting: his outfit or his rolling around on his back, smoking a cigarette, and exposing his knickers to the television audience. Thank God he was wearing some!*

Mark Evans told *Classic Rock* in February 2005 that they never knew what Bon was going to do, until it happened. "Another time was when we performed "Baby, Please Don't Go" live on *Countdown,* and Bon got dressed as this schoolgirl. Again he didn't tell us. So here we were, being filmed live on television, and the music starts up and Bon's nowhere to be found and we're all going, 'Where the fuck is Bon?' As soon as his vocals are about to begin he comes out from behind the drums dressed as this schoolgirl. And it was like a bomb went off in the joint; it was pandemonium, everybody broke out in laughter. Bon had a wonderful sense of humor. He was the archetypal naughty boy."

AC/DC was a phenomenon compared to what everyone was used to seeing on *Countdown*. Their rough-and-ready rocker following was rivaled by all the screaming teenyboppers. *RAM* wrote, "They were everything the Bay City Rollers didn't stand for. Maybe it was the way Angus Young jumped and rolled around the stage like a demented epileptic while not missing a note of his guitar duties. Maybe it was the way Bon Scott leered and licked his lips while his eyes roamed hungrily up and down little girl's dresses." OK, that's one way you could put it. Although Angus was the focal point of the band, Bon's stage presence definitely had a force all its own.

The band stayed busy by playing Heavy Metal Nites at the Hard Rock Cafe and during the day, a special series of concerts at the Hard Rock called, "Schoolkids Week." While not working, AC/DC was known for not hanging out with other bands or musicians. As a matter of policy, they hated other bands...except, of course, for their idols like Chuck Berry or Little Richard. Their attitude was, "If you're not with us, you're against us."

Bassist Mark Evans remembers Bon not always being able to conform to this theory. He was known as "Bon the Likeable," after a character on the television show *Get Smart* who was called Simon the Likable. His secret weapon was that he was impossible not to like. That was evident, even to

Mark's mother, who used to have the band over for dinner. Bon would always ask to help her with the dishes. Needless to say, she adored Bon just like every other woman who would cross his path.

Their single "High Voltage," which missed being included on their album, was released in June. That same month, they played their first headlining concert at the Melbourne Festival Hall with Stevie Wright and John Paul Young supporting. This performance was shot with four cameras, which was unheard of in those days. The intent was to get them some interest overseas. A promotional video of "High Voltage" was taken from that footage, and for good measure, they spliced in applause from George Harrison's *Concert For Bangladesh* album.

Melbourne music fan and roadie, Raymond Windlow, saw AC/DC for the first time when they played the Festival Hall. He was working for the band Fox at the time. He went on to work with The Dingoes, Skyhooks, and briefly with The Little River Band. "There were quite a few bands there that day, but being offered a days work initially with AC/DC was putting money in my pocket. Whilst my musical taste didn't extend to their raunchy, loud, thump, thump, thump music, the appeal of the screaming girls did.

"It was an amazing concert with the stage being surrounded in a crush of bodies, mostly barely legal females. I almost got my marching orders prior to the guys playing a note. Being worldwise, I offered to score for them if they wanted something in the dressing room before they went on. The silence was absolutely deafening. The look from their manager had more than daggers in it and when no one spoke up, I assumed I had 'dropped a clanger,' and left the room mumbling something about checking the sound equipment. One of the management put his arm around my shoulder, and in a gentle fashion said, 'No, mate, don't ever mention drugs around the band.' And he left the whole conversation at that. I believe that the attention the guys were getting at the time may have opened them up to the possibility of being set up for a narcotics bust.

"During their performance, the audience was in a frenzy with a mass of bodies pressed hard into the front of the stage. Girls looked pleadingly at the guys on the side of the stage holding their hands up. Not to grab at Bon or Angus, but for someone to pull them out of the crush. Myself and a couple of others did just that much to the annoyance of the management who admonished us for venturing out onto the stage during their performance. Nonetheless, we survived the night and when the younger members of the band wandered home with their 'minders,' Bon, myself, and a few guys from other bands wandered off to the local post-gig hot spot, the Hard Rock Cafe.

"Bon and I spent quite a few nights playing eight ball at the Hard Rock during their extended Melbourne visits. Bon was a regular at the Hard Rock after a gig. He loved his drink and whilst we were not bosom buddies, we were pool buddies. I was the roadie who did a few gigs for them and he was the lad who made the girls scream at his stage performance. On occasion some members of the public who paid to get in at the Hard Rock would try to smart arse their way into Bon's bad books. Maybe to get the reputation of having been in a fight with him or what, I don't know. What I do know is that if ever a fight was in the making, I would have Bon on one side and 20 or 30 roadies on the other. The music community was tight when it comes to that, and Bon had the look of a classic street scrapper. But the whole time I knew him, not once that I know of did he actually throw a punch. He was a happy, smiling guy with a wit and "rude charm" that endeared people to him and yet distinct from many band singers, he did not have the air of being above smaller bands or guys from road crews. Anyone was welcome to chat, share a smoke, or a drink with him and try to beat his ass at eight ball! Not many did. I still reckon we had the longest run on that pool table as unbeaten pair champs."

By the end of June, a mere four months after its release, the album *High Voltage* was certified Gold in their homeland. The band immediately left for Sydney to record their second record. Angus and Malcolm moved back into their parent's home in Burwood, while the rest of the band and crew stayed at the Squire Inn at Bondi Junction. Right across the street from their hotel was the hottest nightclub in Sydney, the Lifesaver. In 1975, Bondi Lifesaver was the place to be. It was a club and restaurant that most fans frequented more than a couple of nights a week. Bon set up shop there.

Located in the old Boomerang House on King Street was Albert Studios. Radio station 2UW was also housed there. The band recorded in Studio One, which was a small room with bare brick walls. They also used the side room, which had two Marshall stacks and a bass rig. The drums were set up in a room that was once a kitchen. Most of the songs were recorded live, within the first few takes. The guitar leads and vocals were the only tracks that were overdubbed. While recording, Angus would perform just like he was onstage. No sitting still for him!

The studio had become the closet thing to a hit factory in Australia. George and Harry had a 16-track mixing desk shipped over from England and spent every minute in the studio, writing and recording hits. Their main acts were John Paul Young, Ted Mulry Gang, and William Shakespeare (who was a goofy Gary Glitter-type character). It all came together for them when they brought AC/DC in to record. Harry explained, "We tried to capture that energy they had onstage. You had to get them at the right time, when they were really fired up."

This new album would reveal a more polished approach, opening with "It's A Long Way To The Top (If You Wanna Rock 'N' Roll)." It was the only rock song to feature bagpipes, that is until Korn did it almost 30 years later. They re-recorded "Can I Sit Next To You Girl" and added "Rock 'N' Roll Singer," "High Voltage," "Rocker," a cover of Chuck Berry's "School Days," "Live Wire," "T.N.T.," and Bon's ode to venereal disease, "The Jack." *I would like to point out that Bon should be credited with originating the phrase, "You're the man," since he sings in the song "T.N.T.": "...the man is back in town, so don't you mess around!" I'll bet you never noticed that one before!*

George Young had a huge influence on his younger brother's writing style. Angus described, "[George] would take our meanest song and try it out on keyboards with arrangements like 10cc or Montovani. If it was passed, the structure was proven, then we took it away and dirtied it up." This is a formula that has stood the test of time. The band enjoyed the involvement of the Young family, which was working class and very close. Sometimes after gigs, they would all come around to play cards. They were nurtured by the support of George and Harry, and the expertise of former Easybeats tour manager, Sammy Horsburgh (who had married their sister, Margaret).

AC/DC also had the benefit of George and Harry's knack for picking hits. Angus once said that George didn't choose to work with them because they were family, it was because George thought they were good. Bon stated that George was more a father figure to the group, rather than a brother. He didn't tell them what to do, but he helped them get more out of what they were doing. Bassist Mark Evans was quoted in *Under Cover Media,* saying "...George Young fine tuned things. George is an absolute genius. I have never met a more astute person in the studio than George."

Angus and Malcolm were both gifted riff masters, coming up with songs every time they sat down to jam. Malcolm often came up with titles and then they would try to write a song around it. Malcolm and George would work it out on the keyboards, leaving Bon to add the lyrics once the backing tracks were done. Bon always had notebooks of lyrics, all neatly printed in capital letters. Although some of his lyrics were quite simple, phrasing was his strong suit. He once told *Countdown,* "Things fall into place. Sometimes. You gotta keep your eyes open for lines and words and stuff…ideas, just pictures, you know."

They spent the rest of the summer playing Melbourne and Sydney, becoming regulars at Sydney's Bondi Lifesaver. Their plan to play a series of free concerts at Melbourne's Myer department store had to be cancelled when some say as many as 5,000 fans stormed the store on the first day, ripping the place apart, ending AC/DC's set after only two songs.

When a fight erupted later at the Matthew Findlers Hotel in Melbourne, drummer Phil broke his thumb, requiring former drummer Colin Burgess to fill in for him. This could be where Phil got the name, Phil "Left Hook" Rudd. Reportedly, Phil flew off the drums and hit a guy so hard he knocked him out. To which he explained, "This guy was kicking Angus in the head, so I had to now, didn't I?" He did have a point.

Vince Lovegrove concurred by telling *No Nonsense* in May 1999, "In Australia in those days it was pretty wild, a bit like cowboy days, the business was still young and lawless and the band had a reputation for being wild, mainly due to Bon, really. The rest were wild boys, but Bon was unique. He was from another planet."

Australian fan Rob Tognoni remembers seeing AC/DC right after *T.N.T.* was released. He told *No Nonsense* in the August 2001 issue, "Well, the shock that you could have seen on my face and the faces of everyone in the place when the first glimpse of Angus silhouetted by an intense strobe behind him, launched into "High Voltage" would have been a sight. We had never heard such incredible volume before. I made my way to the front row and stood in stunned disbelief of what I was witnessing. All I could think was, 'Fark!!!!' Bon leered from stage left clutching the microphone in one hand and stretching the cable looped in the other."

Personally, this would become my favorite part of the first few times I saw AC/DC live, watching the faces of people in the crowd that had never seen them before. True amazement, followed by disbelief, bordering on mild shock…but in a good way.

In early September, the band played a free show at Sydney's Victoria Park that was promoted by radio station 2SM. This time, Angus would climb up on Bon's shoulders for their first ever "walkabout." Chris Gilby used an advertising campaign for AC/DC which stated, "Your mother won't like them." It worked like a charm. To further piss off mothers everywhere after the Victoria Park concert, Angus was quoted as saying, "That notorious leader of thieves and vagabonds, Bon Scott, to celebrate the success of the show in Sydney, went out and got a new tattoo and pierced his nipples for earrings. The other boys celebrated in other ways."

Bon had been living in the Freeway Gardens Motel in Melbourne where he reunited with his friend Pat Pickett. Pat heard the band was in Melbourne and traveled there to work for the band as one of the road crew. One night during a party at an apartment building, someone offered Bon five dollars to jump off the balcony into the pool. Bon got him to raise it to 10 dollars, and in front of everyone—including a terrified Angus—leapt off the second-floor balcony and made a perfect dive into the hotel's swimming pool. As he told *Guitar World,* Angus grabbed the guy and said, "'Don't ever fucking dare Bon to do something again!' Accepting dares was Bon's favorite party trick. He had no fear when it came to things like that." He also had no fear of any woman who might catch his eye.

Freeway Gardens was where Bon met the infamous Rosie. The band and especially Bon, loved to push each other to do the most disgusting things. When Rosie—a large Tasmanian mountain woman starting showing up at their shows—an ultimatum was presented to Bon. One morning when Pat Pickett woke up, he looked over and saw a rather hefty lady lying in Bon's bed, with a small tattooed arm sticking out from underneath her. Bon's homage to her, in the song, "Whole Lotta Rosie," is proof that he had more fun with her than he expected.

The band was completely amazed at his ability to attract women. One time he managed what Mark Evans recalled a "trifecta" which was bedding three women a day for four days in a row. Now we know who Gene Simmons looked up to! Bon definitely loved the ladies and although he was known to be a street fighter, he usually kept his head about him and would stand back and watch before he got directly involved in a fight. He was also known to travel light, carrying a shaving kit with a toothbrush, toothpaste, a change of underwear, and socks. Each night he would wash out his underwear and hang them up in the bathroom to dry.

The only time Bon really snapped was when they played on the *TV Week* King of Pops awards show. They played live, and Bon had all kinds of problems on stage. When they were done, they went downstairs and broke a lock off a door to get into a bar. Inside was a stack of *TV Week* magazines with Sherbet's singer, Daryl Braithwaite, on the cover. This enraged Bon and he promptly tore up all the magazines. He spent the rest of the night drinking champagne from a frozen turkey. You heard me. And if you knew Bon, you don't have to ask which end he was drinking it from. This is the only time anyone can remember Bon ever being rude to anybody, frozen poultry included.

The "High Voltage" single shot up the charts to Number Six. The album of the same name, had sold more than 70,000 copies and was catapulted to

125,000 copies once the single went on sale. Now that they were getting sales in Australia, it was only a matter of time before they conquered the rest of the world.

Browning signed them to a five-year management deal and started planning a national tour to promote the release of their next album, which was called *T.N.T.* The tour started in Melbourne on their way to Perth and would wind up in Sydney by Christmas. Bon was able to visit his parents and Chick and Isa were finally able to meet the boys. They immediately approved of Bon's new mates.

While on the road, the local band The Keystone Angels opened for them. Vocalist Rick Brewster recalls the first time he ever saw AC/DC: "We supported AC/DC as The Keystone Angels on their south Australia tour in 1975. The Port Pirie Hotel was the first gig and it was the first time I met them and saw them perform live. They were the tightest band I'd ever seen, despite the fact that Phil Rudd had broken his wrist [sic] and was not on the tour. We later saw Phil play with the band many times and he was a machine hammering out one of the hardest of all feels to play well. Malcolm drove the band, called all the shots with minimum effort; Mark Evans played the bass and although he only remained with the band for another few years, I always liked his playing. Bon was right up there with [Bad Company's] Paul Rodgers as one of the best and most charismatic rock singers I'd ever heard. His tongue-in-cheek delivery was infectious and his ad lib version of "She's Got The Jack" [sic]…well, you had to be there. And then there was Angus. I'd never seen anything remotely like Angus. Superb musicianship complemented his over-the-top stage antics…such an incredible combination. He's still one of the finest guitar players I've ever heard and he reels it off in the same manner as a gifted circus clown who makes a difficult acrobatic feat look easy.

"And his act was essentially the same as it is today! The Chuck Berry 'Duck Walk,' the 'Death of a Fly', the schoolboy uniform…it was all there in Port Pirie, South Australia in 1975 and he's spent the next 30 years hammering it home to the rest of the world. I remember Angus telling me in the tour bus on that first tour, 'Yeah…you know if I was a piano player, I'd play with my feet!'"

When both bands played at the Sundowner Hotel in Whyalla, Brewster recalled the funniest thing he ever saw Angus do. "Angus lost his temper with someone in the crowd who must have been yelling the wrong thing. This guy happened to be a six-foot-four biker. When Angus lost it, he threw his SG down and leapt on him with a full-flying tackle from the stage. They went down in a screaming heap and the only reason that Angus is alive today, is that Bon followed him into the skirmish and somehow managed to defuse the situation and coax a screaming and kicking Angus back to the stage to finish the show." Hecklers, beware.

After they got home, Angus, Bon, and Malcolm all told George about The Keystone Angels and Albert Music signed them. The band's name was changed to The Angels and Albert Music guided them to become one of Australia's most successful bands during the Seventies. Eternally grateful, Brewster said, "They saw something in us which I didn't see myself. We weren't very good musically at the time. Maybe they saw 'hungry and determined with potential.' Whatever it was, we were grateful, having already been turned down by EMI (who ironically, distributed Albert's records). After the boys from AC/DC put in the good word for us, George and his partner Harry Vanda came to see us in Sydney, at Chequers nightclub where we used to play from 8 'til 3 or 4 in the morning for $100. We were offered a deal on the spot. One of the best spin-offs from signing with Albert's was working next door to a number of other great acts. These included Rose Tattoo, Ted Mulry, John Paul Young, Flash And The Pan and, of course, AC/DC. It gave us tremendous insight and inspiration."

AC/DC played another headlining date at the Festival Hall in November and were back in Sydney to play the State Theatre on the thirtieth. On December 8, 1975, their next single "It's A Long Way To The Top (If You Wanna Rock 'N' Roll)" with "Can I Sit Next To You Girl" was released, followed by their new album, *T.N.T.* The cover of this album would feature a picture of two railroad ties with the letters "T.N.T." stenciled on them.

Michael Browning's sister, Coral, lived in London and worked for a management company who handled Peter Tosh, Bob Marley, and Gil-Scott Heron. She had traveled to Melbourne to see the band and was very excited to be working with them. In December, Michael flew to London armed with the footage that was taken at the Festival Hall, intent on landing the band a record deal. After showing Phil Carson of Atlantic Records a kinescope [video] of the band playing live, Carson offered them a worldwide recording contract. The first deal was a one-album trial, with an option for Atlantic to extend a longer contract in the future.

Atlantic Records was formed in 1947 in New York City. In the early Seventies, after they had signed Yes and Emerson, Lake, and Palmer—two of rock's biggest acts—Atlantic opened an office in London. The label was crazy for AC/DC and they, in turn, were thrilled to be on the same label as Led Zeppelin and The Rolling Stones. Amazingly, Atlantic outsmarted everyone else who had passed on the band. AC/DC was now on their way to taking over the rest of the planet...one concert at a time.

The band played the Royal Showgrounds in Sydney on Christmas Eve, then celebrated New Years Eve playing a show in Adelaide. The band had the electricity cut off while they were performing and Bon incited their fans to storm the stage in protest. Then he triumphantly appeared in the middle of the crowd on someone's shoulders, playing bagpipes. Power or no power, you can't turn off AC/DC!

By the end of the year, *High Voltage* was certified triple Gold. AC/DC was now the top band in Australia, 24-carat proof that they had conquered their homeland. Considering the nation's birth in 1821 as a dumping ground for the United Kingdom's criminal population, it would be safe to say that they cut their rock 'n' roll teeth on the toughest audiences you could find. The New Year would bring another member change and, finally, a long-awaited trip overseas. The rest of the world had no idea what they were in for!

AC 5 DC

T.N.T. OR FIVE GUYS IN A VAN PILLAGE ENGLAND

To promote the new album, *Countdown* shot a video of the band playing "It's A Long Way To The Top (If You Wanna Rock 'N' Roll)." The song was Number Five on the Australian charts and the band lip-synched their way through Melbourne on the back of a flatbed truck, accompanied by three professional bagpipers, lots of fans, and a camera crew.

Later, they were filmed in a rock quarry in the western suburbs of Melbourne playing "Jailbreak." Paul Drane directed the videos for "Jailbreak" and "It's A Long Way To The Top" with a budget of only $5,000. Drane was quoted in Peter Wilmoth's book, *Glad All Over: The Countdown Years 1974–1987,* "We had a set in a quarry where we could use explosives. Our special-effects guy was thrilled because in those days there wasn't a lot of opportunity for that sort of stuff. Part of the set blew up and you can see me in the clip running away. Bon Scott was in the foreground, just before the bit where he got shot. A make-up artist had put some pellets in his back. Nobody got hurt, but Angus—who was standing on a rock playing guitar—got a bit of a fright during one of those bangs."

T.N.T. sold 11,000 copies in the first week of release. It could have been because the band was so popular, or due to the fact that the album was wrapped in a pair of ladies knickers. We may never know. It reached Number Two on the national charts and within weeks, *T.N.T.* was certified triple Gold with the release of their next single, "T.N.T." with B-side "Rocker."

With all their success, George and Harry were convinced that they needed to get back into the studio to cut AC/DC's third album. In February, they recorded nine songs that would become the gem, *Dirty Deeds Done Dirt Cheap*. Angus came up with the album's title, which was taken from the cartoon, *Beanie and Cecil*. *Do you remember that show? The villain Dishonest John, used to carry a business card that said, "Dirty Deeds Done Dirt Cheap. Holidays, Sundays, and Special Rates." For Christmas of 1963, I actually received a Dishonest John hand puppet from that show. How funny to find out one of my favorite AC/DC songs was inspired by a boy and his pet serpent! Come to think of it, aren't they all?*

Very quickly, they laid down nine tracks, including "Dirty Deeds Done Dirt Cheap," "Ain't No Fun (Waiting Around To Be A Millionaire)," "There's Gonna Be Some Rockin,'" "Problem Child," "Squealer," "Rock In Peace," "Jailbreak," Bon's future anthem, "Ride On," and "Big Balls." The lyrics to "Big Balls" are a fantastically funny display of Bon's use of sexual innuendo. He delighted in the turning of a phrase, and as Malcolm once said, was also obsessed with his balls. Both worthy traits.

While the band recorded their tracks, Bon would take their songs and play them on his cassette player. From there he would figure out what lyrics would inspire him. To enhance that nice raspy edge to his voice, his morning ritual was to gargle with red wine and honey. *I can just imagine singers in AC/DC tribute bands all over the world taking note of this concoction.*

While the band was recording, their manager Browning was finally able to secure a tour through the United Kingdom supporting ex-Free guitarist, Paul Kossoff's band, Back Street Crawler. Browning was offered a deal by AC/DC's first booking agent in England, Richard Griffiths. When Browning walked into the Virgin Agency in 1975, Griffiths remembered seeing the video of AC/DC playing live in Melbourne for the first time. He thought the band was amazing. Soon he left Virgin to form his own booking company called Headline Artists. His first two clients were AC/DC and Paul Kossoff. Booking AC/DC to support Kossoff in England was a perfect way to help them launch their overseas attack.

To celebrate, AC/DC played a farewell concert at Sydney's Bondi Lifesaver. For the first time ever, Angus mooned the crowd. Considering all the grief Australia would give the band over the coming years, mooning the crowd was a most-appropriate send off.

Musician Spencer Jones, whose band ended up covering "Ride On," was at their last show at the Lifesaver. He remembers it changed his life, recalling in *Highway To Hell,* "During the show, a rather large girl got up onstage and stripped naked, while Angus made it all the way to the bar on someone's shoulders to do his Chuck Berry duck walk. Then Bon picked up the naked girl, and put her on his shoulders. The place was packed, and the crowd went crazy." *I like to think their upcoming assault on the motherland was karmic payback for the Brits banishing their criminals to the outback in the first place.*

Before leaving, they attended a Gold-record reception and farewell party in Melbourne where they were presented with three plaques: two for *High Voltage* and one for *T.N.T.* After two years of solid touring, those albums would eventually gain Silver, Gold, and Platinum status in Australia. The night before they flew to England, the band also celebrated Angus's twenty-first birthday. Although according to his press kit, he was only seventeen.

AC/DC arrived in London, England on April 8, 1976, ready to knock the British music invasion on its royal crown. Rock 'n' roll was being infringed upon by the punk movement, which made it the perfect time for AC/DC to invade. The Queen was celebrating her jubilee and The Sex Pistols were enjoying success from their rewritten version of "God Save The Queen."

Browning had slyly kept their departure to England low key, seeing too many bands previously fall on their faces and come home with their tails between their legs. Angus was unaffected by all of this. He was quoted in England's *Record Mirror & Disc,* saying, "Success there [in Australia] means nothing. We left on a peak rather than overstay our welcome, and set out to plunder and pillage." They set out to pillage, riding around in a van with Phil behind the wheel. Being a car fanatic, he preferred to be the band's designated driver.

They played their first gig in England at the Red Cow pub in Hammersmith, where they became fixtures. They also got a regular spot playing a club called the Nashville Rooms. Originally they had been scheduled to play with Paul Kossoff's band, Back Street Crawler. Unfortunately, by the time they landed in London, Paul was dead from ill health due to years of abuse from heroin addiction. Bon was sentimentally quoted as saying in Martin Huxley's *AC/DC: World's Heaviest Rock,* "That cunt Paul Kossoff fucked up our first tour. Wait'll Angus gets a hold of him."

The change of plans didn't slow the band down at all. Once again, they played wherever they could, picking up club dates all around England. The British music scene, as Angus remembers it, was a real throwback. He told Jodi Summers Dorland in *Hit Parader,* "When Bon first walked onstage in a little club in London, the audience was made up of your Johnny Rottens and all of those people. Bon, being older, would go out there and really strut his stuff. Then, I remember seeing Rotten and those punks the next week, wearing the same clothes and haircut as Bon."

Oh yes, they would be noticed in England. Noticed and injured, that is. One of the first things Bon did when he got to London was to visit the pub in Finchley where he bartended during his days in Fraternity. The minute he walked into the place, someone threw a full pint of beer hitting him in the face. He said he walked into the middle of someone else's fight. Bon suffered a black eye and dislocated jaw. In pictures from their first photo session in England, he covered his injuries by wearing dark glasses. On the upside, if there could be one, this forced Bon to have extensive dental work done, which was very much needed since his motorbike accident.

Upon their arrival in England, the British division of Atlantic Records issued a combination of *High Voltage* and *T.N.T.,* making it their first European release. The American/British cover would feature Angus in school uniform, aping at the camera, with a lightning bolt shooting down into his foot. It was actually the Australian version of T.N.T., but with two songs from *High Voltage* on it. "She's Got Balls" and "Little Lover" were included in place of "Rocker" and Chuck Berry's "School Days." If the majority of songs were from *T.N.T.,* then why was the album called *High Voltage? Confused? Good, because I am.*

Whether it was actually *High Voltage* or *T.N.T.,* this album got the attention of BBC Radio 1 disc jockey, John Peel. In June AC/DC recorded a 4-track session in Maida Vale 4 Studios in London for Peel's radio show. That's exactly what the doctor ordered, live AC/DC on the British airwaves. *I don't care how menacing The Sex Pistols were, Sid Vicious had nothing on Bon!*

Although Coral Browning wasn't officially on the payroll, she was offered an office at London's Atlantic Records to help Michael out with the band. She quickly persuaded journalists Caroline Coon and Phil McNeill to come out to see them. McNeill reviewed their performance at London's Nashville Rooms for the *New Musical Express* with the headline, "I Wallaby Your Man." "In the middle of the great British Punk Rock Explosion, a quintet of similarly ruthless Ozzies has just swaggered like a cat among London's surly, self-consciously paranoid pigeons...and with a sense of what sells rather than what's cool, they could well clean up...We're impressed."

The British rock press at the time was ruled by *Melody Maker, New Musical Express,* and *Sounds* (which was the newest paper debuting in 1970). *Sounds* immediately got behind AC/DC and put them at the top of the list in its "New Order Top 20." Behind them were Eddie And The Hot Rods, The Sex Pistols, The Damned, Iggy Pop And The Stooges, Ted Nugent, Rainbow, Motorhead, Judas Priest, and sharing last position, The Ramones and The Dictators.

Their nine-date tour supporting Back Street Crawler, which was postponed due to Paul Kossof's death, opened at the famed Marquee Club in May. [Kossof was replaced by guitarist Geoff Whitehorn.] This was the place to play in London, having hosted acts like Jimi Hendrix; Led Zeppelin; and Emerson, Lake, and Palmer, among many others. Rock journalist Phil Sutcliffe reviewed the show and predicted the band would be huge. He quickly became one of their biggest supporters in print.

On June 4, they played their first headlining gig at the Marquee, launching a 19-date club tour sponsored by *Sounds* magazine, most delinquently titled, the Lock Up Your Daughters Summer Tour. Their set included a live DJ and featured film clips from other bands.

Before the show that night, while everyone was nervously waiting for Bon to arrive, Browning asked a photographer to go outside and take a picture of the marquee which read, "Sold-Out-AC/DC." After the shot was taken, Bon walked in the side door to everyone's relief. A few days later, the photographer brought the pictures around for Browning to see. There was the marquee and underneath it was Bon, all alone, walking past the venue on his way to the gig. There was no entourage and no hired car for the rising rock star. Just very casual—and unpretentious—and so very Bon.

When Malcolm and Angus returned to their birthplace of Glasgow, the audience destroyed the first two rows of seats at the City Hall. A fine welcome for the band, considering most of the audience—according to Bon— was made up of Angus and Malcolm's relatives. *I guess that really shouldn't be a surprise.* While in Scotland, the Young's enjoyed a reunion and Phil and Bon went driving off into the countryside looking for Bon's family roots. There are reports that all they found were two bears shagging in the woods. *I'll bet that delighted Bon just as much as finding a long-lost cousin.*

On June 12, Angus was featured on the cover of *Sounds* magazine...his first of literally thousands of future magazine covers to come. Their single "Jailbreak" with B-side "Fling Thing," was released in Australia. "Fling Thing" was a Scottish traditional song that was not included on any of their albums. One more thing to throw off the most ardent collector. [*For the AC/DC fan that wants to keep all their single releases straight, a master discography is printed at the back of this book.*]

On the last date of their United Kingdom tour at the Lyceum in London,

Atlantic Records arranged a "Best Schoolboy/Schoolgirl" competition. Other sources say it was a contest to look for the "Schoolgirl we'd most like to..." There was no evidence that Bon wore his dress and braids for the event. If he had, he probably would have won. The actual winner, Jayne Haynes from Middlesex, England, won a folk guitar and a night out with bassist Mark Evans. Bon was not happy. Maybe Bon's jealousy was the real reason for Mark's impending dismissal from the band.

Two nights later they celebrated Bon's thirtieth birthday, but he was a no show for his own party. Something that wasn't all that unusual, as he often preferred to go off on his own. He ended up being gone for three days, hiding out with his girlfriend, Silver [Margaret] Smith. Hitting the big 3-0 back in the mid-Seventies must have been traumatic for him. Especially when you recall the popular Sixties phrase, "Don't trust anyone over 30!"

In July, they played their first European tour through Holland, Austria, and five dates in Sweden.

The Swedish tour was arranged by Tomas Johansen, who represented Abba. He originally had trouble getting Abba into Australia, but was able to strike a deal to bring AC/DC into Sweden and Abba into Australia. *As far as I'm concerned, not a fair trade for Australia.* Before the band left for Sweden, they filmed a 20-minute segment for Mike Mansfield's *Superpop,* a British television program which also featured Malcolm's idol, Marc Bolan and his band, T. Rex.

While on tour, Bon was to keep the Australian press informed of their adventures, and/or misadventures, writing home to Debbie Sharpe of the *Melbourne Herald.* He reported that the Swedish clubs dates were more like cabaret, with polkas, folk songs, and beer. *Now I know why they enjoyed Wisconsin so much!*

Bon's favorite Swedish staples were the topless beaches and the swimming pools. And Bon loved to swim. According to Mark Evans, the rest of the band couldn't have cared less about these perks. Angus and Malcolm had tunnel vision. All they wanted to do was play. They were convinced that someday they were going to make it big and everything else was secondary. Malcolm's favorite saying was, "We're just waiting around to become filthy rich."

Somehow the band managed to fit in some recording time at Vineyard Studios in England to lay down "Dirty Eyes," "Carry Me Home," "Love At First Feel," and "Cold Hearted Man." The four-song EP was never released, with each of these songs appearing later in various forms: on albums, as singles, and in the future box set, *Bonfire.* That same month, they made their European television debut playing "Jailbreak" on the *So It Goes* show in London.

Their appearance at the Orange Festival in Nimes, France in August was canceled, but on the twenty-eighth, they filmed a 3-track live performance at the Wimbleton Theatre in London for the *Rollin' Bolan Show* which aired on the U.K.'s weekend television. If that wasn't enough excitement for one month, they played with Ted Nugent, Brand X, and Black Oak Arkansas at the Reading Rock Festival in the U.K. on the twenty-ninth, in front of 50,000 people. The word "whirlwind" should be inserted here. George, Harry Vanda, and Michael and Coral Browning all made the trip to see them play. Supposedly their set didn't receive the usual reaction from the audience, which caused tension within the band and management. *Some sources called this performance a "misfire" for AC/DC, which you and I both know is an impossibility. 50,000 people can be wrong, you know!*

By the end of the summer, AC/DC had became the house band at the Marquee, breaking attendance records by bringing in over 1,400 fans every Monday night. And that's not counting the ones who were left standing outside! This inspiring *New Musical Express* to write, "The only sound coming through the wall was *chunka-chunka-chunka,* while the bar resounded with ribald Aussies telling me to watch for Angus Young to expose himself. When he stripped off to his knickers and leapt on an amp, a well-informed source rose and said, 'My God, he's been wearing the same underpants for four weeks.'"

Exactly the press that their booking agent Griffiths was looking for when he struck a deal with the Marquee booker Jack Berry to let them play there once a week. Plus, all the local magazines ran full-page ads for AC/DC's Marquee dates, including comments from Berry comparing them to Led Zeppelin. When they first started playing every Monday night, there weren't that many people at their shows. Atlantic Records promotions man, Dave Jarrett, started bringing staff out to see them. Before long the band was drawing so many people, that Jarrett himself couldn't get in.

It's fair to say at the time that there were three popular styles of rock artists. The multi-membered orchestral bands, such as Pink Floyd and Yes. Then there were the hippie rock bands or folk singers, like Grateful Dead and Bob Dylan. And last, but definitely not least, were the straight-up fry-your-brain-to-the-speaker-column arena rock like Led Zeppelin, The Who, and Black Sabbath. AC/DC mowed down all of that, including punk and everything else that was in their way.

After the release of the United Kingdom's version of *High Voltage,* author Mark Putterford's review of this album appeared in *Kerrang!* It

deserves to be repeated: "Snotty nostrils a-flarin,' crooked teeth a-gnashin',
and grubby knees a-tremblin,' the crazed Just William exaggeration begins
to nod uncontrollably as his pale, boney hands jerk across the live wires in
his grasp. The simple infectious riff that marched in "It's A Long Way To
The Top" was the leak that would burst the banks of contemporary rock. It
introduced us bewildered Britfolk to the outrageous high-voltage antics of
Australia's youthful delinquents, AC/DC, who were destined to riff all over
the opposition for years to come." *Amen, brother!*

Due to *T.N.T.* still selling 3,000 to 4,000 units per week, Albert Music
delayed the release of *Dirty Deeds Done Dirt Cheap* in Australia until
September 20, along with the first single from the album, "Dirty Deeds
Done Dirt Cheap" with "R.I.P." The album cover was a caricature of Bon
swinging his tattooed arm and Angus flipping the bird. Later, the American
release would feature seven people and a dog standing in the parking lot of
a motel. Everyone's eyes are covered by black boxes, except the dog's, who
was apparently unconcerned for his identity.

The band never slowed down enough to celebrate the record's release
and continued to tour throughout France, Switzerland, Belgium, Denmark,
Sweden, and Germany for 19 dates in support of Rainbow. Aside from
Blackmore's nasty temper, the only downside was a huge replica of a rainbow on stage, which kept falling over during the band's performance.

The *High Voltage* compilation had sold 16,000 copies the first week of
its release in Germany, proving the Germans knew quality rock 'n' roll
when they heard it. Of course it was never easy for any band to have to follow AC/DC's set and one night, Ritchie Blackmore refused to let them do
an encore. The fans were so upset, many of them walked out before
Rainbow came on.

On September 28, 1976, the United States got their first taste of AC/DC
when High Voltage was released to barely a whimper across the airwaves.
How embarrassing...for us Americans, not the band.

Rock journalist Billy Altman wrote in *Rolling Stone* in October, "Those
concerned with the future of hard rock may take solace in knowing that
with the release of the first U.S. album by these Australian gross-out cham-
pions, the genre has unquestionably hit its all-time low. Lead singer Bon
Scott spits out his vocals with a truly annoying aggression which, I suppose, is the only way to do it when all you seem to care about is being a star
so that you can get laid every night. Stupidity bothers me.

Calculated stupidity offends me." *Ouch! Somebody sounds jealous.
Makes you want to cancel your subscription, doesn't it?*

Luckily for Altman, the band had to postpone their tour of the States that fall due to visa problems, considering Michael and Bon both had convictions for pot possession. *Besides, were we ready for AC/DC in 1976? Considering that Captain And Tennille had one of the biggest songs on the American charts that year with "Muskrat Love," I think not.*

Their visa problems were the least of their worries since vice squads were following them all over on tour, threatening to arrest Angus if he dropped his pants. Luckily this wasn't Bon's concern, or half the female population of Australia would have revolted. On the bright side, the ever-so-smarter *Billboard* magazine put *High Voltage* on their "Recommended LPs" list, and wrote, "Australia's newest entry is a cross between Led Zeppelin and the Sensational Alex Harvey Band. Lead singer has a very unique-sounding voice and the twin guitars are front and center from the first cut. Expect airplay on progressive stations."

At the end of October they earned the distinction of being refused the chance to perform at Southhampton University, due to their music containing 'blatant vulgar and cheap references to both sexes.' And that's a bad thing?

Dirty Deeds Done Dirt Cheap was released on November 5 in Britain. A few days later, the band played their first headlining concert at London's Hammersmith Odeon: half the audience arriving in schoolboy uniforms was a sure sign that AC/DC was catching on.

The second week of November saw their return to Glasgow, which was reviewed by the *East Kilbride News* on November 11, 1976. "'High Voltage' aroused the audience to greater heights—but the stage reached its climax when the band burst into 'Baby, Please Don't Go.' Angus, having dispensed with the uniform, fell to the floor, wriggling around like a severed worm. Then he climbed to the top of a column of speakers while Bon Scott mounted those on the other side of the stage. Angus reverted to playing his guitar with one hand, Bon screamed out the lyrics before jumping back onto the stage, and catching Angus as he leapt down—still clutching his guitar. And the incredible thing about the whole routine was that is was executed to perfection without Angus missing so much as a solitary chord. The audience was left breathless."

Breathless, and I'll bet frustrated, taking into account that security wouldn't let the audience get out of their seats. Obviously due to the fact that those crazy Scottish rockers ripped them out the last time AC/DC was in town. (The real story is that they stood on their chairs the first time they saw the band and had broken off some of the backs of the seats. It's just funnier to say they ripped them out altogether.) *Making fans sit still while watching AC/DC live onstage was cruel and inhumane punishment. The one and only AC/DC concert I am not sorry to say I missed. No, I don't mean that. Watching AC/DC while strapped down horizontally on a Thorazine drip would still be a treat for me!*

Their first stateside single—"It's A Long Way To The Top (If You Wanna Rock 'N' Roll)" with B-side "High Voltage"—was released in November of 1976. They played a Christmas show at the Hammersmith Odeon—which would become a yearly tradition—and then headed home to Australia to launch a 26-date tour called A Giant Dose Of Rock 'N' Roll.

AC/DC was met at the airport by hundreds of screaming fans, many already sporting tattoos immortalizing their rock 'n' roll heroes. The opening date of the tour was a sold-out show at the Myer Music Bowl. Although they were gaining more and more fans, their tongue-in-cheek lyrics and "leering at your daughter" attitude continually caused problems. Their Australian tour was fraught with difficulties. Many dates were cancelled or threatened in some way. Due to the obscene images of the band that had been generated by the media, Australia's Parliament actually discussed AC/DC and their possible bad influence on the nation's youth. Too late.

They did get a lot of free publicity when a rich widow started getting phone calls after Bon sings *'just ring 36-24-36,'* in the song, "Dirty Deeds Done Dirt Cheap." Their publicist Chris Gilby had to release a public apology for the band. More coverage followed when the Mayor of Tamworth refused them permission to play his city. The news crew from Channel Nine's *A Current Affair* even flew in to report the tragedy. *My condolences to the AC/DC fans of Tamworth.*

One station, 2SM, a previous supporter that was owned by the Catholic Church, apparently didn't appreciate anything called a Giant Dose of Rock 'N' Roll. Their main beef was Angus exposing himself. This prompted Bon to state in Australia's *RAM,* "You see his backside in the papers more than you see his face—which is preferential as far as I'm concerned."

The station refused AC/DC airplay after 2SM's general manager said, "Members of the Australian punk-rock group AC/DC must decide if they are strippers or musicians. Until they do, the station will not associate with them in any way." *Knowing them, my guess is being called a "punk rock" group upset them more than getting no airplay!*

The newspapers declared, "Rock Band Threatens To Leave Country," which ran a quote from Angus: "It's no good if we drive half way across the country to stage a concert to find that someone has cancelled it because they consider us obscene. It will only take a couple more hassles from the authorities and we will leave Australia."

Further irritation was caused when the 1976 to 1977 tour book was pulled from sale at their second date in Albury for its "obscene" nature. The straw that broke Parliament's back was credited to a comment made by bassist Mark Evans, even though it was actually said by Bon. In response to the meaning of his lyrics to "Ain't No Fun (Waiting Around To Be A Millionaire"), Bon's priceless quote was: "It means that it takes a long time to make enough money to be able to fuck Britt Ekland." Britt was the Swedish sexpot who married the late Sir Peter Sellers, of course when he was still alive. *I think. She also hooked up with Rod Stewart for a while, and somewhere off in the distant future, devoured one of The Stray Cats, if I remember correctly.*

At least someone stood by them when Australia's *RAM* wrote, "Loud seems too tame a description for the volume they inflict on an audience. It's more a 'living sound' that actually penetrates the flesh and bones until movement and rhythm come involuntarily and the audience is swept into the same current...behind the insistency lies an excellent rock/blues outfit with an amazing singer out front in Bon Scott." This could quite possibly be the best description ever written about the band.

On top of everything else, Browning was informed that the American division of Atlantic Records refused to release *Dirty Deeds Done Dirt Cheap* stateside and the band was in danger of losing their American record deal altogether. No thanks to *Rolling Stone* magazine. Luckily, Phil Carson in the London office was able to persuade them to stick with the band. Although, it has also been said that the American division of Atlantic Records wanted to replace Bon and that is why they refused to release *Dirty Deeds* over here in the first place. Silly suits. Except for the rare import, we wouldn't see an official copy of *Dirty Deeds Done Dirt Cheap* sold here in the United States until 1981.

AC/DC appeared live on *Countdown* playing "Dirty Deeds Done Dirt Cheap" on December 5, before enjoying a short Christmas break. Bon celebrated New Years Eve by watching Rose Tattoo perform at a local club. He was so impressed with the band that he helped them get signed by the Alberts.

After the first of the year, the band went back into Alberts studio to record their fourth album. Fortified by three years of constant touring, guided by the dream team of Young and Vanda, this next album would be a real turning point for AC/DC and their sound. They most righteously christened it *Let There Be Rock.*

Malcolm, Phil, Angus, Bon, and the newest AC/DC member, Cliff Williams. © W. Roelen/LFI

Phil, Angus, Mark Evans, Malcolm, and Bon: the original bad boys of rock. (1977) © Hulton Archive/Getty Images

AC/DC performing at the Aragon Ballroom in Chicago, Illinois (September 22, 1978). © Paul Natkin

omotional glossy of AC/DC during the Let There Be Rock tour.

Bon Scott Live at the Stone Hearth in Madison, WI. © Keith Wessel

ngus, victorious after mooning the crowd. © Paul Natkin

Angus doing his famous "walk-about." © Frank Griffin/LFI

AC/DC at the Sunshine Pop Stars concert (1980). © Mazel/Retna UK

Bon Scott in all his glory (1979). © Anastasia Pantsios/LFI

As author Mark Putterford once wrote, "[Angus]...Snotty nostrils a-flarin', crooked teeth a-gnashin,' and grubby knees a tremblin'..." © Paul Canty/LFI

You can't take them anywhere! © Janet Macoska

hil, Angus, Bon, Malcolm, and Cliff relaxing at the record company.

3on, Phil, Angus, Mark Evans, and Malcolm, ain't no fun waitin' around to be a millionaire!" © LFI

Promotional glossy of Angus from their *Powerage* press kit.

AC/DC backstage at Radio Luxenburg (1976).
© Dick Barnatt/Redferns/Retna

Phil Rudd at the Aragon Ballroom in Chicago September 22, 1978. © Paul Natkin

...reviously released publicity picture of the band, which ended up being used for the cover of the *Highway To Hell* album.

AC/DC backstage during the Back In Black U.K. tour, Birmingham, GB (October 22, 1980). © George Chin/WireImage

Malcolm Young, riff-maniac incorporated.
© Deborah Feingold/ Hulton Archive/Getty Images

Cliff Williams, master of the eighth note.
© Deborah Feingold/ Hulton Archive/Getty Images

Brian, Cliff, Angus, new drummer Simon Wright, and Malcolm—bathing beauties at the beach in Ipanema, Brazil (1985). © Dave Hogan/LFI

AC 6 DC

DIRTY DEEDS DONE DIRT CHEAP

AC/DC played 16 Australian dates in January and February of 1977, which unbelievably would be the last official performances by Bon in his homeland. The single "Dirty Deeds Done Dirt Cheap" with B-sides "Big Balls" and "The Jack" was released in the United Kingdom. At the same time in Australia, Alberts released "Love At First Feel" and "Problem Child." Side A was recorded at Vineyard Studios in England the previous summer. On the thirtieth of January, the band played at the old Haymarket warehouse for the Festival Of Sydney. As usual, they blew away the headliners, fellow compatriots The Little River Band.

Completing a tour across Adelaide, Perth, and Melbourne, AC/DC went back into Albert Studios in Sydney and recorded eight new songs. They still play some of these tracks live in concert today, over a quarter of a century later. To say these particular tunes would have longevity is putting it mildly. The album included the title track, "Let There Be Rock." The other seven cuts were "Go Down," "Dog Eat Dog," "Bad Boy Boogie," "Problem Child," "Overdose," "Hell Ain't A Bad Place To Be," and the ever-so lascivious, "Whole Lotta Rosie."

The title of "Rosie" is Bon's nod to Led Zeppelin's "Whole Lotta Love." This song is the epitome of how Bon's female conquests inspired his songwriting. If perhaps she wasn't the most memorable encounter while on the road, she was at least the largest. Later, a trimmer Rosie visited with the band while on tour, much to Bon's disappointment since her measurements no longer fit the song.

Of course, "Bad Boy Boogie" would become the soundtrack for Angus's hysterical nightly strip tease. The biggest joke of all is watching a sweaty pint-size schoolboy strutting around the stage trying to be sexy. Often after Angus pulls off his shirt, he will blow his nose into it, signifying that he laughs hardest at this image of himself.

Malcolm was quoted in *Metal CD* about the recording of *Let There Be Rock*. "Now that was a steamer. I suppose we were a bit more serious and we wanted to get a rawer sound and cut out the commercial choruses like "T.N.T." We knew exactly what we wanted, which was to have three really strong live tracks to flesh out the set. "Whole Lotta Rosie," we knew, would be a surefire winner, and "Bad Boy Boogie" and "Let There Be Rock" were the other two that we felt would really go the distance on stage. Those three have really overshadowed most of the other songs on the album and ended up in the live set for years after."

The cover of *Let There Be Rock* was a picture of the band live on stage, doing what they do best: enthralling audiences. Capturing rock 'n' roll lightning in a bottle only took a couple of weeks and the band again left for the U.K. In Edinburgh on February 18, they launched a 26-date tour in support of *Dirty Deeds Done Dirt Cheap*.

National RockStar wrote on February 26, 1977 about the Edinburgh University show: "The trouble started after the first number "Live Wire" and in the middle of "Eat Dog" [sic]. Some of the audience spilled over onto the stage to sit on the monitor speakers, inches away from their new heroes. Some of the crowd were being held back by the stewards and they didn't like it. Fights broke out all over the front of the hall…It was the presence of 17-year-old Angus Young in black velvet school blazer and shorts and a little leather satchel which sparked off the bizarre audience reaction…AC/DC have it. It's more than just rock—it's provocation. They will be the band of '77."

Let There Be Rock was released in Australia on March 21, 1977. The cover artwork featured their lightning-bolt logo for the first time. Whenever Bon was asked if he was AC or DC, he would laughingly reply, "Neither, I'm the lightnin' flash in the middle!" How right he was.

Their Glasgow University performance was reviewed by Eric Wishart for the *Record Mirror* on February 26: "Angus Young on lead guitar was amazing. Dressed in his standard short pants schoolboy gear he twitched, jerked, and bounded across the stage nonstop, his head whipping back and forth until it looked as if it just had to come flying off…Centerplace was an extended "The Jack," their ode to that dreaded disease which Bob [sic]

Scott introduced with a reworking of "Maria" that would have made the heroes of *West Side Story* think at least twice before approaching Natalie Wood."

Describing their appeal to the fans, Bon told the *New Musical Express,* "The music press is totally out of touch with what their kids actually want to listen to. These kids might be working in a shitty factory all week, or they might be on the dole—come the weekend, they just want to go out and have a good time, get drunk, and go wild. We give them the opportunity to do that." One of AC/DC's best qualities has always been keeping their priorities straight.

Once back in London, Angus and Malcolm moved into an apartment—or a flat as the Brits call it—in Ladbroke Grove. Phil and Mark got one close by and Bon stayed with his girlfriend, Silver. In Clinton Walker's book, *Highway To Hell,* Silver remembered Bon, "As far as my life goes, I don't think anyone loved me as unconditionally as Bon. He had no complaints—they were all on my side. It gave me the guilts for quite a long time. Because Bon was really good to me. He accepted me exactly as I was. He was really attentive too, you know, two or three letters a day bombarding you when he was on the road, and he was always bringing flowers and little presents. I mean, it was full on, right up until we split up." She went on to describe Bon as a very "pipe and slippers" kind of guy, who enjoyed a clean, peaceful home, with dinners on Sundays. Just the way he grew up.

On March 5, Ian Flavin wrote in *National RockStar,* "They sure get down to it. Australia's exiled bad boys came on in strictly $\frac{4}{4}$ time and hammered out a mean dose of street corner rock 'n' roll from start to finish...Malcolm Young, the rhythm guitarist, seemed to be the driving pivot, churning out slashing bashing power chords with the musical finesse of a caged tiger...[Angus] delivered a constant stream of red-hot licks in the best guitar-hero fashion. He's 17. If he's still playing when he reaches 25, that might be something truly amazing to dig." How about still playing at 50 years old?

That spring their single "Dog Eat Dog" with B-side "Carry Me Home" was released in Australia. The B-side doesn't appear on any of their albums, again frustrating collectors worldwide. The single "Love At First Feel" is their last song to chart in Australia until the release of *Highway To Hell.* On April third in London, the band appeared on *Countdown's* fifth anniversary special, playing "Dog Eat Dog."

Their European tour of 12 dates included opening for the legendary Black Sabbath in Sweden. Unfortunately, Sabbath was also becoming legendary for their alcoholism and drug abuse. The band was in disarray and matters only became worse when AC/DC blew Black Sabbath off the stage every night. In retaliation, Sabbath kept shortening AC/DC's opening set. One night, the tension finally exploded and Sabbath's bass player Geezer Butler pulled a flick knife on Malcolm. Of course Mal started swinging and AC/DC was fired off the tour. This night would also be bassist Mark Evan's last performance with the band.

I guess you really haven't lived the rock 'n' roll lifestyle until you can say you threw a punch at one of the gods of rock. To be fair to Malcolm, years later Butler admitted that he had finally given up drinking after head butting someone in an argument in front of his hotel the night before. The next morning he went outside and discovered the object of his intense irritation was a statue. My guess is that the statue refused to move. That story alone should always be included at all AA meetings.

Although in *Q* magazine in the 'Cash For Questions' fan feature it stated: "AC/DC has come clean about a knife-pulling incident during the group's 1977 tour opening for Black Sabbath in Europe." Malcolm's version of the story: "We were staying in the same hotel, and Geezer was in the bar, crying in his beer, '10 years I've been in this band—10 years—wait 'til you guys have been around for 10 years, you'll feel like us.' I said, 'I don't think so.' I was giving him no sympathy. He's had many, too many [drinks], and he pulled out this silly flick knife. As luck would have it, Ozzy walked in. He goes, 'You fuckin' idiot Butler—go to bed!' Ozzy saved the day, and we sat up all night with him."

At the end of the United Kingdom tour, Mark Evans was fired from the band...supposedly over personality clashes with Angus. Some smart-ass was quoted as saying, "His downfall was his being too nice to last." Evans at first accepted a flat payment of $2,000 against future royalties, but 10 years later won a generous settlement from Albert Music.

Angus had his eye on the bass player from Manfred Mann's Earth Band, Colin Pattendon. But Browning had a lead on an English bass player who was working with Bandit. His name was Cliff Williams.

Clifton Williams was born in Romford (Essex), England on December 14, 1949. When he was nine years old, his family moved to Liverpool. Cliff's musical influences were The Beatles, The Kinks, and some blues artists. When he was 13, all his friends had started forming bands. By the time he was 16, Cliff was playing bass...with his only formal training coming from learning some riffs from a professional bass player who lived nearby. There is no evidence that his name was Paul McCartney.

Before music became his vocation, he spent two years working as an engineer in an office behind the Lime Street railway station in Liverpool. Cliff's first band featured singer Mick Stubbs, keyboard player Clive John, guitarist Laurie Wisefield, and drummer Mick Cook. They were called Home. In 1970, Home signed a recording contract with Epic Records and released *Pause For A Hoarse Horse. Don't look at me, I just report the facts.*

While in Home, Cliff supported Led Zeppelin at the Wembley Empire Pool on the second concert date of their Electric Magic tour in November of 1971. The show featured circus acts and rock bands. *One and the same, when you think about it.*

By 1972, Jim Anderson replaced Clive John on keyboards and the band released a self-titled album. That release included their one hit, the song "Dreamer," which made it to Number 41 on the British charts. Their third and final release was *The Alchemist* in 1973.

Home was asked to back Al Stewart on his first American tour in 1974. Mick Stubbs left the band, and the rest of the group became The Al Stewart Band. Cliff didn't last very long playing Stewart's music. He left before the year was out and formed his own band, Bandit, with vocalist Jim Diamond and drummer Graham Broad. They were immediately signed to Arista Records and released a self-titled debut album in 1977.

After placing an ad in *Sounds* magazine, AC/DC auditioned over 50 bass players. Cliff explained to *Guitar School:* "I auditioned. The band was looking to strengthen up their rhythm section, so they came to London where there was a larger pool of players. They had a few records out at that point, were successful in Australia and toured Europe once or twice, but hadn't been to the States yet. They were looking to tour the U.S. behind the *Let There Be Rock* album. Anyway, I got a call from a friend of a friend who thought I might be right for the job, and I ended up auditioning a number of times."

They held the auditions in a tiny room in Victoria and the first tracks they played with Cliff were "Live Wire," "Problem Child," and an old blues number. Just before his audition, a friend had tipped him off that the band preferred their bassists to play with a pick, rather than with their fingers. Cliff was asked to join the band on May 27, 1977, and Angus was quoted as saying that Cliff was hired due to his good looks being able to attract more girls. *On behalf of all us girls Angus, thank you very much!*

The addition of Cliff delighted Bon, since he was closest to Bon's age. (Cliff was three years younger.) Cliff also had a lot in common with Bon. They liked movies, books, and girls. *Although, I doubt in that order.* As soon as he joined the band, they flew back to Australia to work him in.

In June, Angus and Bon appeared onstage with Rose Tattoo at the Bondi Lifesaver. It was time to prepare for their first long-awaited tour of the United States. *Let There Be Rock* was released in the States on July 23, 1977, just four days before they would play the Amarillo World Headquarters in Austin, Texas. The album would eventually peak on the *Billboard* charts at Number 154. Before they left for America, AC/DC played two undercover shows at the Bondi. The first night they used the name The Seedies. The second night they called themselves Dirty Deeds.

In anticipation of their arrival in the States, Atlantic hired a new promotions team to handle the band. The late Perry Cooper's first assignment with Atlantic was to promote AC/DC. "I was working with Michael Klenfner at Arista Records, who was vice president of promotions. I was director of special projects, but I had a bunch of titles. We spent two years at Arista during the early days, we worked with Barry Manilow, Melissa Manchester, Outlaws, Bay City Rollers, it was wonderful. We had a great time. Then when he got offered this opportunity at Atlantic, he took me with him. We were sent over to Atlantic as a package deal.

"Right after we went to Atlantic, Jerry Greenberg came to Michael one day and said, 'We've got this band from Australia, they're doing fairly well and we signed them to a long-term contract. But their lyrics are a little risque and we're not getting any radio play. So could you guys look them over and see what you can do?

So he gave us a kinescope, it was really weird, like a film. It had a cartridge that you put into this machine, and we looked at it. No, actually I looked at it. Michael, who will deny this, told me to look at it because he didn't give a shit. So I looked at it and saw this guitarist doing a duck walk. And I thought, 'Well, he's a little bit copying Chuck Berry,' but we should bring them over here and tour them, because they are terrific live. And that's what we did."

Once Cooper saw the kinescope of AC/DC live, he went back to Greenberg and convinced Atlantic that the band had potential. His idea was to bring AC/DC over to the States. "So they toured their asses off for two years straight. We just said, 'When people see them, they will love them!'"

AC/DC landed in the United States on July 27, 1977. Unlike The Beatles, they were able to sneak into the country without being noticed. Just like The Rolling Stones before them, the band got into a used station wagon and embarked on their first tour of the United States. The first three American dates AC/DC played were opening for the band Moxy, in Austin,

San Antonio, and Corpus Christi, Texas. The band went over very well in the Lone Star state, with Angus exclaiming Texan people, "Really know how to party!" On July 30, they played a free concert at the Electric Ballroom in Dallas hosted by radio station, K2EW.

From Texas, they drove to Florida...starting the long road that would stretch across two years and later become known as their personal "highway to hell." Their first date in Gainesville on August 4 was cancelled. On August 5 and 6, they co-headlined with REO Speedwagon in West Palm Beach and Jacksonville.

A radio station in Jacksonville programmed four or five of the band's songs into their play list. AC/DC had been getting paid five-hundred dollars a night to play a club, but when they got to Jacksonville with Pat Travers opening, they played in front of 8,000 people at the Coliseum. This coastal city would become one of AC/DC's strongest American markets.

After playing 'A Day For The Kids'—a charity date at the Sportatorium in Hollywood, Florida for radio station, WSHE in front of 13,000 people—they made their way into the heartland. Opening for Foreigner and UFO, AC/DC played at Mississippi Nights in St. Louis, Missouri on August 9, and at the Memorial Hall in Kansas City, Kansas on August 10. They appeared at B'Ginnings, a club in Schaumberg, Illinois and opened for Michael Stanley in Cleveland, Ohio. The next two nights AC/DC opened for The Dictators at the Agora in Columbus, before continuing their drive north toward Wisconsin. Bon wrote home to a friend that he, "Enjoyed America very much, especially the chicks."

AC/DC was booked to play a campus bar in downtown Madison on Tuesday, August 16, 1977. Technically the fifteenth date of their first American tour, but actually the fourteenth time they were ever to play here, considering Gainesville had been cancelled.

This historic occasion would fall on the same day Elvis Presley was found dead at the age of 42 in his bathroom at Graceland in Memphis. *The end of an era for many. And the beginning of a new one for me, considering that on that day, Angus, Malcolm, Bon, Cliff, and Phil arrived to play at the Stone Hearth in Madison, Wisconsin—my hometown. Lucky me!*

AC 7 DC

LET THERE BE ROCK

I've tried many times to remember what I was doing earlier that day, but the first memory I have of Tuesday, August 16, 1977 is driving by the newspaper I was writing for. Every radio station in the city [Madison, WI] was talking about Elvis's death. Personally I wasn't a huge Elvis fan, but I did feel sorry for him. Dying at the age of 42—with the talent and sex appeal that he had—was a pure tragedy. If I caught any radio spots advertising the band that was playing downtown that night, I don't recall hearing them.

Just as I was driving by the offices of the paper, something told me to stop and check on getting a new assignment. I had just started writing for the music rag a few weeks earlier, so I wasn't the first person they called when something needed to be covered. I was still fighting for my journalistic territory.

I stopped at the Madcity Music Sheet, *which was in an older building on the east side of Madison. The two writers who had started the paper had adorned the walls with posters of rock bands. Their matching desks were sitting next to each other, with a tent made from Indian-print bedspreads fashioned over the top of them. Very gypsy like. Or what I preferred to call, "Hippy Central."*

As I walked in the door, Gary Sohmers, the editor was just hanging up the phone. I told him that I had stopped in to see if there was anything that needed to be covered. He looked up at me and said someone from Stardate Productions, a large promotions company based in Milwaukee, had just called from the Stone Hearth. They were looking for someone to help out that night, nothing specific, just someone to run errands for the band, or do whatever was needed.

It sounded fairly easy to me, so I said I'd be happy to do it. As I walked out the door to go home and change, I turned around and asked him who the band was. Gary shook his head and said, "I don't know, some band from Australia called AC/DC." Little did I know that after that night, my life would never be the same.

Stardate wanted someone to come down to the club as soon as possible, so I ran home and changed, and took off for downtown around 4 o'clock. The Stone Hearth was a worn-down rock club in the midst of the University of Wisconsin-Madison campus. As soon as I got there, the promoter sent me out to the liquor store for Blue Nun wine for the lead singer.

When I got back, I took the bottle up to the dressing area and helped arrange some deli platters with cheese and crackers. I noticed a three-man road crew downstairs setting up the show. The band was out eating dinner at a local restaurant. Since there wasn't much else to do before they returned, I asked the promoter if he had any press materials about them that I could read. He handed me a single sheet of paper with the band's picture and a short biography on it. Their promotion boasted that AC/DC had start-ed brawls from one end of Europe to the other. Their black and white pho-tos were not very flattering. I was starting to wonder what I had gotten myself into!

Feeling a bit out of place, I went downstairs to watch the road crew. There were only three of them: two older-looking gentleman and a younger one with long, caramel-colored hair. While they were setting up the gear, they were laughing about what they thought of the United States. Apparently they weren't too impressed with us Yanks. I got closer and listened to them talk about how soft we Americans were and how we sent our children to school armed with calculators to learn math. I've always been a pretty opin-ionated person myself, so it wasn't a stretch for me to walk up to the young one and say, "Hey, the airport isn't that far away. Can I give you a lift?" Slightly shocked and a little bit amused, he turned around and asked me who I was. I introduced myself and as we shook hands, he said his name was Barry Taylor. Not only was he cute, but I could have listened to that English accent all day. Funny how accents can do that to a girl, huh? Anyway, we started talking about how America compared to his home in England and I had to agree with some of his observations. Before long, we were laughing and insulting each other and I felt like I had just made a new friend.

Barry had just started working with rock bands when he was hired to go out on tour with AC/DC. The other two roadies were Ian Jeffery and Keith Evans. (Although Keith's nickname was "Plug," I thought they were calling him "Plum" because most of what they said was barely intelligible due to their accents. I can imagine my Midwestern twang wasn't any easier for them to understand either.) Barry and Keith were teasing Ian because he had just been made "tour manager," which didn't mean much except for the fact that he had to be more responsible...especially if something went wrong.

Once again I was sent out to buy another bottle of Blue Nun wine. The band was due back at the club at any minute, so I ran upstairs to make sure the deli platters looked good and that everything was in its place. After seeing their mug shots, I didn't want to piss anyone off. Just as I was getting ready to leave, the band started to file through the door. Considering their apparent penchant for brawls, I figured the further away from the band I was, the better. So I started to back out of the room, telling this strange group of guys that if they needed anything, to just come downstairs and get me.

Right then a rather intimidating guy with shaggy dark hair and tattoos up and down his arms walked right up to me, shoulder to shoulder, looked me in the eye and yelled, "Sit!" I immediately grabbed the first object I could find, which luckily was a chair, and sat down. So much for slinking out of the room unnoticed. Then he walked over to the table and poured two glasses of Blue Nun wine. He walked over to me, handed me a glass, and said as he extended his hand, "Hi, I'm Bon Scott, you must be Sue." I asked him how he knew who I was. Malcolm, who had walked in and sat down on a couch, laughed and said, "The promoter told us all about you. He said you would give us anything we wanted!" That got a huge laugh from everyone in the room. His humor broke the ice and we sat and visited while I desperately tried to decipher their accents.

Once I saw them in person, they didn't look all that scary. Bon was about my height, five-feet-five inches with long, dark layered hair, lots of tattoos, a twinkle in his eye, and a cute little smile. Even if he wasn't saying anything inappropriate, you could just tell by looking at him that he was thinking about it!

Malcolm had long dark hair, parted in the middle, and was no more than five-feet-four inches tall. Malcolm has a very distinctive voice, which you can hear really well when he's singing backup on "Dirty Deeds Done Dirt Cheap." His younger brother Angus had long reddish/brown hair, blue eyes, and was built just like a little boy. He couldn't have been more than five-feet-two inches tall. Angus didn't talk much and spent most of the early evening playing around with his guitars.

Their drummer, Phil Rudd, was five-feet-six inches or so, had shorter dark blonde hair, piercing blue eyes, and a mischievous smirk. They weren't *all that bad looking after all. At least that's what I was thinking when Cliff walked through the door.*

Cliff was their new bass player and from the first time I saw him, I couldn't have cared less if he knew how to play an instrument or not. He was the tallest in the band, perhaps five-feet-eight inches tall. He had long dark shaggy hair, fringy bangs, dark eyes, and the thickest eyelashes I have ever seen on a man. Maybelline should have signed him up! Plus, he had a dreamy English accent. At least I could understand him a little easier than I could the Australian accents. The rest of the band started to tease me about being nice to Cliff, because he had just joined the band. Oh yeah, you bet I'd like to be nice to Cliff...

After bantering back and forth with the band, Cliff asked me to go downstairs with him to get something from the bar. He asked for Smarties and the bartender thought it was a drink. After several minutes of trying to explain to him what they were, Cliff gave up and went back upstairs. Years later I would learn that Smarties were the English equivalent to our M&Ms. The poor man didn't want a drink, he just wanted some chocolate!

The Hounds, a lackluster band from Chicago, opened the show. The cover was three dollars and I don't think there were more than 75 people in the place, including bartenders. The Hounds had never impressed me much, so I spent their set hanging out in the dressing room with the boys from down under. Since I hadn't yet heard any of AC/DC's music, I had no idea what to expect from them as a band. As they started to get ready to play, I went downstairs and found a spot next to the soundboard. Up until this point, I was pleasantly surprised at how nice and engaging they all were. I didn't give it much thought that they would be anything other than your run-of-the-mill rock 'n' roll band. After all, a Led Zeppelin or a Black Sabbath doesn't come along every day. Not until that Tuesday evening in August of 1977, anyway.

*As the lights went down, the band took the stage. All of a sudden Phil started in with a steady beat on the high hat, accompanied by Cliff's pounding bass. After a few bars, Malcolm joined them and when Angus came in jamming, the whole band launched into "Live Wire." Their sound took on an unearthly volume. Bon was standing on the edge of the stage dressed in tight blue jeans, with no shirt on. He looked up into the spotlight and start-*ed to scream..."Well, if you're lookin' for trouble, I'm the man to see, Well, if you're lookin' for satisfaction, satisfaction guaranteed. Cooler than a body on ice, I'm hotter than the rollin' dice, send you to heaven, I'll take you to hell, I ain't foolin', can't you tell? Live wire, I'm a live wire..."

'Oh my God! What is this? Who knew a band could be this loud? Not only do Malcolm and Cliff sing backup, but the guitar player has gone mad! He hasn't stopped running from one end of the stage to the other since the song started. Oh no, he fell down! He's rolling around on his back and he hasn't missed a note!' By the time AC/DC got to the end of the song, I had backed all the way up against the wall across from the band. The hair on my arms was standing straight up, my body was covered with goose bumps, and I felt like I had just stuck my finger into a light socket. I had listened to a lot of rock 'n' roll in my lifetime—even saw The Who live—but AC/DC made it sound like they had invented it!

The last time I felt this way about a band I was eight years old. It was a Sunday evening and Ed Sullivan had just introduced four lads from Liverpool called The Beatles. Even at that age, I knew I was witnessing a phenomenon. I felt exactly the same way that night at the Stone Hearth.

In front of 70 or 80 extremely stunned Midwesterners, the band slid from "Live Wire" into a bluesy, sexy version of "She's Got Balls." Any man who wrote a song about a woman having balls, was a man after my own heart. Not only could these guys blow rock with the force of Led Zeppelin on speed, they wrote songs about chicks having balls! By the end of the first song, I was more than impressed. I was so overwhelmed, I couldn't move from the spot I was standing in. And I couldn't take my eyes off Bon.

After letting everyone catch their breath, the train kept rollin' into "Problem Child." These lyrics were inspired by Angus, who Bon thought of as 'a bit of a juvenile delinquent.' "What I want I lick, and what I don't I kick, and I don't like you..." *What's not to love? The band continued playing at a volume audible in other dimensions and the sheer energy coming off the stage could have been cut with a knife. Within the first three songs, I decided that Malcolm, Cliff, and Phil were the best rhythm section I had ever heard. In my opinion, they still are today. Angus is an incredible guitar player, able to run all over the stage in a super-human way without missing a note, but have you ever really noticed what Malcolm, Cliff, and Phil do? They are a relentless powerhouse of rhythm.*

By now, everyone in the bar was standing there staring at the band...just in time for Bon to announce that the next song was called "The Jack." While Angus started the song, playing a few notes that fed back, the whole band teased us with a few power chords. Then, Bon started singing, "Gonorrhea, I've just had my first dose of gonorrhea..." *to the melody of "Maria" from the Broadway hit,* West Side Story. *Who knew Bon sang show tunes? Supposedly, he loved Broadway musicals and enjoyed listening to their soundtracks often.*

The band is wailing and Bon is complaining about a chick that gave him the clap. Now Bon's ad-lib lyrics in this song have to take the cake for being the most outrageous of all AC/DC songs: "She gave me her mind, then she gave me her body, but it seems to me she gave it to anybody, I made her cry, I made her scream, I took her high and curdled her cream. But how was I to know that she had been there before, she told me she was a virgin, she was number nine ninety-nine on the critical list, and I fell in love with the dirty little bitch, she's got the jack, she's got the jack..." *These are the words he sang that night but are not, of course, the same lyrics that are on the recorded version of the song. At this point, the whole club is singing along and I don't think it's all that easy to get a bunch of dairy farmers to sing about venereal disease. Who the hell are these guys?*

For the next hour or so, we stood mesmerized by the band. The sound, the beat, the power, the force, and the flash in Bon's eyes were riveting. I had been wrong...once or twice in a lifetime a band like Led Zeppelin or Black Sabbath does come along and thank God I was lucky enough to be there to witness it.

At the end of their set, Bon dedicated their last song to Elvis, "Who should have played some good hard rock." And that was that. There weren't that many people in the club, but I do believe every single one of them went upstairs to the loft to meet AC/DC. The band was more than cordial and stood around for quite a while visiting with everyone who wanted to meet them. I held back, waiting for the room to clear out. I wanted the band's— especially Bon's—full attention.

As I walked over to him, Bon was sitting on one of the couches relaxing, when he looked up at me, and I said, 'God, Bon! You blew my socks off!' He screwed up his face and said, 'I did wha?'

And I replied, 'Oh, I'm sorry. "Blowing my socks off" is a slang term. What I meant is that you were incredible! The band is absolutely amazing!' That he liked, and he smiled and thanked me. I could barely contain my enthusiasm and I told the whole band that someday they were going to be internationally famous. That statement got a lot of laughs and generated a few smart comments that I couldn't really make out. I continued, 'You will be. It will take two to three more years, but you're going to be huge!' Then I blurted out, 'Someday you're going to be as big as The Rolling Stones!' I actually remember the moment I said that, and as it was coming out of my mouth I thought that that wasn't the band I wanted to compare them to. Little did I know that they idolized the Stones and someday would become the only band in history to ever co-headline concerts with them. When I said that, Angus laughed, pulled off his shoe and stuck his foot in my face. Looking up at me, he said, "Does that mean then someday I will be able to buy me some new socks?" Yes, Angus, someday you will not only be able to buy yourself some new socks, but your likeness will be embroidered on them as well.

While I was gushing over the band, their road crew struck the show and loaded the gear into the back of a truck. They were on their way to the next venue. The band was going back to the Holiday Inn out on the edge of town. I believe Bon was the one who invited me back to the motel with them. I politely turned him down, thinking there was no way I was going to get too close to any of the band members. This was one of the best bands that I had ever heard and I knew they were going to be extremely successful. I wanted to keep them as friends and going back to the motel would ruin my image as a serious rock journalist. Pretty good foresight for a 21-year-old, if I do say so myself.

As I said goodbye to everyone, the roadie Barry came over and asked me for my name and address, saying that he would keep in touch with me. I found a scrap of paper and as I wrote my name, number, and address out for him, I was silently thinking I would never hear from him again. Barry said they were on their way to Michigan, when they were actually playing in Milwaukee the next night. At least he was headed in the right direction! Before he left, he gave me the only piece of AC/DC merchandise he had, which was a small pin with a picture of two bluebirds hovering over a heart with a lightning bolt through the middle. Not very rock looking, but the image itself actually resembled the tattoo Bon had on his lower stomach. I know what you're thinking. The first time I actually saw it was in a photograph!

From that night onward, I told everyone who would listen about this band called AC/DC. Unless they had been at the club that night, most people couldn't understand what all my raving was about. I continually stated that when they got the chance to see them live, they would fall in love with the band as I had.

The next night in Milwaukee, AC/DC played at the Riverside Theater opening for Head East. From there, they drove back through Ohio and on the night of August 22, their concert at the Agora Ballroom in Cleveland was recorded live by a local radio station and broadcast on the QFM 96 Sunday night special. If you don't already have a copy of this show, you need to find one. It is a rare recording of one of AC/DC's first concerts in the United States. Plus, it's worth it, if only for Bon's hilarious ad-lib lyrics in "The Jack."

Two days later they made their New York debut as guests of The Dictators at the Palladium, and then opened a midnight show for The Marbles at CBGB's. The funniest part of this show is the fact that Bon met the head of Atlantic Records outside the club while he was peeing into a jar. If you have ever used the bathrooms in CBGB's, this makes perfect sense.

CBGB's is an extremely small club on Bleeker Street in Greenwich Village with tons of graffiti all over, no doors on the bathroom stalls, and a small stage for the band to play from. *I'd love to hear from someone who was in the crowd that night. I can't imagine AC/DC's power being contained within those four walls. It must have been like detonating an atomic bomb in a telephone booth. I bet you could still probably scrap DNA off the plaster from all those who were blasted up against the walls that night!*

The New York fanzine, *Punk,* interviewed Bon and Angus and asked them the very deep question, 'What's the meaning of life?' To which Bon replied, "As good a time and as short as possible."

Thanks to modern miracles, Angus was extremely happy trying out his brand new wireless guitar system. On their way to California, they played at the Masonic Auditorium in Detroit opening for Johnny Winter and .38 Special.

Two weeks after seeing the band's Stone Hearth appearance, my first postcard arrived from Barry. The picture was an aerial view of Hollywood, postmarked August 31, 1977. They were booked to play three nights at The Whisky-A-Go-Go in West Hollywood on the twenty-ninth through the thirty-first. This would be their California debut. It is also where Gene Simmons first saw them and invited them to open for Kiss in December.

We've almost finished over here. I must admit I'll be glad to get home even if it is only for two days. Things have been going really well for us. L.A. is quite a strange place, the people try to be a little too cool. We're here for three days and then on to San Francisco, I might even go home with a tan! We'll definitely be back in November, hope to see you then, good luck with the paper.

Clearly I had underestimated this shy, young Englishman. Barry Taylor would continue to faithfully call or write to me from all over the world, every week, for the next three years.

AC 8 DC

AIN'T NO FUN (WAITING AROUND TO BE A MILLIONAIRE)

After AC/DC's performances at the Whisky in L.A., they played two nights at the Old Wharf in San Francisco, then went straight back to Fort Lauderdale to play a benefit with radio station WSHE at the 4 O'Clock club. I believe the band got to fly to the gig, but the roadies still had to drive the gear back.

Roadie Barry Taylor later wrote in his book *Singing In The Dark,* "In that first tour we covered some 40,000 miles, zigzagging the country. One day it was Chicago, a couple of days later Miami. There were times when we could have killed the booking agent, but we certainly got a taste of the diversity of the American lifestyle."

AC/DC's performance in Ft. Lauderdale was the first chance Atlantic's Perry Cooper had to see the band live. "We had brought them to a convention in Florida and they played a party for the Atlantic—actually the WEA (Warner Elektra Atlantic)—people. The first time I saw them was in Fort Lauderdale where they were opening for somebody. I have a picture of all of us backstage: Barry Bergman, Michael Browning, Michael Klenfner, the band, and myself. [When I first saw them live] they were incredible! They were exactly what I thought they would be. No, wait, they were better!"

In early September, the band flew back across the ocean for the European leg of their Let There Be Rock tour. They were scheduled to play 20 dates in Finland, Sweden, Germany, Belgium, and Switzerland.

The band played the Thierbrau Sportshall in Kontich, Belgium on October 9 and the police stormed the stage—one with a machine gun—trying to stop the show. This lack of respect for rock 'n' roll incited a riot. The event also inspired the song, "Bedlam In Belgium." Even military action couldn't curtail the band's creativity!

Their single, "Let There Be Rock" with B-side "Problem Child" was released in the United Kingdom on September 30. Right after playing their dates in Europe, the band headed back to England for 20 more. The album, *Let There Be Rock,* was released in the U.K. on October 14 and became AC/DC's first album to chart there, peaking at Number 75.

Phil Sutcliffe gave them four stars in his album review in *Sounds* on October 22, 1977. He wrote, "So it's just as well I first heard *Let There Be Rock* in the bath: very handy for washing my mouth out with soap. Because I could hardly [deleted] usually believe the [deleted] audacity of the mother [deleted], the sheer [deleted] simplicity and [deleted] directness of the little [deleted]. They [deleted] me totally...You know what AC/DC do live. Blow roofs off. Destroy walls. Steamroller the debris into a fine powder. Well this is the first time I've heard them pack all of that into a record. They broke the master after they pressed Ron [sic] Scott." *Phil, you took the [deleted] words right out of my [deleted] mouth!*

The following week Sutcliffe continued his support with a review of their show at Mayfair in Newcastle: "The crowd was pogoing, roaring, and chanting, 'AC/DC, AC/DC' after that first number. They basked in their own hell heat while soaking in Angus's flying sweat and snot as if it were Holy Water...With a superbly produced instrumental sound, you could hear exactly how effective they all are. Phil Rudd on drums straight and loud, new bassman Cliff Williams unorthodoxly strumming a growling under-thrum, Malcolm Young emerging as a riffmaker of the most ferocious intensity, and Angus continuing to play hard and ever-imaginative lead while shaking himself about as if he had no further use for his head...Bon is vital. He's the spice and flavor with the heavy hardtack. An appealing rogue and buccaneer, give him a wooden leg and a parrot on his shoulder and he'd be the image of Long John Silver."

John Howe recommended *Let There Be Rock* on October 22 in *Record Mirror,* "This is a great album, the best heavy metal I've heard in years. AC/DC have knocked the Sabbaths, Quos, Aerosmiths *et al* for six. I urge you to buy it." In the same issue of *Record Mirror,* Selma Boddy also reviewed their appearance in Newcastle. "They are a kind of new wave on the old sea. Quo and The Sabs were last seen leaping for the lifeboats...Crude they may be, but they've both humour and truth in what they write: 'they hit you where it counts—between the eyes and legs.' They rock crazily on the raging guitar sound of the Young brothers, riffmaniacs incorporated."

The band played their first sold-out shows at London's Hammersmith Odeon on October 25 and 26. Within a few days, they would mark their one-year anniversary from the first night they headlined there. Amid the punk-rock movement in Britain, with the press raving about them, AC/DC had blown the competition out of their own country.

The next night they filmed their appearance at the Golders Green Hippodrome in London for broadcast on the *Sight And Sound* program for the BBC, with an FM simulcast on Radio One. The concert aired on October 29, 1977.

As predicted, the band was back in the States in mid-November for the second leg of their American Let There Be Rock tour. They supported Rush for the first three dates in upstate New York. From there, AC/DC traveled south through Tennessee to co-headline three dates with UFO, this time with The Motors opening. From Tennessee they drove further south down to Atlanta to play the Capri Theatre. For some reason only known to insensitive booking agents, they had to turn around and drive back up north to appear at the Roxy Theater in Northhampton, Pennsylvania. *Can you say, routing, anybody? Barry and I used to joke about it, but once you really look at how much driving AC/DC did, their original three-man road crew should also have been inducted into the Hall Of Fame!*

Journalist Marc Mayco wrote a brilliant article about the band in the November issue of *Trouser Press:* "Suddenly Hurricane Angus explodes from the east wing, head bobbing wildly, feet pounding the boards in time, ridiculous school clothes falling off in pieces. Wearing a large Gibson and a wireless mike, Angus begins at one edge and crisscrosses the stage as often as he can. Occasionally traveling out into the audience, he never misses a beat, shaking and bobbing as if his brain were wired to the drum kit."

After seeing them live at the Palladium in New York at 9 pm, then again at CBGB's for a midnight set, he wrote, "AC/DC may well be the world's rudest, most tasteless band. Angus is probably not 18 years old as press releases claim, but no matter. If any desire to hear rock 'n' roll at its most vulgar remains in America, AC/DC might become a heavy singles threat. All they need is to keep touring and getting the response shown this time around. Keep an ear out and your legs crossed."

AC/DC's first Chicago appearance was at the Riviera Theater on December 1, and this time Detective opened for them. Al Rudis wrote in the *Chicago Tribune* that the band made a stunning debut: "The band's material is mostly all-out, wall-of-noise hard rock, with Scott's shrieks skipping over the top. It's not new and it's not subtle, but it's done with conviction and flair and the audience reaction was pure pandemonium. Welcome to another generation."

AC/DC was only three days away from Wisconsin and I was counting the hours! While they had been in Europe, I left the first paper I was writing for and helped launch another. It was a bi-weekly music newspaper called the Emerald City Chronicle, à la The Wizard of Oz. *By our second edition, we were the coolest rock rag this side of the* Illinois Entertainer. *This was the late Seventies and the press enjoyed a very powerful position within the music industry. It was before MTV, with fewer radio stations available for airplay. Print was mighty and for a rock journalist, these were the salad days. Just ask Cameron Crowe.*

The band was scheduled to play the Electric Ballroom in Milwaukee on December 4, 1977. My two girlfriends, Katy Sticha and Terry Thompson, were coming along with me and we booked a room near the venue at the Ambassador Hotel. Barry would be setting up the show in the afternoon, so we agreed to meet at the club around four o'clock. I was very excited to see them again, even though I was exhausted. I had been awake for the entire 24 hours prior to this, partying with Kiss at the Edgewater Hotel in Madison. But that's another story...no, actually it's another book: Rock 'N' Roll Fantasy.

When we arrived at the Ballroom, Barry was finished with his duties for the meantime so he was able to come back to the hotel with us. We ate dinner and enjoyed visiting with each other for a while. Quite a change from the day-to-day rush while on the road.

Back at the club, trouble was brewing. Tour manager Ian Jeffery and roadie Keith Evans were running around and the band was walking around talking with each other. There was some concern over the electrical system and the club's manager wasn't sure they should play. The band wanted to do nothing but. Bon could be heard saying, "We came here to play, and that's what we're going to fucking do!"

The band gathered upstairs in the dressing room, while the opening band decided to pack up and walk out. That's right. Detective, five guys from England fronted by the eventual B-list actor, Michael Des Barres (also future spouse of the reigning queen of groupies, Miss Pamela Des Barres). Des Barres was fearful of the electrical problems and decided not to play. AC/DC went on as scheduled.

The band again opened their show with "Live Wire" and proceeded to turn every person in that club into a rabid fan. This time I knew what to expect and I wanted to stand as close to the stage as I could get. It would become one of my favorite AC/DC memories...watching the band tear up the stage, then Angus on Bon's shoulders doing their soon-to-be famous "walk-about." That stunt used to amaze me since it required Barry or one of the roadies, to follow them through the crowd, keeping Angus's guitar cord from getting caught on anything! Although that hazard had just been eliminated with Angus's new Schaefer cordless guitar system.

The band had hurried through their set and decided against an encore when smoke came rolling out of one of the air vents behind the stage. Not good. After everyone cleared the club and no fire was found, I went upstairs with the band to record an official interview for the Emerald City Chronicle. *The band had blown Milwaukee away and were on their way to becoming as big as The Rolling Stones. I couldn't wait to tell the world—or at least the southern half of Wisconsin—about them.*

When I listen to the recording of this interview now, it's very funny to hear how laid back I was. I think after a few drinks, I was a little too relaxed, if you know what I mean. Since the band had just come off stage, it was a good combination. I politely questioned them and they blatantly propositioned me throughout the "interview." From the time the tape started rolling, all five band members have their way with me...journalistically speaking, of course. I couldn't get them to answer a question straight-faced if my life depended on it. Thank God it didn't. Listening to Bon is always bittersweet. He is so alive on the tape, but has been gone for so long now. His antics during this interview always make me laugh out loud. Panasonic, I salute you!

Two days after they left Milwaukee, AC/DC arrived in New York City on December 7 to record a live set at Atlantic Recording Studios. Perry Cooper had conceived the idea that the band should utilize the record label's recording facilities and track some songs. Hoping to capture their live energy on vinyl, Atlantic planned to press 5,000 promotional copies and distribute them to radio stations across the country.

What a great job to have, introducing AC/DC to an unsuspecting country! Cooper explained, "I was in a good position at Atlantic where I could encourage the publicity staff to be much more enthusiastic than they were. When Michael and I came over, Atlantic was a very close-knit family group. This was my first band, and Michael and I just decided to make this our cause. So we went crazy. We put a lot of pressure on the Atlantic staff to make sure they would promote it, merchandise it, and sell it. Do everything they could.

"I had come up with the idea of the *Live At Atlantic Studios*. I'm an old radio man and I said, 'Wait, we've got these studios up on Broadway. How about if we put out promotional albums and broadcast live?' So we decided to put out a series of *Live at Atlantic Studios* and, of course, the classic AC/DC first record came from that. We decided to broadcast on MMR from Philadelphia which became one of the mainstays of AC/DC.

"While they were performing, everyone from some of the maintenance staff to people next door tried to get into the studio to see where all the racket was coming from! After we did the recording, you could feel the vibe there. I felt so good about putting it together. I just knew these guys had it. They had it, they had it, they had it!

"The recording was very raw and we were up all night mixing it. Five thousand copies were printed up and sent out to the radio stations. I also got pictures of that, with Scott Muni, Ed Siacky, and Bob Pittman [MTV Founder] with the band. What a great night that was and nobody had ever heard of them!"

The band spent the rest of December playing dates opening for Kiss, Blue Oyster Cult, Styx, Aerosmith, and Cheap Trick. On December 13, their opening date was reviewed—*or should I say, trashed*—by writer John Finley when he wrote an article for the *Courier Journal* in Louisville, Kentucky. "...AC/DC relying on a lot of athletic prancing around by its lead guitarist, who strips from a Little Lord Fauntleroy outfit down to shorts and does a lot of falling down while continuing to perform...It's hard to see where groups like Kiss and AC/DC can go from here." Nothing like a visionary.

Angus remarked about playing with Kiss to *Guitar World* saying, "We toured in a station wagon. [Kiss] had everything behind them, the media, a huge show and stuff. And here we were—five migrants, little micro people. It was tough to even get into the show with that station wagon. Many a time they wouldn't let us into the venue 'cause they didn't see a limo!"

While AC/DC was performing with Kiss, my name came up in conversation. It wasn't my name actually. I think Mr. Simmons's direct quote was, "There's this crazy blonde journalist in Madison, Wisconsin. Sometime you've got to meet her!" Barry said Gene laughed like hell when he heard they already knew me! This prompted Barry to call me from Indiana's Market Square Arena where they were opening for Kiss. With the band blasting in the background, Barry tried to ask me, "What the hell did you do to Gene Simmons?" His question really epitomizes the phrase, "small world."

I told him that it was a long story, but I did reveal that I ran away from Gene...that probably put me in a whole new category with him. In fact, that would be the "crazy category." Not many women ran away from Gene Simmons in those days. It was probably the dead Tarantula encased in plastic as a belt buckle—which came up to my eye level—that struck the fear of God into me. But as I said, that's another book.

The band co-headlined some of their dates with Cheap Trick. Their tour manager Kirk Dyer—also notoriously known as the Wheel—worked with Cheap Trick for 14 years. He recalled the first time they played with AC/DC. "I remember it was someplace in North or South Carolina [Greensboro, North Carolina on December 18], after we finished the Kiss tour, we started co-headlining. I was in the dressing room with the band and I opened the door and these little squirts went by and I said, 'What the hell?' They were five of the shortest guys I had ever seen. So I couldn't figure out what was going on, what were these guys doing? And I saw they were headed up to the stage, so I walked out to the soundboard. I watched one song and ran back to Cheap Trick's dressing room and dragged them all out to the soundboard to hear these guys. It was the first night of the tour. They just rocked. Personally, they just blew me away! They have been my favorite band ever since, still are."

AC/DC ended a groundbreaking year by going back home for Christmas. Barry was hoping to visit the States during his time off. According to his letter dated January 13, 1978, Cliff, Barry and the rest of the road crew were stuck in England. They were trying to get to Australia for a few performances before hitting the studio to record their next album.

Cliff (the bass player) and I went to the Australian embassy to get our visas on Monday, but they said that they couldn't give Cliff a visa without contacting Melbourne first, because he had to have his visa extended the last time he was in Australia. So we've been delayed for at least a week which in effect means that we will have to go directly to Australia because they have to start recording pretty soon or they won't get the album finished in time.

It would take a month for the visa situation to be resolved. This mess of red tape would make it impossible for AC/DC to play a few dates around Australia before going into the studio. Sympathies, as Phil put it, to "the birds they hadn't seen in a while."

At the end of February, the band and road crew finally checked into the Corban Hotel on Coogee Bay Road in Sydney to ready themselves for recording AC/DC's fifth album. Energized from their whirlwind tour of America, they would come closer than they had ever been to capturing their raw power on vinyl. This patch of electrifying songs inspired AC/DC to hook up the perfect title, they called it *Powerage*.

POWERAGE

In the studio, George and Harry were once again guiding the creation of their next album and in a letter from Coral Browning, dated February 28, 1978, I heard about the next collection of tunes:

From all reports in Sydney, the boys are putting down the best rock ever. They'll be in Alberts Studios for another month, then go to England in April and hopefully the U.S. tour will start in May.

The Australian government refusing to issue work visas to the road crew cost AC/DC the Australian tour and a tour of Europe. Once the new album was recorded, the strategy was to tour England briefly before coming back over to the States by late May. That was the plan, anyway.

The collection of nine songs they loaded into *Powerage* were "Rock 'N' Roll Damnation," "Down Payment Blues," "Gimme A Bullet," "Riff Raff," "Sin City," "What's Next To The Moon," "Gone Shootin'," "Up To My Neck In You," and "Kicked In The Teeth." *All masterpieces in my opinion.* Many of these songs are still part of their live concerts today.

Malcolm commented in *Metal CD* about *Powerage:* "That album was more of the same. We were happy to stay in the same area as *Let There Be Rock* because all that stuff was going down so well on stage. "Sin City" was the big one on *Powerage* and we're still getting some mileage out of it when we play it live even now."

Without work visas to allow a proper tour, AC/DC played two concerts at the Bondi Lifesaver under the name, The Seedies. The news leaked out and over 4,000 people tried to get into the club over the two nights they were there.

While *Let There Be Rock* had sold only 25,000 copies in Australia, it was selling 10 times that internationally. The demand for AC/DC in countries all around the world was starting to increase. As soon as the recording of *Powerage* was finished, they were off to have another shot at pillaging England. God save the Queen!

I received a letter from Barry upon his return home to Buckden for a few days. It was postmarked April 12, 1978 from Huntingdon, Cambs, England.

Hello there, I must say that it's great to be back home again. It certainly does feel like a long way from home down there. The new album is finished and should be out on the 1st of May. It's the best they've come up with yet. I'm quite sure you'll like it. We are starting a U.K. tour in a couple of weeks. It was originally only eight or nine gigs, but there's quite a demand for the band and we are now doing 28 concerts. So we won't be hitting the States until the first week of June, it seems to get further away all the time! We are starting in Texas and working up. I'm pretty sure that Chicago will be on the list and hopefully Madison, we'll have to see. We're going to be in the States for quite a while this year, I think. We'll be doing some festivals in Europe at the end of August and then back to the U.S. for another 12 weeks, can't be bad! There's a talk of a live album this year, too. There are plans to record and film a couple of gigs here in England and two in the States. I think San Antonio and Jacksonville are penciled in, we're quite popular down south, y'all!

He also enclosed four photographs taken of the scenery around where they had stayed while in Sydney. It looked very beautiful, sunny with white and gold cliffs jutting out over a turquoise ocean.

I received another letter from Barry dated April 27, 1978 written in

London, but postmarked from Wolverhampton. He included four postcards from Godmanchester, England and Hinchingbrooke Castle.

The band arrived from Australia today, so I got a letter of yours that arrived after I left...I'm staying with a friend of mine here in London for a couple of days getting a few things prepared for the tour. We've got two days of rehearsals this weekend to warm up...Actually we've just been out with Cliff, Malcolm, and Ian to a gig at the Music Machine, a newly opened, very clique, and very boring place in trendy Camden Town-a bit of a punk area of London...Our British tour is selling very well, I think the London gig is already sold out. We're playing 28 dates, which is quite a few for Britain. It's going to be a pretty grueling tour; I dare say the exercise will do me good...I found out that we start in the U.S. on June 14. It gets further away each time I ask, perhaps I should stop asking.

Powerage was released in the U.K. and the first single, "Rock 'N' Roll Damnation," entered the British charts at Number 51. The British leg of the Powerage tour started on April 26 in Wolverhampton England, but the first night was cancelled.

The band's appearance in Glasgow, Scotland on April 30 was captured live by a mobile recording studio and used for their next release, *If You Want Blood (You've Got It)*.

A couple of weeks later, I received a letter from Barry while they were in Colchester.

We're playing here in Colchester today, it's an old Roman town pretty close to the east coast of England, not very far from where I live, in fact. There are some amazing old houses around here, lots of little villages around and about the city which have been virtually untouched for hundreds of years.

We had to cancel a couple of concerts last week, Angus has been ill but he's back in business once more. However, it does mean that the tour will be lasting a bit longer, they've rescheduled the cancelled dates and added a couple more, yet another delay. But things look pretty certain for the second week in June, so I'm keeping my fingers crossed.

Having a couple of days off, Bon and Cliff went to Paris to visit Bon's friends in the band, Trust. He was very happy about the fact that Trust had just gotten banned from French television due to his lyrics in their cover of "Love At First Feel." Bon victoriously claimed, "So I've struck again!" Meanwhile, Angus was sent to Australia to promote *Powerage* and their new single. He commented, "We drew straws to see who'd come, and I lost."

On May 15, their single "Rock 'N' Roll Damnation," reached Number 24, making it their first hit in the U.K. Ten days later, (*drum roll please*)...*Powerage* was turned on in the United States. The cover of the album had a picture of Angus on it with wires exploding out of his jacket sleeves in place of hands. On the back cover there is a great—if slightly menacing—group picture. You may notice that Phil is showing off his southern solidarity by sporting a Lone Star state T-shirt.

Around this time, Coral Browning sent a package to me at the Chronicle, which included a Powerage *T-shirt, along with the new album. Attached was a note that said, "Hope you like the album! Cheers, Coral P.S. PLAY LOUD." I did many, many times. To this day,* Powerage *remains my favorite AC/DC album. That puts me in the same category as Malcolm Young and Keith Richards, which ain't a bad place to be.*

In June, the band traveled to Munich to appear on the German television show, *Rock Pop,* performing "Rock 'N' Roll Damnation." That same week they played it again on the English television show, *Top Of The Pops.* Finally on the nineteenth, Australia joined the rest of the world in feeling AC/DC's power rage.

As soon as their U.K. tour was done, Barry got a short break, and actually wrote a letter from home.

Our British tour finished officially on Monday in Dundee, Scotland, however we had a couple of cancellations earlier in the tour which we have to do next week, but we have a few days off. The tour has been really successful, great reactions from the audience everywhere. British audiences usually tend to be somewhat reserved and don't usually let themselves go too much, but they seemed to go pretty crazy at most gigs on this tour, so there is some hope yet. We had a meeting with Michael, the band's manager, a couple of days ago about the States and stuff. We should be flying to New York on the nineteenth of June...maybe a couple of days earlier. We start in West Virginia on the twenty-sixth with Alice Cooper, which should be fun. Michael asked me about you at the breakfast the other morning, I don't know why, it came straight out of the blue...but he reckons that he's going to fix up a couple of gigs up your way, which I won't complain about, and we're definitely going to Chicago...We should have another couple guys with us this time out to do the lights and another roadie to take care of Angus. I'm supposed to be taking care of Phil and his drums, but I dare say I'll still manage to run around with Angus. I've carried him around on my shoulders a couple of times on this tour which was fun.

The American leg of the Powerage tour started on June 24 supporting Alice Cooper in Norfolk, Virginia, before winding through Kentucky, Alabama, and Tennessee. *Powerage* peaked on the *Billboard* charts at Number 133. For this tour, the band was enjoying a new sound system and equipment to play through and this would be their first tour to officially feature AC/DC T-shirts, posters, and patches for sale.

The 67-date tour continued from Tennessee, down to Florida, through Texas, and west to California. Along with Alice Cooper, they also opened for Bob Seger, Mahogany Rush, Journey, Ronnie Montrose, Blue Oyster Cult, Savoy Brown, Thin Lizzy, and Aerosmith. As Atlantic's Perry Cooper recalled, "They got out on the road and opened for a lot of bands and did some real shitty shows. Shows that I wouldn't have wanted to be involved in, but they did them! And we developed little pockets of airplay. I believe Cleveland was one, San Francisco was another. Then Florida, there were like four or five pockets that really loved them and started playing them. And they toured for two years straight!"

On July 23, AC/DC performed in front of 70,000 people at the Day On The Green Festival #3 in Oakland, California with Aerosmith, Foreigner, Van Halen, and Pat Travers. Even though they played at the very unrock-like hour of 10:30 am, the band had no trouble raising the entire crowd to their feet. Any time AC/DC got the chance to play in front of massive crowds with major headliners, they always gave the other bands a real run for their money.

Of course, it didn't hurt that Cooper was dreaming up publicity stunts that the band was always happy to cooperate with. He recalled, "I had this radio station broadcasting live. The deal was Angus was going to go up the stadium and they would drop a microphone down and talk to him while he was playing. Angus is walking up there—on the shoulders of one of the roadies—and they're walking up to where the press box is, and they're dropping a microphone down. They did whatever we asked them to do. They really did. They were great guys, they hated the record company telling them what to do, but certain people in the record company they would listen to. If we asked them to do something, they'd do it." Take note rock star wannabes.

Cooper, who traveled with the band often, was closest to Bon. "I was better friends with Bon than anybody, because of our age. We were older than the rest of the band. And Bon and I, from the beginning, we bonded. I think that's why we got friendly, we were about the same age, so we would room together. You should see this naked picture I have of him. [Laughs] It's funny, we were sharing this room in some hotel, and he had just come out of the shower. And I used to take pictures of everything; I was a bad boy. And he came out of the shower and he's standing there and I just said, 'Smile!' And all he did was look at me [while holding his...] and laugh. It's a brilliant picture, typical Bon Scott. As if, 'Look at this girls!'"

From California, the band traveled north to Canada and then south through Oregon and Montana, before playing an Evansville, Indiana date on July 29. AC/DC was scheduled to play Alpine Valley in East Troy, Wisconsin opening for Aerosmith on Thursday, August 3.

AC/DC took the stage that night at Alpine Valley around 7:30 pm and swept the crowd right up into the palm of their hands. They opened their set with "Live Wire" and hammered the audience with "Problem Child," "Sin City," "Gone Shootin'," "Bad Boy Boogie," "High Voltage," "Whole Lotta Rosie," and "Rocker." Go ahead Aerosmith, follow that! Their time onstage felt like a hit and run, leaving thousands of people standing there with stunned looks on their faces.

The next two shows were in Chicago. On Friday, August 4 AC/DC opened for Alvin Lee at the International Amphitheatre. On Saturday, August 5 they performed in front of 40,000 people in Comiskey Park for the Summer Jam, supporting Aerosmith, Foreigner, Van Halen, and Cheap Trick. The band was very well received by the audience.

From Chicago they traveled to Nashville to perform at a Record Bar Convention on August 8. The next two nights they played in Salem, Virginia at the Roanoke Civic Center and the Cumb County Arena in Fayetteville, North Carolina supported by Cheap Trick and an up-and-coming rock band called Nantucket.

Nantucket guitarist Tommy Redd has written about his experiences playing with AC/DC on his own website and thoroughly enjoyed recounting for this book some of his fondest memories of the band: "We played with AC/DC two times with Bon Scott. One of the dates was Fayetteville, North Carolina with Cheap Trick. The other was in Salem, Virginia which is right out by Roanoke, also where Wayne Newton is from. The first time I saw them, I thought they were a great band. They had a great show with a lot of energy. They weren't into all that flashy deal, like the glitter bands that were around at the time. Angus was the only one who had his little get-up on."

Redd still has great affection for the band, especially the Young brothers. "Angus was always drinking a big glass of chocolate milk or coffee, and Malcolm used to walk around with Jack Daniels in a bottle that was as big as he was. You know they're both about four feet tall.

"When we played in Lake Charles, Louisiana, Angus mooned the crowd and a local cop—who looked like Jackie Gleason—didn't take kindly to this and they got into a spat and told them it was time to leave town. Someone came backstage and told Malcolm that Angus was in trouble. Malcolm showed up and told the police to, 'Piss off.' The police—not knowing who he was—treated him like some little boy who came backstage from the crowd.

"Nantucket was traveling around in an old bus we bought from a gospel band which had to be started with a screw driver. AC/DC used to really laugh at us riding around in this. One time when the windshield wipers wouldn't work, we had to take the panel off in the front of the dash. When we did, we found about 10 bags of pot, and I mean, really old bags of pot. That must have been the 'get rid of it!' spot on the bus. And we're talking southern Baptist gospel band!

"AC/DC had two buses...one of them being called 'the worm.' It was two buses that had a link in the middle, like you see on a train. It was made in Belgium or something and they hated it. We were coming up from West Palm Beach and we stopped at the bar called the Kiki, where we auditioned for Epic. So we were like an hour or so behind AC/DC who took off on highway 95.

Way out in the middle of Florida, somewhere around Daytona, we saw these lights flashing on the shoulder of the road; they had broken down. Here we were with an old 1960-something bus, it looked like the bus Marilyn Monroe was on in the movie, *Some Like It Hot*. It had a big round back and a huge steering wheel like Ralph Kramden's bus on *The Honeymooners*. So we pulled up and opened the doors and Ian [Jeffery] and everyone was jumping up and down. It was like stopping at a school bus stop full of kids. We said, 'Well this old bus looks pretty good now, huh?' We took them to the next exit and they made some phone calls. Then they rode with us up to Jacksonville. Here they were riding on this old bus, the one that they always wondered if it was going to make the tour at all."

Once again, the band drove south to Atlanta, Jacksonville, and Miami and then back up north through Pennsylvania, New York, Massachusetts, and New Jersey. Most of these dates were supported by Cheap Trick, the power-pop quartet from Rockford, Illinois who had just released their first self-titled album. The two bands got along so well together that Cheap Trick was the only opening act that was welcome to come out onstage at the end of the night to jam with AC/DC. Some of these shows they actually co-headlined, and many were sold out.

Cheap Trick tour manager Kirk Dyer remembers: "Every night they played together, they would always watch each other's set. We always made sure that we made room for them onstage when we were playing. By the end of that tour, we were jamming together. Every night there was an encore that involved both bands. At the end of the tour, Bon Scott was becoming famous for putting Angus up on his shoulders, so I got Rick Nielsen up on my shoulders and we had a chicken fight the last night [that we played with them] in Omaha at the Music Hall Civic Center. It turned into 30 minutes of pure hell, it was just crazy. It was a real "break your guitars, beat people up" chicken fight. It sort of disintegrated from a song or two into this literal guitar-swinging war and everybody was just laughing their asses off. I said, 'These guys are going to be the next big thing,' and sure enough, they were."

Bon's friend Vince Lovegrove saw the band on August 11 when they co-headlined Symphony Hall in Atlanta with Cheap Trick. Lovegrove was quoted as saying, "[That he found himself] quite nostalgic watching Bon onstage, struttin' across the boards like the eternal Peter fuckin' Pan that he was." *Maybe J.M. Barrie was inspired by one of Bon's ancestors, and not some little kid named Peter. Hey, it's possible!* During a drinking session after the show, Bon confessed to Lovegrove that he was tired of touring. At that point, he had already been on the road for the past 13 years.

Through the fall of 1978, the never-ending turns of the "highway to hell" took them from New York, through Rhode Island, Connecticut, Maryland, and all the way across the country again to Seattle and Portland. While still on the east coast, they opened for Rainbow at the Palladium in New York City on August 24. *I'll just bet that made Ritchie Blackmore's day.*

AC/DC appeared at the Day On The Green #5 in Oakland, California on September 2 with Ted Nugent, Journey, Blue Oyster Cult, and Cheap Trick. Dyer remembers that a pyro technician was knocked unconscious while he was over 90 feet in the air, on top of one of the PA stacks. "All of a sudden we heard this loud boom and realized one of the pots went off and blew him literally unconscious. They had to climb the PA and bring him down. He lived, but I don't know how badly he was injured."

Four nights later, the band appeared live playing "Sin City" on ABC's late-night concert series, *The Midnight Special*. The show was hosted by Ted Nugent and Aerosmith. For fans sitting at home in front of their television sets, it was starting to sink in how AC/DC was taking over the planet. It was very exciting for the band, record label, and fans. From there, the band would head to the Riverside Theater in downtown Milwaukee to open for UFO on September 12. AC/DC clearly slayed the Milwaukee audience and left them wanting more.

From Milwaukee, the band headed east to Michigan. AC/DC had 14 more cities to play here in the States before wrapping up the Powerage tour in Europe and the U.K. When they played Cobo Hall in Detroit on September 29, the band was shut down due to excessive volume.

Supposedly, Malcolm waited until they got paid before he punched out the promoter. *They don't call him the brains of this outfit for nothing!*

In the September 1978 issue of *Circus,* rock journalist Kurt Loder reviewed *Powerage*. "AC/DC's first album was so aggressively witless that any response to it beyond a slack-jawed stare would have seemed gratuitous. The band's forte at that point was a particularly bland brand of third-rate boogie with metal pretensions; distinguished only by the lewd wheeze of lead singer Bon Scott and the lone "visual interest" of guitarist Angus Young's drooling-schoolboy routine — a dead-end shtick if there ever was one...*Powerage* shows AC/DC to have evolved from ineptitude to full-blown competence...But thanks mainly to Angus and his brother Malcolm, who maintain a deliciously fat and nasty two-guitar sound throughout the album. AC/DC does have real power now...If they add nothing new to the catalog of time-tested rock moves, at least AC/DC rehashes them all with a catalytic energy that makes them sound fresh again. These days, that alone may be enough to take them to the top of the hard-rock heap."

Brad Balfour's article in *Creem* magazine celebrated AC/DC's dedication to playing rock 'n' roll. Angus was quoted as saying, "The only hero I may have besides Batman, is meself, 'cause I'm the one out there doing it. Why, when we played Belgium and the police came to shut our concert down because of the 11 pm curfew, they arrested me for starting a riot. They couldn't get me off the stage any other way."

Manager Michael Browning stated, "We have pockets of fans from San Antonio to Jacksonville, Florida where we headline. We plan on working until it happens for us. Because this band is so young, they're willing to do what they have to do to make it, like traveling 600 miles to a gig, getting there 15 minutes before the show, and hitting the stage on time."

Less than six months after *Powerage* came out, Atlantic Records released their sixth album in the U.K. on October 6. It was a live concert that had been recorded in Glasgow, entitled *If You Want Blood (You've Got It)*. Once again, it was produced by George and Harry and featured 10 songs from *Let There Be Rock* and *Powerage:* "Riff Raff," "Hell Ain't A Bad Place To Be," "Bad Boy Boogie," "The Jack," "Problem Child," "Whole Lotta Rosie," "Rock 'N' Roll Damnation," "High Voltage," "Let There Be Rock," and "Rocker."

The cover is a surreal picture of Angus being impaled by his own guitar. Considering the grueling schedule they had endured since early 1974, giving blood was the least of it. Despite their passion evidenced in the *Creem* article, Bon was drinking heavily and the original road crew was beyond exhaustion. *While at the Alpine Valley gig, Barry—one of the roadies—had discreetly confided to me that Phil was suffering from panic attacks and that they had to call in a psychiatrist to treat him on the road. If you want blood, you've got it, all right.*

On October 10, AC/DC launched their 16-date European tour through Sweden, Germany, Holland, Switzerland, France, and Belgium. Postmarked October 20, a card arrived from Barry with a picture of a castle and a bridge in Heidelberg, Germany.

Europe has gone crazy for the band since we got back and the tour has sold out which can't be bad. We have a new stage set and show which is amazing. We're still working very hard. But it's not for too much longer.

Once they finished the European leg of the tour, the band immediately traveled back to the U.K. to play 17 more dates. November 2 and 3 were sold out shows at Mayfair in Newcastle. Postmarked November 3, 1978, I received another card from Barry with a picture of the beautiful Scottish hills covered in amethyst heather.

Only 14 more gigs before our work is done for this year. I must say that I am looking forward to the break. Our European tour sold out and the U.K. tour had done the same. The new live album has also gone right into the charts at Number 10. It looks like they've finally made it. It's got a little out of proportion though, we have 16 crew and two trailers on this tour, slightly different to our U.S. trip.

AC/DC closed their tour of the U.K. with two sold-out shows at the prestigious Hammersmith Odeon. *Barry was right, it did look like they had finally made it.*

Malcolm stated in *Metal CD* in 1992, "*If You Want Blood*...was exactly where we were at that stage in our career. That record summed the band up perfectly and it was recorded at one of the last gigs from that tour, at the Glasgow Apollo." Although while performing in Glasgow, Bon got lost during their "walk-about" and ended up outside the venue. Since he didn't have a ticket or pass to the show, security wouldn't let him back in until he convinced them he was indeed in the band! Luckily, not having a shirt on in the November cold did the trick.

If You Want Blood (You've Got It) was released in the U.S. on November 21 and in Australia on the twenty-seventh. By Christmas, it peaked on the Billboard charts at Number 113. After living in hotels for the past three years—finally getting home to Perth for the holidays—Bon stated in the *Melbourne Sun,* "I haven't seen them [family and friends] in three years. I hope they recognize me."

Favorable press, sold out shows, and constant touring still wasn't enough though and it failed to gain them the kind of airplay that could produce a hit single. It would take a change of producers and the release of their seventh album for AC/DC to gain the respect they had worked so hard for. Against their record company's wishes, the band decided on the phrase that they had used to refer to their unrelenting U.S. tour. The new album would be called *Highway To Hell.*

AC**10**DC

HIGHWAY TO HELL

By the end of 1978, *Powerage* had sold 150,000 copies making it AC/DC's first Gold album here in the States. The record reached Number 13 in Britain and, for the first time, made it into the Top 50 on the American charts.

David Fricke from *Circus* magazine interviewed Bon in January 1979 and Bon stated, "There's been an audience waiting for an honest rock 'n' roll band to come along and lay it on 'em. There's a lot of people coming out of the woodwork to see our kind of rock. And they're not the same people who would go to see James Taylor or a punk band." When asked how he was withstanding the constant touring, Bon replied, "It keeps you fit—the alcohol, nasty women, sweat onstage, bad food—it's all very good for you!" When Fricke asked what he would do if his voice ever gave out, Bon shot back, "Then I'd become a roadie."

As the band recorded rough tracks at Albert Studios, Atlantic Records was hatching a new plan. They felt that George and Harry weren't producing radio-friendly records, so they put pressure on the band to work with legendary producer Eddie Kramer. He had previously worked with Jimi Hendrix, Led Zeppelin, and Kiss. The suggestion was not met with much enthusiasm from the band, especially since they were not used to recording anywhere but Albert Studios. It also must have been a hard pill to swallow being told to fire your own brother: The one person who had stuck by the band from the very beginning and had produced their first six albums.

It would turn out to be a good move for the band, but in a roundabout way considering more than one person would lose their job over it. Although George and Harry weren't at all happy, Angus claimed George gave them the go ahead. However, George told them, "Don't let them mess with what you are. Always remember you're a rock 'n' roll band."

The original plan was business as usual: record an album within three weeks, then tour Japan in February. A farewell party was organized for the band at the Strata Inn in Cremorne where Bon, Angus, and Malcolm jammed with George on bass and local musician Ray Arnott on drums.

Right before the band was to leave for their first tour of Japan, work visas were denied and the tour was called off at the last minute. Instead, AC/DC flew to Miami to meet their new producer and record the next album at Criteria Studios. The change of plans and pressure of working with someone new didn't stop them from blowing off some steam during their off hours. Tommy Redd from Nantucket recalls running into Bon and Malcolm while at a club, The Tight Squeeze, in Hollywood, Florida. Ironically, they would see a local band that night also called Tight Squeeze. When Bon ripped off his shirt and got up on stage to sing with the band, Malcolm looked over at Tommy and said, "Oh, now he's showing off again."

While trying to record with Kramer, who kept urging the band to add keyboards, Malcolm made many frustrated calls to Browning. Hearing things weren't going well, Atlantic sent Michael Klenfner and Perry Cooper down to Florida to hear the rough tracks. "Michael and I loved the band," said Cooper. "After I got them to come over and tour, he [Klenfner] decided that Eddie Kramer would produce their next album. So they came to Florida to rehearse and get ready to record with Eddie. Michael and I got a call to come to Florida. We fly down there and Michael's listening to it. I go into the bathroom and Angus, Malcolm, and Bon follow me in there. They say, 'What do you really think of it?' And I say, 'It sucks.' I really did. I said, 'It sucks, and something ain't right. I can tell you're not having a good time' and they said, 'Ah, thank God!' But I was not a major player then. And we walked out of the bathroom and later on we went back to New York and Eddie Kramer was fired. It just wasn't working; the vibe wasn't working. Klenfner got fired right after that. He had been adamant about Kramer producing their next album. Up until this point, their brother had produced everything for them. And you don't want to go up against your brother. They were forced into using Eddie, and they don't like being forced to do anything."

While trouble was brewing in Miami, Browning was visiting Clive Calder, who represented a Rhodesian-born producer named Robert John "Mutt" Lange. Coincidentally, Lange was staying with Calder when one of

Malcolm's distraught calls to Browning came in. After hearing a demo of the new album, Lange agreed to take on the project. Lange had previously worked with City Boy, The Boomtown Rats, Graham Parker, and The Motors. AC/DC would be his first heavy-rock band. Bon was quoted in *RAM* as saying, "Three weeks in Miami and we hadn't written a thing with Kramer. So one day we told him we were going to have the day off and not to bother coming in. We snuck into the studio and on that one day we put down six songs, sent the tape to Lange and said, 'Will you work with us?'"

Lange was impressed with the recording, which had Bon singing and filling in on drums. Although Lange had never worked with such a heavy band before, his decision to sign on was good for all involved. Previously, the band had never spent more than three weeks on recording an album. This time, AC/DC spent nearly three months at London's Roundhouse Studios.

Highway To Hell would wind up being a groundbreaking record for them all. Lange added harmonies and double tracking and pushed Bon to sing more, instead of scream. Angus told *Musician* magazine, "I think the thing about *Highway To Hell* was that Mutt knew what FM stereo sounded like and we didn't. Every week he'd be there with the Top 10 of America, listening to the sounds. And he's got a great set of ears. He could hear a pin drop. I know Bon was very happy with him. Mutt taught Bon to breathe, bring in from your stomach. After we'd done the album, Bon said to Mutt, 'I like what you've done. Do you think it would be worth it for me to go off and learn with somebody?' Mutt said, 'No, I don't. This is you.' And I think Mutt learned something from us as well. I think he was impressed that we could play and knew what a song was, as opposed to just a riff."

The new album contained some of their best work up to this point. The 10 incendiary tunes were "Highway To Hell," "Girl's Got Rhythm," "Walk All Over You," "Touch Too Much," "Beating Around The Bush," "Shot Down In Flames," "Get It Hot," "If You Want Blood (You've Got It)," "Love Hungry Man," and "Night Prowler."

"Night Prowler" features Bon's best Robin William's impression of Mork, his television character from the show *Mork & Mindy,* where you can hear him say at the end of the song, "Shazbot…nano, nano." Talk about the power of TV catch phrases!

Malcolm summed up *Highway To Hell* in *Metal CD:* "That was a definite change for AC/DC. Atlantic Records in America were unhappy because they couldn't get the band on the radio and they were desperate for us to come up with something more accessible. We'd had our own way for a few albums, so we figured let's give them what they want and everyone will be happy.

"Back then Mutt Lange was still an unknown—I think he'd just produced The Boomtown Rats before he came to us. Mutt seemed to know music and he looked after the commercial side while we took care of the riffs and somehow we managed to meet in the middle without feeling as though we compromised ourselves. In fact, there was no way we'd back down on anything. We were a pretty tough band for any producer to work with.

"'Touch Too Much' was a hit off that record, but the one song that stands out head and shoulders over everything else was the title track. If certain people had their way, it wouldn't have been called 'Highway To Hell' because the bible-belt was very strong in America at the time and they made a fuss once the record came out. But even though we were under pressure, we stuck to our guns."

In 1979, I had left the paper and started working for Cheap Trick. Their manager was based in Madison and I got a job handling all of their fan mail. As soon as I mastered the art of dealing with thousands of fan letters, without a computer, I wrote Coral Browning a letter asking about AC/DC's fan club. She replied on March 26, 1979 from their new offices at 250 West 57th Street in New York City.

Thank you very much for your letter. Sounds like you are keeping busy with the Cheap Trick fan club. I have passed your letter on to our official fan club president in England, her name is Sandra Munday. She will send you an application form in due course. AC/DC are in London recording and will be there until the end of April. The U.S. tour will start in May. They won't be doing the California Music Festival as they have to finish the new album. I will pass on your regards to the band.

By the end of April, the band was ready to hit the road again for 53 dates, this time supporting *If You Want Blood (You've Got It)*. As luck would have it, the first night of their tour opened in Madison, Wisconsin. *Coincidence? What do you think?*

AC/DC opened for UFO at the Dane County Coliseum in Madison on Tuesday, May 8, 1979. They pummeled fans with "Live Wire," "Problem Child," "Sin City," "Gone Shootin'," "Bad Boy Boogie," "High Voltage," "The Jack," "Whole Lotta Rosie," "Rocker," "Rock 'N' Roll Damnation," and the mother of all rock songs, "Let There Be Rock." It was clearly a struggle for UFO to keep the audience's attention after AC/DC had left the stage.

Afterwards, I hung out with the band backstage for a while. Their spirits were high and it was obvious they were happy to be back onstage again. Later on, I ended up sitting in Phil Rudd's hotel room across the highway from the venue. Phil was very excited about the new album and told me they were convinced that this was going to be the record that would put them over the top. He eagerly popped a cassette into his boom box and we sat and listened to Highway To Hell, *from front to back. Talk about rare rock 'n' roll privileges! I was stunned by the new songs and the polished sound of the record. Lange had amazingly brought out the best in them, surprising everyone...especially the band.*

Phil also told me all about the photographs that were taken for the album. One night they went out on this road in England to film the band hitchhiking. The artwork was to show the band getting into a car and the cover picture was going to be the band riding in the backseat with the devil behind the wheel driving as he smiled at them in the rear-view mirror. Kind of creepy, actually. Phil also mentioned how upset the record company had been over their choice of album titles. Seems the bible thumpers were not going to be pleased.

From Wisconsin, AC/DC drove south down through Iowa, Ohio, Indiana, Tennessee, and Georgia supporting UFO. On May 27, they played Rock Superbowl VII at the Tangerine Bowl in Orlando with Boston, Poco, and The Doobie Brothers. The more they played, the larger and more animated the crowds got.

Throughout May and June they played almost every night of the week, driving back up through New York, Iowa [yeah, that's close], Illinois, Pennsylvania, New York again, and then Texas. Actually, the phrase "highway to hell" is pretty tame when you think about it. Of course, with Bon at their side, there was never a shortage of road humor and harmless pranks. AC/DC played hard and, off stage, played even harder.

Cooper spent so much time with them on tour, that they used of have a spot on the stage marked "PC," so he always had a place to stand and watch them. He fondly recalled how much fun they were. "They were the best guys in the world; you just wanted to be around them. They were funny, but they were never malicious. They would never hurt anybody."

AC/DC was scheduled to play on the Fourth of July at the Winnebago County Fairgrounds in Pecatonica, Illinois, which is right outside of

Rockford. Naturally, Cheap Trick was the headliner in their hometown to be supported by AC/DC, Molly Hatchet, and The Babys.

As has been mentioned before, Cheap Trick and AC/DC got along very well together...especially Bon Scott and Cheap Trick's bassist, Tom Petersson. *Let's just say the two partying together were a lot like squirting gasoline onto a fire. Although I'm not sure who was the gasoline and who was the flame.*

Right before they went on stage, Cheap Trick tour manager Kirk Dyer had quite a time of it getting Petersson ready to perform. He and Bon had been drinking together most of the day. I marveled at Kirk's calm demeanor while trying to lead Tom up to the stage. It would have been much easier to just throw him over his shoulder, which at almost six-feet-five inches tall, he could have easily done. Once Tom was up there, he did a fine job. To be fair to Tom's miraculous recovery and future success, these were the days of pure debauchery and both Tom and most tragically, Bon, paid a dear price for their revelry.

At the end of Cheap Trick's set, Bon, Angus, and Malcolm came up onstage and joined the band for an encore of "Sin City" and Chuck Berry's "School Days." This special treat was highlighted by Rick Nielsen climbing up on the shoulders of one of their roadies. Cheap Trick was the only band to share the same stage with AC/DC, who didn't mind following them. When the Highway To Hell tour was booked, AC/DC was turned down as an opening band by Van Halen, Sammy Hagar, and Foreigner. To which Bon stated, "Our aim is to make the headliners work for their money."

Reportedly, AC/DC's constant touring put a strain on the Alberts finances, which put pressure on Michael Browning. The band was being courted by bigger management companies and when Leber and Krebs expressed interest in the band, Browning accepted a settlement for the last year of his contract.

As part of a very successful New York management company, both Steve Leber and David Krebs had previously worked for the powerful talent agency, William Morris, before forming their own company in 1972. During the Seventies, they handled some of the biggest acts in rock, such as Ted Nugent and Aerosmith. Since Nugent's drawing power was declining and Aerosmith was on a downward spiral into drugs, drinking, and diminishing record sales, signing AC/DC at this time was a major coup. Steve Leber and David Krebs had clearly just snagged a band who were well on their way to becoming superstars. It was a great move for both parties really, and the company appointed Peter Mensch as AC/DC's personal manager. Browning went on to form Deluxe Records, the successful Australian record company who signed the Nineties rock sensation, INXS.

Right in the middle of AC/DC's American tour, they flew over to Holland to appear on the Veronika TV concert in Arnhem, Holland at the Rijnhallen on July 13. This could possibly be where Angus met his future wife, Ellen. Their performance was filmed for the television show, *Countdown*.

The band immediately flew back to the States and resumed their never-ending tour. Eight days after filming in Holland, AC/DC performed in front of 60,000 people at the Day On The Green festival at Oakland Stadium in California with Aerosmith and Ted Nugent.

A week after that, they played for another 80,000 at the World Series of Rock at Brown Stadium in Cleveland supporting Aerosmith, Ted Nugent, The Scorpions, Thin Lizzy, and Journey. This event was sadly marred by a lone gunman in the audience who shot a fan dead and seriously wounded another. There were also numerous arrests and nine people suffered stab wounds.

AC/DC spent the rest of July and the first part of August touring through Indiana, Ohio, and Pennsylvania. On August 4 they opened for Ted Nugent at Madison Square Garden in New York City. This was their first appearance at this Big Apple rite-of-passage venue. Their popularity started to explode when *Highway To Hell* was released in the States on July 30. Songs like the title track, "If You Want Blood (You've Got It)" and "Shot Down In Flames," are still audience favorites today.

If You Want Blood (You've Got It) had hit the quarter-million mark and this new album would skyrocket AC/DC even further. There had definitely been hell to pay for this particular release, considering it cost George, Harry, Michael Browning, Eddie Kramer, and Michael Klenfner their jobs. With Lange's more lush production and the band's radio-friendly choruses, *Highway To Hell* would wind up being paved in Platinum.

When I received a promo copy of the album, I was shocked to see the cover photo. Apparently the band had won the battle over the album's title, but lost the war over the cover pictures. Instead of using the shot of the devil driving a car while smiling in the rear-view mirror at the band in the back seat, the record company used an already-released publicity shot of the band. The only change they had made to it, was superimposing horns and a tail on Angus. This is the first time AC/DC's marketing portrayed Angus as the little devil. Contrary to popular belief, the necklace that Bon is wearing in the picture is not satanic. Yes, he is wearing a pendant with a pentagram on it, but the pen-

tagram is pointing up, which means white magic, or positive energy. Bon was a rock 'n' roll outlaw, but certainly no Satan worshipper. One shot from the original photo shoot was used for the album's back cover.

Just as I had predicted at the Stone Hearth two years earlier, AC/DC had become internationally famous and on August 17, they headlined over The Police, The Pretenders, and The Specials at the Festival De Bilzen in Bilzen, Belgium. The next night they were invited to open for The Who, Nils Lofgren, and The Stranglers at the Who And Roar Friends festival at Wembley Stadium in London. The future for AC/DC couldn't have looked any brighter. Or, so we all thought.

AC 11 DC

KICKED IN THE TEETH

Highway To Hell was released in the U.K. at the end of July 1979 and made its way into Britain's Top 10, stopping at Number Eight. The album continued to sell like wild fire in Germany, Holland, and Scandinavia. The record also hit the Top 20 in the States, peaking at Number 17.

After the Festival De Bilzen, AC/DC played five dates in Ireland and France before appearing live on the German television show *Rock Pop* playing "Highway To Hell." While in Munich, the band also filmed five promotional clips for their brand-new about-to-break-through album.

On September 1, the band was honored to open for The Who, along with The Scorpions, Molly Hatchet, and Cheap Trick at an open-air festival in Nuremberg, Germany. Kirk Dyer vividly recalled AC/DC's set that day. "I remember Nuremberg 1979. We were playing in Hitler's war stadium, where he used to have his war rallies. It was a two-day event and AC/DC followed us and then The Who. During our set, all the band guys are watching us play. Pete Townshend and all the AC/DC guys are trying to get us to screw up, that kind of thing. Which is normal, band guys will sit on the sidelines mooning each other, just like a football team or something. Just a bunch of practical jokers. Anyway, it was time for AC/DC to go on and no one could find Angus. You can hear him, but no one can tell where he is. All of a sudden you see that he's up on a security guard's shoulders all the way in the back of the crowd—85,000 deep! About a quarter of a mile away from the stage, starting the song. I'm standing onstage with Pete Townshend and Rick Nielsen—right next to them—

and they're talking and Pete was just blown away. He couldn't believe how great they had just rocked. I don't think he had ever seen them before that. They just came out and did a killer set, I mean it was unbelievable. [AC/DC] came out and just blew the crowd away and The Who guys are looking at each other and Pete Townshend said to the rest of the band, 'How are we going to top this?!'

"It was a hell of a memorable weekend. They had put all the bands in the same hotel and the bar scene that night after the gig was like a who's who of major rock stars. It was Cheap Trick sitting with AC/DC sitting with The Who...We took pictures of me, Bon Scott, Bun E., and Robin Zander playing pool. The next day we're all on the airplane and it hadn't started to move. We started to pull out and all of a sudden the plane stopped and here comes Bon running across the apron of the airport—with no shoes on—half a bottle of Jack Daniels already down his throat at eight o'clock in the morning! He had forgotten his shoes and was already in the bag the next morning after the show. So all the guys on the plane were razzing him when he got on."

Bon had written home to his ex-wife, Irene, that he planned to eventually buy a place in California where he could settle down. All the years of traveling exacerbated his drinking, which wasn't helping him withstand the rigors of the road very well. After a two-week tour of Europe, AC/DC landed back in the States playing the Auditorium in Oakland, California on September 5.

Journalist Sylvie Simmons wrote after seeing them play the Arena in Long Beach, California on September 10, "I'm drawn to this depraved quintet simply because they're here once again, and because amid this ever-changing universe, they can be relied on to be much the same as last time." Decades later, another shrewd journalist would state that there were only three things one could count on in life: death, taxes, and AC/DC.

From the west coast of America, the band traveled through Nevada into Texas. Somehow Bon missed a flight in Phoenix and ended up drinking and playing pool all night with the locals. He reportedly made it to the Civic Center Arena in Amarillo in plenty of time for their performance. Over those two weeks, AC/DC played 10 nights in Texas with Molly Hatchet opening several sold-out shows for them. All 10 dates were in different cities and all back to back with barely three days off in between.

They wrapped up September with a gig on the twenty-sixth at the Auditorium in Memphis supporting Sammy Hagar and two sold-out shows with Molly Hatchet in Charlotte, North Carolina and Greenville, South Carolina. From there they traveled back down south to Jacksonville,

Florida over to Alabama, and back up to Atlanta playing the Fox Theatre with Pat Travers opening.

Creem published a recap of all the ruling rock bands of October 1979. AC/DC was included along with Angel, Rainbow, Queen, Nazareth, Rush, Van Halen, Judas Priest, Whitesnake, Molly Hatchet, UFO, Mahogany Rush, The Runaways, and The Godz. They hilariously described AC/DC as: "All Aussies ever do is sit around on their stupid little beaches, drinking Obtuse Aborigine Beer, and belting each other around with surfboards because there's barely enough surf to even paddle out in. They need good drowning music down there and this band contains no lifeguards. Bearing down with mangy curtains of cancerous sludge, AC/DC make Black Sabbath sound like nerf Heavy Metal. Great stuff, comparable to cleaning out a septic tank with a toothbrush." *Those last two lines shows why* Creem *was always my favorite rock magazine.*

The afternoon of October 19, I drove to the Aragon Ballroom in Chicago. At the time, my boyfriend John was rehearsing to record an album for CBS Records, so I invited his manager and the singer from the band as my guests to see AC/DC that night. The show was sold out and the excitement around the band had reached a fever pitch. Highway To Hell *had taken off and the band was performing like a well-oiled rock 'n' roll steamroller. The audience went completely berserk over their new songs, especially "Highway To Hell" and another personal favorite, "Girl's Got Rhythm." It was such pandemonium that Angus had to get on the shoulders of a very large security guard to make his way through the crowd. Chicago fans couldn't get enough of the band and AC/DC's set was over far too soon. Afterwards, they wanted to pack up and get on to the next city. Since I had guests with me, I chose not to go backstage to see the band. They were exhausted and only had two nights left on the American leg of the tour before they were off to England.*

After the band was settled backstage, Barry—one of AC/DC's roadies and my friend—came out and led me to their tour bus. He said he had a birthday present for me. Yeah, I know, that's what I thought. A cute guy with an English accent finally takes me to the AC/DC tour bus and all I get is a blue and white stone necklace that he bought on a Native American Indian reservation in Arizona. Pretty and very thoughtful, actually. But not what I expected! When I jumped up and kissed him on the lips, he blushed and backed away from me. So much for any AC/DC tour bus action. We said our goodbyes and I sent my love and thanks to the band. Seeing AC/DC live, getting to know them, and hanging out backstage whenever I wanted was an incredible privilege for me. Not to mention that I had more fun with them than I could ever possibly put into words!

On the drive back to Wisconsin, I cried without really knowing why. Was I getting too attached to Barry after all this time? I looked up at the stars and prayed that they would all stay safe on the road and that it wouldn't be too long before I would see them again. Looking back, somehow I must have known that it would be the last time I would see Barry working with the band and the last time I would see Bon alive.

Two nights later on October 21, the band played at the St. John Arena in Columbus, Ohio. Perry Cooper was traveling with them and he delighted in telling me about the evening before they flew to New York to accept their first Platinum award. It seems the celebrating started a bit early. "Once we were in Columbus where they were playing the day before they were supposed to fly to New York to receive their first Platinum album. Well, that night we got really ripped and it was a bit of a rowdy night. We had a great time and later on we were all running around the hotel doing bad things. Bon was there, it was great. Their first album *Highway To Hell* had gone Platinum and they were going to meet all the executives at WEA [Warner/Elektra/Atlantic], it was going to be a big day. Well, we kind of wrecked the hotel. We blocked doors; we did some bad things. The next day I go downstairs in a suit and tie and complain about the noise from the night before. Here were all these State troopers coming in the front door! I went to a phone and called Ian [the tour manager] and told him to get the band out of the hotel—now! Leave the roadies, let them get arrested, but get the band out of there. Somehow we all made it to the airplane, got to New York, and they got their Gold [and Platinum] records. We were very bad boys, but we were having a really great time!"

The band collected their precious metal for *Highway To Hell,* which had sold over 500,000 copies. The record had been out here in the States for just 12 weeks. Their rock 'n' roll futures really couldn't have looked any brighter. It was now a fact that Malcolm and the boys were well on their way to realizing his dream of becoming filthy rich.

David Fricke wrote for *Circus* in November 1979, "The boogie beat and aggressive clash of electric guitars on *Highway To Hell* and *If You Want Blood (You've Got It)* is so relentlessly hard and loud that Angus's stage antics provide both visual emphasis and comic relief in one fell entertaining swoop."

Producer Mutt Lange was also quoted in the article, saying that the band was much more refined offstage than they were on. He marveled at the fact that they were famous for being rowdy, but would still stand up when his wife walked into the room.

Angus's penchant for jumping out into the crowd to paste a heckler gained them the constant supervision of the local vice squad. Angus also stated in *Circus*, "They were on tour with us, all the way. But the thing is, we don't do anything offensive. It's more of a party. The only damage we do is to the eardrums."

Their contentious relationship with the Australian government was what kept the band from touring there more often. *Highway To Hell* was released down under in early November, making it to Number 13. The first time they had made it onto the Australian charts in three years. Yet once again, they flew out of New York and headed for England, the country who had opened her arms to AC/DC early on. The Brits readily appreciated good rock 'n' roll. God knows they'd produced enough of it.

The British leg of the *Highway To Hell* tour was supposed to start on Thursday, October 25, but had to be postponed due to a fire in the venue. *I think it's rather spooky that it broke out in Brian Johnson's hometown and it's also the same venue where Bon would perform one of his last two concerts with AC/DC.*

From November 1 to 4, AC/DC played four sold-out shows at the Hammersmith Odeon, now called the Apollo. Just three years after their maiden British invasion, the band had earned England's royal seal of approval...not from the monarchy of course, but from London's rock 'n' roll royalty. *Although it wouldn't surprise me if someday they find a picture somewhere of a young Lady Diana Spencer at an AC/DC concert.* Just six weeks later, the band would play two more sold-out shows at the Hammersmith, "back by popular demand!"

AC/DC closed the U.K. leg of their tour on November 9 with a sold-out show at the Hall de Montfort in Leicester. Without as much as a 48-hour break, they continued on to Europe playing more than 30 dates in Belgium, Germany, Switzerland, Holland, and France.

Barry, the conscientious Englishman managed to send me an early Christmas card dated November 19, 1979, written from Passau, Germany. The cover of the card depicted a religious scene and the inside greeting was in German. My guess is that it said, 'Merry Christmas and Happy New Year.'

This may reach you a little prematurely, but I don't know how reliable the Deutsche Bundar Post is! We have just finished the load out, in thick snow, the first this year, looks like winter is now here for real! Passau is a small bavarian town on the German-Austrian border, it's really picturesque. Lots of cobbled streets and crooked houses. We are zigzagging across Germany, they really know how to organize tours in this part of the world. At least we have a bus this time, so that makes life a lot easier. And speaking of organization, we have 14 shows in France which is a lot for that country and two of them have raindates and yet the French promoter assures us that the shows are not open-air, leaky roof perhaps?!

The band have moved a little closer to earth on this part of the tour, nobody is too concerned with rock 'n' roll stars on the continent, so they have to be alright to the crew because there is no one else that they can talk to. I have a sneaking suspicion that Angus could be getting hitched pretty soon, he seems pretty deeply involved with his Dutch girlfriend and he visited her parents a couple of weeks ago, without his horns! Well, I trust you will have a happy Christmas and joyful New Year. I hope that I shall see you fairly early in 1980. I just have to clear up a few things over here and then I'm off.

AC/DC played two shows in France at the Pavillion De Paris, on December 9. Once at four o'clock and again at eight o'clock with Judas Priest. Their second performance was another sold-out show, captured live on film. Later released as *Let There Be Rock,* the movie, this is an incredible documentation of what it was actually like to hang out with AC/DC at the time. A pre-MTV *Behind The Music,* if you will. (Although *Behind The Music* actually airs on VH-1, for those about to get technical.)

What I love most about this video is that it captures AC/DC exactly the way they were when I met them. I never carried a camera with me in those days, not wanting to intimidate some of the bands I interviewed and got to hang out with. Let's face it, not everything was meant to be captured on film. Especially backstage! The movie, Let There Be Rock, *is a perfect way*

*for me to remember the band when we were all wild, young, and innocent.
And quite good looking too, I might add.*

By the middle of December, the band was back in London playing two
sold-out shows at the Hammersmith Odeon, with four more sold-out performances with The Pirates. Every day, more and more fans turned onto the
highway to hell and "Touch Too Much" and "Girl's Got Rhythm" were
climbing the charts around the world. At last, it looked like the band had
cleared that final hurdle. All their shows were selling out and their fight for
ever-elusive American airplay had been conquered. Little did anyone know
that in just a few short weeks, AC/DC's dream would turn into a nightmare
and their innocence would be lost forever.

After a short break in Australia for the Christmas holidays, AC/DC was
back out on the road by January 17, playing in France and the United
Kingdom. On January 25 and 27, they played two last dates at Mayfair in
Newcastle and Southhampton Gaumont. As soon as they wrapped the
Highway To Hell tour, the band went right into the studio to lay down basic
tracks for their next album. Mutt Lange would again be their producer, with
the recording taking place in London. They all found flats, with Bon making his home near Buckingham Palace in a section called Victoria.

On January 20, 1980, the band appeared at the Cannes Midem Festival
to accept a number of album awards. *If You Want Blood (You've Got It)* was
certified Gold in France and the U.K. and *Highway To Hell* was certified
Silver in the U.K. and Gold in France and Canada.

On February 7, they appeared live on *Top Of The Pops,* playing "Touch
Too Much." Two days later, AC/DC made their first Spanish television
appearance on the show *Aplauso* in Madrid, playing "Highway To Hell,"
"Girl's Got Rhythm," and "Beating Around The Bush." The next morning,
the Spanish were treated to a rare—and always amusing—AC/DC press
conference.

Barry's forecast concerning Angus's love life was right on when he married his Dutch girlfriend, Ellen (a former model) in London. I was happy to
hear that he had finally found a blonde wife to come out on tour and help
take care of him. Perry Cooper told me that at one time, Ellen had a special
kitchen brought out on the road with them, so she could cook for him as
soon as he got off stage. *Now if he had married me, all he would have gotten are some very large room service bills.* Angus and Ellen's nuptials barely made a dent in their schedule and the Young brothers went right back into
the studio.

Before heading to London, Bon stopped in Paris and recorded a version of his future anthem, "Ride On," with the band Trust. This recording wouldn't be heard by the public until 1998. While Bon worked on lyrics, he boasted to photographer Robert Ellis, as quoted in Mark Putterford's book, *Shock To The System,* "All he kept talking about was how great this next record was going to be. He carried this pad full of lyrics around with him, and he'd read them out to you whenever he could. He just kept on about the new album, how it was going to be the best thing AC/DC had ever done, and he was so fired up about it...you couldn't help but believe him."

On the night of February 18, Bon had an early dinner over at Ian Jeffery's [their tour manager]. Then he went back home and made three phone calls. One to his ex-girlfriend, Silver Smith; one to Coral Browning, who was living in Los Angeles; and one to the woman he was dating at the time (Japanese girlfriend, Anna Baba). When Bon spoke with Silver, he asked her if she wanted to do something together. Silver already had plans, but when her friend Alistair Kinnear called to ask her to see the debut of a band at the Music Machine [later called the Camden Palace], she suggested he ring Bon instead. Kinnear ended up fetching Bon to go to the club around midnight. For a couple of hours, both Bon and Kinnear partied heavily at the Music Machine, drinking at the free bar backstage, as well as the bar upstairs. Kinnear later said he saw Bon drink at least seven double whiskeys that night.

By the time Kinnear drove Bon back to his flat in Ashley Court in Westminster around 3 am, Bon had already passed out. Reportedly, Kinnear went looking for Bon's girlfriend, Anna Baba, who wasn't home. He opened the door to flat number 15 on the fourth floor using Bon's keys, but was unable to rouse Bon enough to help him inside. Leaving the apartment door ajar, during his struggle to get Bon out of the car, Kinnear managed to lock himself out of the lobby. The next day, a note was found by the caretaker reporting that Bon's door was left open and a set of keys were found on the inside mat.

Calling Silver for help, she told Kinnear to take Bon back to his own flat at 67 Overhill Road in East Dulwich, South London. Once he got home, he wasn't able to move Bon at all. Taking Silver's advice, Kinnear laid the front seat down, so Bon could lie flat. He then covered him with a blanket and left a note so when Bon woke up, he would know which apartment to come up to.

The next morning around 11 am, a friend by the name of Leslie Loads awakened Kinnear. Kinnear was so hung over, he asked Loads to check on Bon. When Loads came back claiming the car was empty; Kinnear went back to bed. That evening at about 7:45 pm, Kinnear went down to his car intending on visiting his girlfriend. He was shocked to find Bon still lying there—in the same position he left him in—not breathing. Kinnear immediately drove him to King's College Hospital where Bon Scott was pronounced dead on arrival.

Kinnear gave Silver as Bon's closest kin in London, so the hospital phoned her first and told her to come immediately. When she arrived, they ushered her into a little room and gave her a cup of tea. When Silver realized that Bon was dead, she gave them Peter Mensch's phone number. She also called Angus, although she claims she doesn't remember it. He was quoted as saying, "Peter, our manager, got to the hospital as soon as he could to find out exactly what had happened and identify him, because everyone was in doubt at the time. I immediately phoned Malcolm 'cos at the time I thought maybe she had got the wrong idea, you know, only thought is was Bon. And Ian, our tour manager, said it couldn't be Bon 'cos he'd gone to bed early that night. Anyway, the girl gave me the hospital number, but they wouldn't give me any information until the family had been contacted. Anyhow, Malcolm rang Bon's parents 'cos we didn't want them to be just sitting there and suddenly it comes on the TV news, you know."

Malcolm would say in an interview on VH-1's *Ultimate Albums* in June of 2003 that this was the worst phone call he has ever had to make. Bon's mother, Isa, recalled how at first she thought the voice on the other end of the phone was Bon's. When she realized what Malcolm was trying to tell her, she just screamed. Isa would also say that at least her beloved Ronnie knew not to die on her birthday, which had been the day before.

Ian Jeffery went with Peter Mensch to identify Bon's body. Bon's death certificate stated that his demise was caused by acute alcoholic poisoning, or "death by misadventure." Without anyone looking, a few months short of his thirty-fourth birthday, Bon Scott slipped away…all alone in a cold, dark automobile in the early morning hours of February 19, 1980. Gone was one of rock 'n' roll's most original, unique, and endearing front men.

The BBC Radio London would confirm, "Body of 33-year-old Bon Scott was found dead last night in a parked car in Dulwich, South London."

The next afternoon as I was driving to the hospital to pick up my mother who was battling terminal cancer, a lone AC/DC song blasted from my car radio bringing me a welcomed bright spot in my day. Right after the song ended, the disc jockey said, "And that was in tribute to the late Bon Scott, who was found dead earlier today in a car in London." I couldn't believe my own ears. All I could do was pull my car off to the side of the road and sob. How could this have happened? After all their hard work, the years of touring, countless performances, and the legions of fans that kept growing and growing...what would the band do now?

As I sat there wondering what would become of them, my heart broke for the band and especially for Bon and his family. It was simply unbelievable that he would leave us so suddenly and in such a seemingly mindless way. The man who entertained millions, would die all alone. Even though Angus, Malcolm, Phil, and Cliff would suffer one of the greatest losses of their entire lives, they would pull themselves up by their boot straps, raise the rock 'n' roll torch, and come roaring back with a vengeance. AC/DC would be back all right...back in black.

AC 12 DC

BACK IN BLACK

As soon as I was composed enough to drive, I found a phone booth and called my boyfriend John. Choking back tears, I blurted out that Bon was gone and that I didn't understand how something like this could have happened to him. I begged John to turn on the television and radio, to find out if it was true. When I finally made it to my mother's hospital room, she was ready to come home for the last time. Even though I didn't want to burden her with the news, I couldn't hide my devastation. We ended up crying together over Bon. After my divorce, I lived with her for almost a year. She had only seen them performing on television, but had taken many phone calls for me from Barry and the boys. Even though my mom was dying, it was she who comforted me that day. Six weeks later, I would lose her too.

In 1980 we didn't have 24-hour television news channels, so getting any details about Bon took quite a while. I barely remember talking to Barry, AC/DC's roadie, over the phone; we were both so completely in shock. Barry had just quit working for the band and was now living in Hollywood.

For several days, the band turned off their phones and sat in stunned grief. For a time, they actually thought about giving it up. Losing Bon was not just the loss of a singer in the band, but the loss of a brother: someone they all loved, admired, and looked up to. When Bon came along, being older and road worn, he just swaggered into AC/DC with his own rock 'n' roll style. He captivated their audiences and forever defined the band's playful personality.

Angus later said in *Musician* magazine, "It was just like losing a member of our own family, maybe even worse, because we all had a lot of respect for Bon as a person, 'cause, even though he did like to drink and have a bit of a crazy time, he was always there when you needed him to do his job, and I think in his whole career there's maybe only three shows he ever missed, and that was 'cause his voice wasn't there and we didn't really want him to sing. But I think it's more sad for the guy himself, you know, 'cause he always said he would never go unless he was famous. Malcolm and I were really looking forward to getting Bon in the studio. More than we'd done with any album before, because after the success of the last one, it was going to be a really big challenge, you know. That the best thing he'd ever done on record, I think that's the real loss for everyone, especially the fans, 'cause they would've had a chance to hear him at his peak. That would have been the crowning glory of his life."

Malcolm was quoted in *Classic Rock,* August 2005, "We were so depressed. We were just walking around in silence. Because there was nothing. *Nothing."*

An autopsy performed on Bon on February 22 revealed half a bottle of whiskey in his stomach. There have been many rumors and innuendo about what really happened to Bon that night…everything from murder to a heroin overdose. The real tragedy was the fateful decision to leave him alone in the car. The autopsy report showed no drugs were found in his system. Bon's ex-girlfriend Silver was involved in heroin and Bon once overdosed after trying it for the first and only time years before in Australia. After that scare, he stuck with his trusty JD. Bon rarely drank heavily before his performances and only really partied after his responsibilities for the band were met.

As for drinking until he passed out, Ian Jeffery once said that he roomed with Bon for five years on the road and never once saw him sleep in a bed. No matter how hard Bon partied the night before, he was always up and ready to make it to their next gig. The fact that he died all alone in a dark, freezing car in the middle of the night is completely unfathomable.

Kinnear was interviewed the next day by the police, but for the past 25 years, no one has been able to track him down. Finally, in the fall of 2005, *Classic Rock* gained an exclusive interview with Kinnear himself, who has been living in Costa del Sol, Spain since 1983. Kinnear denied previous reports that Bon choked on his own vomit and was wrapped around the gearshift of his car. When he found Bon, he was lying in the same position he left him in.

Kinnear went on to state, "The next day Silver came around to see me.

She told me for the first time that Bon had been receiving treatment for liver damage, but had missed several doctors'appointments. I wish that I had known this at the time...I truly regret Bon's death. Hindsight being 20/20. I would've driven him to the hospital when he first passed out, but in those days of excess, unconsciousness was commonplace and seemed no cause for real alarm...what I'd like to pass on from this unfortunate experience is the idea that we should all take better care of our friends and err on the side of caution when we don't know all the facts."

Condolences and tributes to Bon Scott came in from all over the world. Cheap Trick and Angel City did a version of "Highway To Hell." Santers, a Canadian trio, covered "Shot Down In Flames." Bon's friends in the French band Trust dedicated their album, *Repression,* to him. The Scottish band Girlschool, added "Live Wire" to their set, and over here in America, Nantucket—the band that played with AC/DC many times—chose to cover "It's A Long Way To The Top" as the lead track for their new album of the same name. The London pub Bandwagon held a Bon Scott benefit night and Ozzy Osbourne and the late Randy Rhoads wrote the song "Suicide Solution" for him. The international media ran stories and George and Harry ran a full-page ad in *RAM* that said, "A great singer, a great lyricist, a great friend, one of a kind. We'll miss you."

Bon's body was shipped back to Perth in Western Australia for cremation and burial. Bon's family, the band, and a few select friends attended funeral services at a church in Fremantle, Australia. Bon's ashes were laid to rest with little fanfare in the Memorial Garden, under the gum trees, in the Fremantle Cemetery on March 1, 1980. Perth, Australia was just too far away for most fans to travel. Bon's mother expressed true appreciation that the fans that were present were very reverent. Angus described it: "The funeral itself was more or less quiet, though there were a lot of kids outside. It was better being quiet, because it could have been very bad if a lot of people had just converged there."

During the services, Bon's father, Chick, leaned over to Malcolm and told him they would have to find another singer and keep going. Bon would have wanted it that way. Damn straight he would have!

The band spent some time with Bon's parents, who were adamant that they keep going. Chick also told Angus, "You must continue with AC/DC. You are young guys, you're on the brink of major success, and you can't afford to give up now." Angus told *Classic Rock* in August 2005, "But to be honest with you—we weren't really listening; we were wrapped up in our grief. Bon's dad kept repeating his assurances. He told us time and time again: 'You should keep going, you've still got a lot to give.'"

In a press release from their record label, Atlantic wrote, "Bon Scott was always the top joker in the AC/DC pack. The stories of his sexual and alcoholic excesses are legion and that part of his enormous fan mail that didn't involve tempting offers from young female fans invariably berated him for 'leading poor Angus astray.' Sadly, Bon is no longer with us after he tragically went just one step too far on one of his notorious boozing binges. But if there is a crumb of comfort to be found in such a needless and premature death, it is that Bon probably went out the way that he would have chosen, never flinching as he went over the top just one more time."

During all my research on Bon, I was unable to find a bad word said or written about him anywhere. Even his ex-wife and girlfriends still cared for him and there aren't that many guys you can say that about! He was a born rock star and loved people. And as Angus once said, Bon wasn't your typical rock 'n' roll singer. He started out as a drummer and always acted like one of the band…never the star. In the movie, *Let There Be Rock,* he was asked if he felt like a star. Bon laughed at the interviewer and said, "No, but sometimes I see stars though!"

At the time of his death, Bon was writing lyrics for the new album. While Angus and Malcolm were hammering out the basic tracks, Bon did come into E'Zee Hire, the rehearsal studio that they were working in. He didn't record any vocals, but a week before he died, he popped in and offered to play drums for them, claiming, "I like to keep my hand in, y'know." Jamming to one of their trademark riffs, together they created "Have A Drink On Me." Later, Bon also helped formulate the drum intro for "Let Me Put My Love Into You." Agreeing to meet the following week, with more lyrics written, Bon said his goodbyes and left. It was the last time Angus and Malcolm would see him.

There has been much speculation about what happened to Bon's notebook of lyrics along with the rest of his personal effects after his death. Ian Jeffery has been quoted as saying he possessed a notebook of Bon's that contained lyrics for 15 songs for *Back In Black.* To this day, no one has ever seen the notebook, nor has it been substantiated that Bon's family received it. Angus heatedly denied these rumors in the August 2005 issue of *Classic Rock,* "No, there was nothing from Bon's notebook. [After his death] all his stuff went direct to his mother and his family. It was personal material—letters and things. It wouldn't have been right to hang on to it. It wasn't ours to keep."

After Bon's service, everyone around the band started to suggest finding another singer. Angus and Malcolm weren't as optimistic, but eventually agreed that they should hold auditions. After several weeks of moping around their separate households, Malcolm called Angus and suggested they work on songs...to keep busy and stay together. Without concern for managers, the record company, or anyone else, Angus and Malcolm locked themselves in their studio and poured their grief into their music. Angus told *Classic Rock,* "I guess we retreated into our music. At the time we weren't thinking very clearly. But we decided working was better than sitting there, still in shock about Bon. So in some ways it was therapeutic, you know."

When it came time to talk about finding a replacement, Angus stated, "After a while, when we felt we were close to having all the songs together, we knew we had to confront the question of a new singer. But it wasn't like we put an advertisement in a music paper that said: 'AC/DC wants a new front man.' No...that would have been too over the top. It was subtler than that. People like Bon are unique. They're special. And we didn't want someone to come in and copy him. If anything, we wanted someone who was his own character."

Perry Cooper was stunned when he heard the news of Bon's death. "I was so hurt when Bon died. I actually got a Christmas card in February, after he died. It was a dirty double entendre card and he wrote, 'I never knew who to send this to, then out of the blue I thought of you, Merry Xmas Mate, Bon.' He had been dead for almost a month when I got it, so that was very upsetting. And I said to myself, how are they going to replace him?"

Apparently Bon didn't put enough postage on his 1979 Christmas cards and they were somehow delayed and delivered in late February. No matter how busy he was while on the road, he cared very much about his family, friends, and fans, and always made the extra effort to show them. Not surprisingly, even after his death, Bon would get the last word in.

When AC/DC started to line up possible singers to audition, many big names came up among the possibilities. They considered Terry Wilson-Slesser, who fronted ex-Free guitarist Paul Kossoff's band Back Street Crawler; Gary Holton, from the Seventies band, The Heavy Metal Kids; Steve Burton, an English vocalist; and Jimmy Barnes, the singer in their cousin Steve Young's band, The Starfighters. Auditions were held at a rehearsal studio in Pimlico, England, where they had narrowed their sights on a young Australian singer Allan Fryer, from the band, Fat Lip. George and Harry went as far as saying Fryer was the new lead singer for AC/DC. That was until AC/DC's management received a cassette tape of a band from northern England called Geordie.

The AC/DC folklore claims a fan from Chicago sent their management that tape of Brian Johnson's band. However, I have also read that the fan was from Cleveland. Regardless, it is quite interesting that it took a cassette sent from across the ocean to alert AC/DC to someone right there in England…a singer who had performed in front of Bon, and at one time, was even recommended by him. Impressed with Brian's performance the night Bon's band Fraternity opened for Geordie, Bon supposedly once told the band that if they ever needed to replace him, Brian Johnson would be a good choice. As Angus recalled in *Classic Rock,* "Bon was a big Little Richard fan—he believed that anyone singing rock 'n' roll would have to match Little Richard. I remember Bon saying that Brian was a great rock 'n' roll singer in the Little Richard mold."

Once AC/DC listened to the tape, they immediately located their lead singer Brian Johnson in Newcastle and rang him up to come in for an audition. He was so taken aback by the telephone call, he hung up the first time, thinking it was a practical joke. When he finally agreed to come in, he still laughs to this day over what happened after he got there.

When Brian arrived at the rehearsal studio on March 29, 1980, he immediately started playing pool with a couple of the band's friends, thinking they were auditioning, as well. He assumed when the band was ready for him, they would come downstairs and get him.

Brian is about as genial of a guy as you will ever meet and waiting for the band to invite him in epitomizes his personality. An hour and a half later Malcolm came downstairs, frustrated that the singer they were waiting on had apparently stood them up. They all had a good laugh when they realized Brian never got past the pool table! The band brought him up to the studio and he performed only a few songs with AC/DC: "Whole Lotta Rosie," "Highway To Hell," and Ike and Tina Turner's hit, "Nutbush City Limits."

A few weeks later, after the auditions came to a close, the band's manager rang Brian and informed him that he had the job. Malcolm stated that he made up his mind about Brian on the spot, "Brian sang great. It [Johnson's audition] put a little smile on our face…for the first time since Bon." Angus remembers that when Brian walked through the door, they were all happy. "He more or less fitted in straightaway. The thing was, we wanted to find someone who was a character, and that's exactly what he is." Johnson wasn't so sure. He figured if things didn't work out, he could tell his mates he was in AC/DC for a few weeks and get a holiday in London out of it. His "holiday" has lasted 26 years and counting.

Fifteen months younger than Bon, Brian Johnson was born on October 5,

1947 in Newcastle Upon Tyne in Northumberland in northern England. He was the son of Alan Johnson, an army sergeant major in the British Army and his Italian wife, Esther. As a child, Brian sang in the church choir and performed Gang Shows with the Scouts. [The Gang Show was a theatrical production performed by the Scouts. The creation of producer Ralph Reader, it has become a worldwide Scouting tradition.] He also once starred in a television play. Quitting school, Brian became an apprentice as an industrial fitter in a local turbine factory while singing at night in local bands.

In 1972, at the age of 25, Brian joined the rock 'n' roll band, USA. Together with guitarist Vic Malcolm, drummer Brian Gibson, and bassist Tom Hill, they changed their name to Geordie. [Geordie is an English slang term for a hard-working, hard-drinking man, which pretty much covered most of the male population of Newcastle.]

Their first single, "Don't Do That," was released at the end of the year by EMI, climbing to Number 32 on the British charts. A few months later, their second single, "All Because Of You," reached Number Six, and their third, "Can You Do It," also made it into the Top 20. Riding on glam-rock's coattails, Geordie's fourth single, "Electric Lady," only reached Number 32 in August of 1973.

Over the next three years, Geordie would release three albums: *Hope You Like It, Don't Be Fooled By The Name,* and *Save The World.* They also released a compilation album in 1974, *Master Of Rock.* Right after *Save The World* came out, Geordie decided to call it quits. Brian once told *Musician* magazine about following the milkman around at 5 am and stealing half-eaten meals from other people's plates in local restaurants. "I gave it up [the band] in about 1975 because it was all wrong. So I left and I didn't think I'd join a professional band again. Ever."

Five years later, right before he got the call from AC/DC, Brian had just convinced his ex-band mates to reform Geordie and give it another try. After getting back together, Geordie had signed a deal to record a single for Red Bus Records when Brian got the ultimate job offer. Recruiting Terry Schlesser to take Brian's place, Geordie carried on, freeing Brian to accept the most promising position a working-class rock 'n' roller could ever hope for. Five and a half weeks after Bon Scott's death, Brian Johnson became AC/DC's new lead singer.

At the time, Brian was married with two daughters, living in Newcastle and earning a wage running his own business installing vinyl roofs on cars. For the past five years, he had provided for his family, virtually giving up the hope that he would someday make something of himself in the music business. Becoming a member of AC/DC must have been beyond his wildest dreams! As soon as he was hired, the band advanced him some money to square away his debts. AC/DC even compensated Geordie for any lost income they might suffer and immediately swept Brian off to rehearse for the new album.

Instead of recording in London as they had planned, the band decided to take advantage of the tax benefits of recording in the Bahamas at Compass Studios in Nassau. This was the recording studio that had been built by Chris Blackwell, the owner of Island Records. Not only did it take the band out of the glare of the media, it also provided a quiet, relaxing place for the band to work Brian in. Evidently flying off to a tropical island wasn't all that it was cracked up to be. When the band arrived, violent thunderstorms were thrashing the island. Brian remembered, "It wasn't a tropical paradise. It wasn't all white beaches. It was pissing down, there was flooding, and all the electricity went out—nae television."

The accommodations weren't exactly secure, either. Brian stated, "This big old black lady ruled the place with a rod of iron. We had to lock the doors at night because she'd warned us about these Haitians who'd come down at night and rob the place. So she bought us all these six-foot fishing spears to keep at the fucking door! It was a bit of a stretch from Newcastle, I can tell you."

Malcolm recalled in *Classic Rock,* August 2005, "It was the best place to do that album because there was nothing going on. We'd sit through the night with a couple of bottles of rum with coconut milk and work. That's where a lot of the lyric ideas come from."

Along with AC/DC, some of rock's biggest stars also paid Mr. Blackwell's studio a visit in 1980. Keith Emerson of Emerson, Lake, and Palmer had recorded there before and enjoyed it so much he made his home in the Bahamas for several years. "What happened with us, with ELP, is we were recording in Switzerland and I didn't like the place very much, because there wasn't a lot happening. So ELP moved to the Bahamas in 1978 or 1979 to start work on their *Last Beach* album. The reason why we chose the Bahamas, because it was kind of a tax-exile place, which is probably why AC/DC chose it. In England at that time, it was being run by the Labor government who charged an exorbitant amount for people who were making large amounts of money. I think we paid 80 to 90 percent of our earnings. We all got out of that one. So a lot of British bands were leaving England."

Emerson agrees that Compass Point was a hotbed for rock stars. "It was an interesting time. Ringo Starr arrived with the singer [Harry] Nilsson. It was about the time that they were both doing a lot of drugs. So there was all this hilarity coming from the next studio. I remember one night around 11 o'clock; I popped around. Ringo is a very friendly guy and even when I see him today, we always have something to talk about. He's a lovely guy. On that particular occasion, which I very much doubt he can remember, we got to chatting and he couldn't remember where he was supposed to be staying. Apparently, his accommodations had been organized by Chris Blackwell, who wasn't there. I happened to know where the lodges were for people who were recording. It was probably less than a quarter of a mile away and it was pitch-black dark. The only transportation I had was a 750 Norton motorcycle, which was outside. So Ringo said, 'I'll climb on the back of this and you can take me where I have to go.' So we drove down the coast along Love Beach and I took him back to his accommodations. It was only after I had dropped him off and went back to the studio, was when I realized, 'Good Lord, I had one of The Beatles on the back of my motorbike!'"

Emerson remembered running into Grace Jones who was also working at Compass, right before AC/DC arrived. "Then we came to realize that a band from Australia was coming down. I didn't know much of the history of the band, but there was always an excitement when you knew a band from England was coming. When AC/DC arrived, they had all their English gear on, leather jackets...And of course, you know what we wore on the island was a pair of shorts and a shirt, if that. Brian was the first guy I spoke to and he was trying to get used to the weather. It was very hot and by the time they arrived, I had bought a 21-foot sports fisherman boat. It wasn't vastly glamorous, but it enabled me to get out and fish and water ski, scuba dive, it had a stereo on board, an ice freezer on it, something manageable for one person to skip around the island with. When I mentioned this to Brian, he said, 'Oh God, I would love to come out with you!' And most of the other band members said the same thing. I asked them if they wanted to come out with me and fish. They'd arrived somewhere in the spring and in April the tuna fish were pretty abundant around the islands...as long as you knew where to go. I had a lot of education in fishing from the locals, so I was pretty confident we'd catch something. I think we left mid-afternoon and sure enough, all the birds were flying out from the mainland and were converging on a particular area of the sea, so we just put the rods in and we had a fish on in about 10 minutes! Which of course, they got very excited about that. I was relieved because if we didn't catch anything, my credibility as a fisherman is, well it would be like Ernest Hemingway."

"I think it was a great excitement for them and kind of introduced them to my way of the Bahamian life. I think they grew to like it and settled into their recording at Compass Point. I ran into Brian a while later on the beach and he told me he had a little bit of difficulty putting his vocals on, after he had been sunbathing. Right after he had been on the beach, he would go directly into Compass Point Studios, which is right across the street from the beach. Wearing his shorts, he'd just put the headphones on and have to do this rip-roaring vocal, and it just wasn't happening. He was singing his heart away and it just didn't have that power. So he had this idea. He told them he was going to go back to the hotel and then he'd be right back. He was gone for about an hour when he came back wearing his stage gear. He walked into the vocal booth and said, 'Right now, roll the tape.' And, of course, it came out, like rip-roaring, you know? He just couldn't sing in his shorts, that's what it was."

Back in 1980, Emerson wasn't quite familiar with AC/DC's music, so I asked him what he thought of them as people, since I've always thought they were very down to earth. Laughingly, he replied, "Oh, absolutely! There were no egos, there was no, 'Hey, listen, I'm a rock star and I can't get any salt water on me. And I certainly cannot deal with this ballyhoo bait that you got here in this stinking bucket! Basically all the guys just mucked in and thoroughly enjoyed the experience. I was just happy to have a bunch of guys on my boat! In other words, there was no, 'Don't you know who I am?' attitude. I would have recognized that straight off and I would not have invited any of them on my boat! They were very keen and very interested and it was certainly great for me to have their company."

With Mutt Lange once again at the helm, AC/DC embarked on recording their eighth album with their new lead singer. As for working with Lange again, Angus told *Classic Rock,* "It was very good—for both us and him—I think. After he made *Highway To Hell* he was in big demand, but I thought it was good for him [to record with AC/DC again]. Especially after what happened to us. It's to Mutt's credit that he still wanted to be involved with us after Bon's death."

Not only did Brian have to fit in with the band, but he also had the daunting task of coming up with his own lyrics. Brian explained in VH-1's *Ultimate Albums* that he was paralyzed with fear. Praying for guidance, Brian revealed that he experienced a supernatural event regarding Bon that he was reluctant to go into detail about. Judging from the future success of this album, I think it's safe to say Bon must have heard his prayers.

In memoriam to Bon, the band decided on an all-black cover with a most

ian thankful that Angus doesn't weigh much, in Providence, Rhode Island (November 22, 1985). © Ebet Roberts

AC/DC at a party in New York City on June 13, 1985, while they were in town shooting the video for *Fly On The Wall*. © Ebet Roberts

AC/DC performing at the Rosemont Horizon in Chicago, Illinois (November 9,1983). © Paul Natkin

aying their only British date for that year, AC/DC headlined Monsters Of Rock at Castle Donington in Leicestershire. (August 22, 1981).
Ross Halfin/Idols

ngus being lowered to the stage at the Hammersmith Odeon in ondon during the Back In Black tour (1980). © Ross Halfin/Idols

Brian Johnson at AC/DC's first time headlining Madison Square Garden in New York (December 2, 1981). © Frank White

Brian Johnson, as Perry Cooper said, "picking up the mantle." © Ross Halfin/Idols

C/DC rocking the Castle Donington at Monsters Of Rock (August 22, 1981). © Ross Halfin/Idols

Malcolm, Angus, and Brian during the video shoot for *Fly On The Wall*, at the World's End Club in Alphabet City, New York City (1985). © Deborah Feingold/Hulton Archive/Getty Images

Brian and Angus—always on the move. © Ken Friedman/Retna

Double the trouble—Brian and Angus. (1986)
© Bliss Morris/Corbis

They do look innocent, don't they? Brian and Angus (1990). © Martyn Goodacre/S.I.N./Corbis

Angus becoming "one" with his guitar at Madison Square Garden, New York City (December 2, 1981). © Frank White

Angus doing his infamous duck walk at the Civic Center in Providence, Rhode Island (November 22, 1985). © Ebet Roberts

fitting title, *Back In Black*. The 10 songs included on this historic album were "Hells Bells," "Shoot To Thrill," "What Do You Do For Money Honey?" "Give The Dog A Bone," "Let Me Put My Love Into You," "Back In Black," "You Shook Me All Night Long," "Have A Drink On Me," "Shake A Leg," and "Rock And Roll Ain't Noise Pollution."

The opening track features the haunting sound of a church bell chiming the death knell, signaling the beginning of "Hell's Bells." To create the proper mood for the song, the band decided to record an actual church bell. They also commissioned a $14,000 replica of the four-ton Denison bell, to take out on tour with them. Luckily for the roadies, they settled on a lighter version at one-and-a-half tons. [The Denison bell is named after Edmund Beckett Denison, who designed and made the bell that hangs in Westminster, known as "Big Ben."]

Engineer Tony Platt took the Manor Mobile recording unit out and surrounded the Carillon [bell tower], which stands in the middle of Loughborough's War Memorial in Leicestershire, England. Armed with 24 microphones, they were still unsuccessful. The live recording had to be scrapped and the band decided to capture the sound of the bell right in the foundry. Steve Cake was interviewed about the recording of "Back In Black," and he stated, "[My father] worked at the John Taylor Bell founders back in 1980 when AC/DC called from the Bahamas." Cake explained, "The traffic and birds chirping made [Tony Platt's original] recording unusable. So the work [on the AC/DC bell] was speeded up and what you hear on the album was definitely recorded at our factory." [The person who forged the bell actually rings it on the album.]

The lyrics to "Hells Bells" were inspired by a comment Lange made to Brian in the studio one night. Brian recalled in *Ultimate Albums* on VH-1 that when he wrote "Hells Bells" there was a terrible storm booming over the island. Lange suggested 'rolling thunder' which prompted Brian to continue, *"I'm a rollin' thunder, pourin' rain, I'm comin' on like a hurricane. My lightnin's flashin' across the sky, you're only young but you're gonna die."*

The title track for the album came from a guitar riff that Malcolm played for Angus somewhere in a hotel room. Angus told *Guitar World* in April 2003, "I remember during the Highway To Hell tour, Malcolm came in one day and played me a couple of ideas he had knocked down on cassette, and one of them was the main riff for "Back In Black." And he said, 'Look, it's been bugging me, this track. What do you think?' He was going to wipe it out and reuse the tape, because cassettes were sort of a hard item for us to come by sometimes! I said, 'Don't trash it. If you don't want it, I'll have it...In fact, I was never able to do it exactly the way he had it on that tape. To my ears, I still don't play the thing right!"

Within six weeks, the band had miraculously created an album that would herald the second phase of AC/DC's career. Brian was so relieved when the recording was finished, he told *Classic Rock* in August 2005, "It was about three in the afternoon, it was a beautiful sunny day, and I went outside down to where the huts were. I sat on this wall and I got a ciggie out and sat among the trees. I was so happy that I had done it. But I hadn't really heard one song. I'd go in and do a couple of verses, pop back and do a chorus. That's the way Mutt keeps you interested, you know." The only complaint Brian had were the high notes on "Shake A Leg" claiming, "Oh, that was fucking way up. Some of those notes will never be heard by man again."

For some reason, it took *Creem* magazine until their May issue to acknowledge Bon's death, "At press time, Bon Scott, 30-year-old [sic] vocalist of AC/DC was reported dead in England. Found in the car of friend Alastair Kinnear, the Australian belter of "Highway To Hell" and similar screechers died of apparent "alcohol poisoning." What's especially ironic is the Australian band's career was just taking off in the States after great success in England. As yet, Atlantic Record's no comment on the incident or the band's future plans, although their next album was in the final mixing stage and will doubtless be released soon."

The less than enthusiastic press was the least of Brian's worries. After he joined the band, he once stated, "I was a bit scared because I didn't know what to expect. I was more scared of the crew than I was of the lads, because the crew were reeling off names like Yes and Rick Wakeman...these fucking huge bands they've worked for. But the lads made me feel dead comfortable. The band's the fucking best! The biggest bonus about being in the band is the fact that I can get into their gigs without paying for a fucking ticket and I've got the best seat in the fucking house! Honestly! I could just sit up there and watch that band because they're fucking great. A great band and a great bunch of lads. I know what they were going through when Bon went, wondering about going on and all that — it's only natural. But they never made me feel left out. Luckily, these guys are so much like a fucking family." Brian received more assurance, when Atlantic Records declared the new album "brilliant."

The month of June was spent rehearsing in London before launching the Back In Black tour with six warm-up dates in Belgium and Holland. On June 29, 1980, Brian Johnson appeared with AC/DC for the first time in

Namur, Belgium at the Palais Des Expositions. Bon's successor was immediately welcomed with open arms by AC/DC, and especially Bon's fans. Brian was quoted as saying, "That poor boy was loved by thousands of people worldwide. When we did a warm-up gig in Holland, this kid came up to me with a tattoo of Bon on his arm and said, 'This bloke was my hero, but now he's gone. I wish you all the luck in the world.' I just stood there shaking. I mean, what can you say when people are prepared to put their faith in you like that? Since then, I feel like I've been singing for that kid and so many others like him."

Brian also told Tommy Vance from the BBC, "I think Bon Scott had a bit of genius. It annoys me that nobody recognized that before. He used to sing great words, write great words. He had a little twist in everything he said. Nobody ever recognized the man at the time. Oh great, when the man died they were startin' to say, 'Yeah, the man was a genius.' That was too late; it's not fair. I think he was so clever, and I think he had such a distinctive voice as well. He was brilliant."

Not everyone was so sure AC/DC could go on without Bon. Atlantic's Perry Cooper said, "They called me up and said, 'We've got this new singer and we're going out on the road. We want you to come out and see him.' And I flew out to see them somewhere in Canada and went on the bus with them from somewhere to Calgary. And I'm sitting there on the bus and there was Brian. He came up to me and said, 'I was told I had to make friends with you. You are the key to Atlantic.' And I said, 'What the fuck are you saying? I can't understand you!' And all he did was tell jokes the whole way, he was so wonderful. He's the best guy in the world!"

In the beginning of July, AC/DC filmed video clips for *Back In Black* in Breda, Holland. From July 13 to 28, they played 11 dates in Canada before making it back to the States. The new album was released in the U.S. on July 21, 10 days later in the U.K., and in Australia 11 days after that. Within six months, *Back In Black* peaked at Number Four, staying in the *Billboard* Top 10 for five months.

Brian's first gig here in the States was on July 30 at the County Fieldhouse in Erie, Pennsylvania. Nantucket opened. Guitarist Tommy Redd remembered it very well, saying that Brian was so nervous that night, his knees were literally shaking. "The first night in Erie, we were supposed to be playing with Humble Pie, but they didn't show up. The second night they showed up at the Spectrum [Philadelphia], and it was sold out. When they showed up, they got into a spat over the sound and lights. Steve Marriott, who was a great singer, was drinking really bad. They didn't want to accept that they weren't the headliners and couldn't call the shots on the lights and sound. But that's when their part of the tour came to an end. So Nantucket started out playing just 30 minutes and that was expanded to an hour. As the tour went on, other bands joined in, like Wet Willie and REO Speedwagon. Most the time it was just the two bands, and they were very generous with the lights and sounds. Some bands only give you one or two lights. They [AC/DC] didn't care."

AC/DC headlined a sold-out show at the Palladium on August 1 with Humble Pie and another English band by the name of Def Leppard trying to follow closely in their footsteps. On the seventeenth, AC/DC would play their last supporting set ever when they opened for ZZ Top at the Toledo Speedway Jam II in Toledo, Ohio.

Over the next four weeks, Nantucket would have the honor of opening many sold-out shows for AC/DC as they traveled through Virginia, North Carolina, Georgia, and Tennessee. Redd is proud to say that he turned AC/DC onto North Carolina BBQ

Onstage cocktails were another band favorite. Redd laughed about the bar that always stood onstage right behind the curtains. It was called 'Hell's Bar.' "It had two arms that swung out, like doors," said Redd. "Each door had about three gallons of liquor hanging upside down, so you could get a shot. It had an ice drawer in it and all these cups…everything you needed to make a mixed drink. We would always run out of our beer along with the radio people, friends, and people coming backstage. We always ran out and I would end up onstage mixing Brian Johnson drinks. He would come around the corner and say, 'Tommy, got anything?'"

Redd described other stress relievers while on tour, "We used to play dart tournaments after sound check, and everyone put money up. You could win some good money. They were like ace dart players, so you had to be partners with one of those guys to get into the ballpark. One night in Savannah, Georgia, we got into a dart tournament at a happy hour in some bar, and they really killed those guys. The local yuppies had no idea who they were playing against. There were roadies along because AC/DC never separated themselves from the road crew."

Nantucket also has the honor of being the only supporting band that was given, by George Young no less, an AC/DC song to cover. It ended up being the first song on their third album *Long Way To The Top,* which was released in 1980. Not only did they cover "It's A Long Way To The Top (If You Wanna Rock 'N' Roll)," but they actually performed it while opening for AC/DC. Redd explained: "Their brother George brought this song to

Epic as a suggestion for us to record. It came off good and they hadn't yet released that song in America. We were real hardcore AC/DC fans and it went over. The only time we had a rough time playing that song was at the Cow Palace in San Francisco. That was the roughest. We played it on the rest of the tour. One time, Angus came back to the dressing room and we played it for him. We asked him if it was all right for us to perform and Angus said, "It's OK with me mate, but you don't have any bagpipes!"

Once they had traveled all the way out to California, the band flew back to the Midwest to play dates in Nebraska, Minnesota, and finally, Wisconsin.

On Sunday, September 14, 1980, AC/DC returned to Madison, Wisconsin to play a sold-out show at the Dane County Coliseum, with Blackfoot opening. Tour manager Ian Jeffery generously set me up with tickets and backstage passes. My boyfriend John and I got to the Coliseum early so we could visit with Ian a bit and be there when the band arrived. About an hour before show time, AC/DC was ushered in the back door. As they were taken to their respective dressing rooms, I could see Angus jumping up and down trying to wave at me. He was motioning for me to follow the band, which I did. Once they were settled in, Angus came out and said that he wanted me to meet Ellen, his new wife.

Ellen was taller than Angus, like most of us, and about the same height as me. She was very pretty, with straight, long blond hair and blue eyes. We had a very pleasant visit talking about Angus and how he didn't fit his stage persona at all. We both laughed when she confessed that she didn't appreciate his mooning the crowd. She seemed more resigned to it when I explained that I thought by now, the audience expected it. After mentioning that Angus had been fighting off a cold, she grabbed him by the arm and pulled him out of a chilly draft of air. I smiled to myself when I realized that Angus had finally found what he was looking for: a blond wife to come out on the road and take care of him.

As they got ready to go on stage, we found a great spot to watch the band on stage right, about 30 feet behind Phil Rudd. Since I hadn't heard anything off the new album yet, I didn't know what to expect. As the sold-out crowd got restless, the lights went down and the audience started to scream. Piercing the darkness was the mournful wail of a bell chiming the death knell, as a gigantic church bell slowly descended from above the stage. The band broke into the opening phrase of "Hells Bells" as the lights came up and the audience literally exploded into a deafening cheer. To this day, I don't think I have ever witnessed anything like it!

Brian Johnson walked out to the center of the stage wearing a black T-shirt, blue jeans, and his trademark flat cap pulled down over his eyes. After swinging at the bell with a mallet, he started singing, "Rollin' thunder, pourin' rain, I'm comin' on like a hurricane..." with a gale-like force that has to be heard to be truly appreciated. By the time they broke into their second song, my eyes filled with tears and I could feel Bon standing right next to me. At that moment, I was certain that AC/DC would go on to become one of the greatest rock 'n' roll bands in the world.

With their amazing new songs, mixed with the best of Bon's, the audience wholeheartedly embraced them. Brian sang with every molecule of his being, giving justice to Bon's memory. There was no doubt that the band sounded stronger than ever, but the loss of Bon had deeply impacted them. The boys had changed. We all had.

Forever the prophet, Bon always said he wouldn't go until he was famous. *Back In Black,* the record that nearly didn't get made, would ultimately become one of the best-selling albums in history and all these years after his death, fans still remember Bon Scott.

AC 13 DC

FOR THOSE ABOUT TO ROCK

The Back In Black tour continued to sell out across the country. Not only were the fans curious to see Brian, but they were also grieving for Bon right along with the band. Divine providence had struck AC/DC twice: once when Bon joined them and again when Brian stepped into his shoes to carry on.

The band played the Rosemont Horizon in Chicago with Blackfoot the following weekend. Again the audience started going crazy when the "Hell's Bell" made its descent toward the stage. Their new songs, "Back In Black," "Hells Bells," and "You Shook Me" were becoming instant rock anthems. Any doubts the band may have had over Brian being the right choice evaporated with the roar of the audience.

Perry Cooper had his own doubts about anyone replacing Bon. "I said to myself, 'How are they going to replace him?' He had such a weird voice. Nobody ever said if it was good or bad, but it was different. And then I met Brian and just fell in love with him. He is such a nice guy. Bon was, too. Yes, he liked to drink, he liked to party. But he was the sweetest man in the world. I really, at one time, considered him my best friend. From what I hear, in his passport, where you have a next of kin to call in case of an emergency, he had my name in it. This is what I was told. I miss him to death. Brian just took it up, when he took over in *Back In Black,* he just picked up the mantel. And I never thought anybody could ever pick up the mantel. And he did, he really did. And that's been the reason for the band's success all these years."

For Perry and many fans, the music is timeless. Perry declared, "Angus and

Malcolm come up with such classic riffs. They [the songs] are anthems, absolute anthems. Now when can you watch a football game or a baseball game and not hear "Hells Bells" or any of those? They're anthems!"

Though the mood may have been somber at times, humor still played an important part in keeping the band's morale up while on the road. Tommy Redd from Nantucket still laughs over all the fun they had on tour together. "One night in San Antonio, we went into the dressing room and I heard all this snickering and I looked underneath the stalls in the locker room and saw about 15 Texas/Mexicans, all with AC/DC T-shirts on. They didn't know who we were. It was still the afternoon and they thought I was going to throw them out. I brought them out and got them beers and gave them passes. They all ended up in the front row. It was cool to watch them jump around while we played."

The last night Nantucket got to open for AC/DC is one of Redd's favorite memories. "I remember that it was someone's birthday or anniversary, so we knew something was up. While performing, we understood why we had been forewarned. The drummer's drumsticks had all the tips sawed in two, so when he hit the drum heads, the sticks immediately broke apart. They [AC/DC] also filled his high hat with shaving cream, so the first time he hit that, the cream sprayed everywhere. If that wasn't enough, the bass drum had two-sided duct tape on it, so eventually the drum pedal just stuck to the drum. I guess there was also a huge cake they wanted to drop on my head, but I never did look up!" While Nantucket fought to get through their set, Phil Rudd and some of the road crew were on the side of the stage, doubled over with laughter.

By mid-October, AC/DC flew back to England to play 24 sold-out shows. Whitesnake and Maggie Bell opened for them.

AC/DC wrapped up the year touring Denmark, Sweden, Germany, France, Switzerland, Spain and Belgium. The singles "Rock And Roll Ain't Noise Pollution" made it to Number 15 and "You Shook Me" made it to Number 20 on the U.K. charts. The radio airwaves in America were saturated with songs from *Back In Black* and AC/DC firmly—and most deservedly—established themselves as one of the greatest rock 'n' roll bands in the world.

Fred William's of *Record Mirror* wrote, "Bells toll in black before the band begin and that's about the only memory of Bon Scott allowed. From here on in it's a trip to the edges of insanity, conducted by vocalist Brian Johnson lurching around like a punch-drunk sailor. Angus Young not so much gripping his guitar as gripped by it, moving around in a fit of demented hysteria in which the only function he's capable of is playing his guitar."

Some of their critics weren't as kind. *Rock-USA* columnist Andy Secher wrote, "AC/DC became successful because they'd broken down the barrier between themselves and the crowd. They *were* the crowd, up onstage. Bon Scott was great at doing that; he had rapport, he'd always toast the audience with a drink and tell little stories. He communicated with the crowd a lot better than Brian Johnson does. I find that sad." Angus retorted, "I don't think of Brian as Bon's replacement. There were people who could imitate Bon, but we didn't go for someone like that. We wanted somebody who could match Bon's capabilities, but we didn't want a carbon copy. Brian's an individual; he's his own character."

Let There Be Rock, the movie, was released in Paris on December 10. The ominous year of 1980—which, by the way, also took Led Zeppelin's drummer, John Bonham and legendary Beatle John Lennon—would close with all of AC/DC's albums released in France being certified Gold. Just five months after its debut, *Back In Black,* selling two-million copies in France alone, was certified Platinum.

After a very brief holiday, AC/DC played in France throughout January. The last date of the tour was at the Forest National in Brussels, Belgium, where the band invited Atlantic Records executive Phil Carson up on stage to play bass on the song "Lucille."

AC/DC eventually made it to Japan for four dates from February 1 to 5. On February 13, almost one year to the day of the first anniversary of Bon's death, AC/DC played in Perth, Australia. It was their first time performing there in over three years. Many of Bon's family and friends were present, making Bon's heir feel like a member of the family. Brian was also completely surprised by the audience's reaction. He said, "I remember the first night after we played. I'm not an emotional person by any stretch of the imagination. But the kids had this 40-foot-long banner right across the audience, and it had, 'The king is dead; long live the king.' And it was smashing. It was great." That night, Brian dedicated "High Voltage" to Bon's mum, Isa.

Commenting on singing Bon's songs, Brian said, "The amazing thing about the older stuff is that when we do a song like "Let There Be Rock" onstage, sometimes it seems like Bon's ghost is right up there with us. It's a very strange feeling. But we're sure that Bon would have wanted us to keep playing those numbers and when you see the reaction from the fans, you know that they want us to keep playin' 'em too."

Angus also described how it felt to work with a new front man. "I'd got so used to having Bon there, but Brian's an individual and that's helped a great deal because he's a pretty natural person. Sometimes Bon would tend to pull back a bit more and then come forward at others. Brian's very much like me—he's got a lot of energy and he's always up front."

Their high-voltage energy was in such demand that Atlantic decided to cash in on the craze and release their 1976 recording, *Dirty Deeds Done Dirt Cheap*. The album came out on March 23, 1981, not only in the States, but also in Canada and Japan. Not wanting to confuse their fans, AC/DC demanded that the record be sold for a cheaper price than a new album, with a sticker on the cover stating, "All selections recorded in 1976 by Bon Scott, Angus Young, Malcolm Young, Phil Rudd, and Mark Evans." *Circus* magazine poked fun at the band for making money off music that was already five years old.

In the March issue of *Kerrang!* rock journalist Sylvie Simmons, using her pen name, Laura Canyon, had visited the boys while in Indianapolis. "AC/DC is still the best hard-rock band in the world and if you dispute that, you can't deny that they're at least the hardest working. Johnson stomping, flexing his muscles, wearing the boards down to blotting paper, punching the air, striking macho poses, hands on his hips and screaming, a fine man to have around if you're getting mugged. A firm, solid thudding rhythm section. And Angus, nutty Angus, head down, rocketing across the stage, falling to his knees, shaking sweat over the madmen in the first 10 rows."

Visiting the band backstage, Canyon commented on all the girls running around. Brian explained, "Most of the audience is fellas in America as well, but since we started this tour there has been a lot of girls. I don't know, I think it's because we're on the radio so much. I don't think it can be me good looks!" Their audience that night in Indianapolis was 17,000 compared to 4,000 only one year earlier.

Dirty Deeds Done Dirt Cheap went Platinum within 10 weeks and peaked at Number Three on the Billboard charts, staying there for three consecutive weeks. The re-release also sent the title track to the top of the charts. Thanks to massive airplay, some of their more enterprising fans started dialing "36-24-36," causing a telephone nightmare for an Illinois couple who filed a lawsuit against the band.

John Doran further praised the backbone of the title song in *Metal Hammer* as, "...that killer riff that's heavier than a statue of Black Sabbath being sucked into a black hole." Now, *that's* heavy!

The June issue of *Kerrang!* voted "Whole Lotta Rosie" as the top Heavy Metal song. The May-June 1981 Year End Report in *Circus* declared, "If AC/DC could achieve such fame in 1981 with no touring until mid-November and some recorded leftovers, imagine what's going to happen next year when they're on the road behind the new record. Even Jeanne Dixon could probably predict this one right for 1982: Look for AC/DC to be at the top of the hard-rock heap once again."

Creem came through with a humorous article in July called AC/DC Book of Lists by Rick Johnson. One of the best was The Three Most Popular "Real" Meanings of AC/DC. 1. According to certain religious fanatics, the lightning bolt in their logo symbolizes the devil. Either that or it has something to do with Blue Oyster Cult. 2. In American heterosexual slang. It means half/heaven half/heartache. 3. In International Distress Code, it stands for "Rub my puppet, bucko." *See, I told you* Creem *was funny.*

Obviously pleased with how things were going, Atlantic Records re-released *High Voltage* in July. It eventually peaked on the *Billboard* charts at Number 146. That's because everyone was still spending their money on *Back In Black,* which by now had sold 12-million copies worldwide. That would be, on average, about one million copies sold per month.

AC/DC played their only British date for that year on August 22, when the band headlined Monsters Of Rock in front of 65,000 people with Blackfoot, Slade, Whitesnake, and Blue Oyster Cult at the Castle Donington in Leicestershire. Further proof that it may be a long way to the top, but if you tour non-stop for seven years, you can get there.

During that summer, the band went back into the studio once again with Mutt Lange. After three weeks of rehearsals in an old factory outside of Paris, they moved into EMI-Pathe Marconi studios to record but couldn't capture the sound they were looking for. After two weeks of futile attempts, they moved back into the old factory and brought Mobile One Studio—a mobile recording unit—over from England. That took care of the backing tracks and the lead vocals were later recorded in Paris at Family Sound Studios.

AC/DC eventually nailed 10 songs for the new album, including the title track, "For Those About To Rock (We Salute You)," "Put The Finger On You," "Let's Get It Up," "Inject The Venom," "Snowballed," "Evil Walks," "C.O.D.," "Breaking The Rules," "Night of the Long Knives," and "Spellbound."

The cover of their ninth album had a picture of a cannon and the words, "For Those About To Rock," in black against a gold background. Released on November 23, 1981, it immediately sold over one-million copies in the first week. It took *Back In Black* five months to be certified Platinum. It only took two months for the new album to go Platinum. At the same time, *Kerrang's* All-Time Top 100 Heavy Metal Albums listed no less than seven AC/DC records.

The Bell and Cannon Tour, if you will, started in October of 1983 in Seattle. The band played 28 dates headlining arenas throughout the U.S. and Canada.

On December 2 the band headlined Madison Square Garden in New York City for the first time. *For Those About To Rock (We Salute You)* had entered the *Billboard* charts at Number One. This was their first album to do so and it stayed there for three weeks.

Angus explained where the inspiration came from for the title track, "We had this chorus riff and we thought, 'Well this sounds rather deadly.' And we were trying to find a good title. And there's this book from years ago about Roman gladiators called, *For Those About To Die We Salute You.* So we thought, for those about to rock…I mean, it sounds a bit better than 'for those about to die.'"

After successfully slaying the dragons of doubt with *Back In Black,* how were they going to top a one-and-a-half ton bell? Coming back with something bigger and better was a no-brainer for this bunch. AC/DC knew that if they were going to give those about to rock a proper salute, they were going to need some cannons. Some very, very big cannons.

Delighting fire marshals around the world, AC/DC would roll out two cannons for their encore, "For Those About To Rock, We Salute You." It was a constant battle to get the clearance to use them each night. Sometimes the road crew would be backstage handcuffed during the song and at other times, Ian Jeffery would provide the cannon blasts courtesy of a Prophet Synthesizer. Perry Cooper laughed about what happened in Connecticut in December. "I remember when the fire marshal came up and said they couldn't fire the cannons. Well, they did and we got arrested that night. At least they gave us a good talking to. Years later, the roof caved in on that place!"

While appearing for two nights at the Capital Center in Largo, Maryland on December 20 and 21, AC/DC was recorded and filmed live. This footage produced promotional videos for "Let's Get It Up," "For Those About To Rock," "Back In Black," and "Put A Finger On You."

The French turned *For Those About To Rock* into Platinum just two weeks after they were given a chance to buy a copy. Further proof that AC/DC had taken over the world, *Kerrang!* published a Reader's Poll which voted AC/DC 'Top Band,' Angus was 'Top Guitarist,' Cliff was 'Top Bassist.' Brian came in as the third top male vocalist, Phil was the second-best drummer, and Angus came in second as 'Male Pin-Up.' AC/DC also won for producing the 'Best Live Gig' and "For Those About To Rock" won for Best Single.

After taking their traditional holiday break, AC/DC was back out for 28 dates in the States, starting with Birmingham, Alabama on January 17. The New Year also brought an American Music Awards nomination for Best Rock Band. Air Supply won the award, apparently disguising themselves as a rock band.

AC/DC took time off from February to June, making it the first real break since 1974. Malcolm and Phil went back to Australia, Angus spent time at his home in Holland, Cliff was in Hawaii, and Brian had settled in Florida.

Reviewing their American tour, *Circus* wrote, "For Those About To Rock (We Salute You)" burst forth from a green-lit stage, accompanied by explosions from the cannon with which AC/DC now travels. Angus Young duck-walked, crab-crawled, and piggybacked his way around the arena in his spiffy maroon uniform."

Newsweek wrote, "Middle-aged critics hate them, moms and dads blanch, the kids cheer on. AC/DC is the latest musical weapon in the war between the generations. Some say they're faceless—but try to convince your 13-year-old cousin."

Enjoying the band's huge success, Angus told *Circus,* "This popularity is what we wanted right from the start. We wanted to be millionaires. Let Mick Jagger worry about image and all that stuff. The most important thing is that the kids remember the difference between us and a group like Styx. Styx? That's not rock 'n' roll. That's show business."

From June 7 to 10, AC/DC appeared for the second time in Japan. It would take the band another 19 years to make a third trip. Around this time Ian Jeffery, their tour manager, became their personal manager when the band stopped working with Leber-Krebs. Their European dates for August and September were cancelled without any explanation. Those close to the band knew the cancellations had to do with Phil's drug problems, which had become severe.

At the end of September, AC/DC launched a 19-date tour through the U.K. and Ireland which included four sold-out dates at the Hammersmith Odeon and two sold-out shows at Wembley Arena. Most of December was spent playing 10 concerts in Germany, France, and Switzerland, although three of their French dates were also abruptly cancelled.

On one of their night's off, Angus jammed with some of Bon's friends from the band Trust at the Rose Bonbon Club in Paris before heading back to Australia for the holidays. At home in Newcastle, *Circus* reported that Brian and his wife, Carol, had the members of Cheetah over for post-concert cocktails. Cheetah was an Australian band that were managed by

George Young and Harry Vanda. After a shaky performance, Brian saved the day by inviting them back over to his place. Cheetah's vocalist Lyndsay Hammond said, "Brian's liquor cabinet has a lot of things in it, but as we discovered, he likes John Barleycorn the best."

By the end of 1982, AC/DC had received 27 Gold and Platinum albums in eight countries. *For Those About To Rock* did amazingly well in sales, but some of the band's critics weren't as keen. Malcolm told *Metal CD* in 1992, "Christ! It took us forever to make that record and it sounds like it. It's full of bits and pieces and it doesn't flow properly like an AC/DC album should...When we wrote it, we wanted another big song to play live like "Let There Be Rock" and "For Those About To Rock" which have stood the test of time and become our main encore. But by the time we'd completed the album, it had taken so long. I don't think anyone, neither the band or the producer, could tell whether it sounded right or wrong. Everyone was fed up with the whole record."

Taking a two-month break, AC/DC planned to meet at the Isle of Man in the United Kingdom in March of 1983 to rehearse before recording their next album, *Flick Of The Switch*. What wasn't part of the plan, was the unexpected departure of yet another band member.

AC 14 DC

FLICK OF THE SWITCH

AC/DC began rehearsals in March 1983 at the Isle of Man in the U.K. before traveling back to the Bahamas to record at Compass Point Studios. This time, Angus and Malcolm decided to produce the record themselves. Angus stated in *Guitar Player,* "We wanted it raw. We always were raw sounding, we just wanted it more free of the reverbs and the effects. You like a natural drum sound—you don't want this gigantic echo going on. A lot of people go, 'What is that?' because sometimes it sounds like oil drums or something. We tend to go for keeping the raw idea of it all, because that's really what rock music is meant to sound like...We always do all the back tracks together—the two guitars, the bass, and drums. That's the only way you can get that feel happening."

While the band was hard at work on the album, Phil's drug problems had gotten steadily worse. Perry Cooper revealed that he had shared a room with him while on tour, right before Phil left the band. Perry was shocked at his behavior, which included hiding things around his room and seeing people that weren't there. Phil's situation was also compounded by an unplanned pregnancy, involving one of Malcolm's relatives. Things came to a head with Phil and Malcolm in a punch-up, and Phil being put on the next available plane back home to Rotorua in New Zealand.

Angus told Mark Putterford in his book, *Shock To The System,* that Phil hadn't really gotten over Bon's death...that he felt their tightness of the "family" unit had died with him and he was hell bent on living the high life, whatever the consequences. "If he hadn't stopped, he'd have gone overboard and done something

131

drastic to either himself or someone else." Although they weren't done recording before Phil left the band, his drum tracks did make it onto the album.

Flick Of The Switch, with its pencil drawing of a tiny Angus reaching up to pull down a huge switch, featured "Rising Power," "This House Is On Fire," "Flick Of The Switch," "Nervous Shakedown," "Landslide," "Guns For Hire," "Deep In The Hole," "Bedlam In Belgium," "Badlands," and "Brain Shake." Thirteen tracks were actually recorded, but three of them were never released. AC/DC finished the record with Procol Harum's drummer, Barry J. Wilson, laying down some drum tracks for them...although they were never used.

Tony Platt engineered and mixed the album, with production credit to Malcolm and Angus. The Young brothers did give a nod to George and Harry by listing them in the credits as the "Dutch Damager" and "Gorgeous Glaswegian."

Mark Putterford's review in *High Voltage* stated, "Listen to the start of "Guns For Hire" and you'll hear that pale boney hand jerk across the live wires. You'll visualize that screwed-up brat face and the ever-present schoolboy uniform that accompanies it. You'll be able to feel the rising power as the legs twitch and the head nods faster and faster."

As soon as the band got back to England, they placed an anonymous ad in *Sounds* magazine, which read, "'Heavy rock drummer wanted. If you don't hit hard, don't apply." Angus quipped that the ad really said, "Any drummer under 5'2"." After dozens of auditions at Nomis Studios in London, 20-year-old Simon Wright, who had previously played with Tytan and A to Z, was chosen for the position. It was a dream come true for the kid who was in the audience in Manchester in 1979 when AC/DC played there with Def Leppard.

As Simon remembers it, "I saw an ad in a British music paper that said, 'Rock group looking for a drummer.' I never dreamed it would be AC/DC. I made a phone call and then I went to a rehearsal—there were Brian, Angus, Malcolm, and Cliff. I couldn't believe my eyes. We went through a first rehearsal and things went very well. They invited me back and the second time I was very nervous. But they obviously liked what I played, so I got the job."

Released in August 1983, *Flick Of The Switch* eventually reached Number Four on the U.K. charts, but only made it to Number 15 here in the States. Malcolm defended the album in *Metal CD,* "We did that one so quickly and I guess it was a reaction to *For Those About To Rock.* We just thought, 'Bugger it! We've had enough of this crap!' Nobody was in the mood to spend another year making a record, so we decided to produce ourselves and make sure it was as raw as AC/DC could be."

Their 28-date tour of the U.S. was postponed and in October, the band filmed three videos: "Flick Of The Switch," "Guns For Hire," and "Nervous Shakedown." The shoot took place in Los Angeles, with Paul Becher directing. By the end of the month, Simon Wright officially took over the drum throne when the tour opened in Vancouver, Canada.

Starting out with just two cannons, their stage design has evolved with every tour. Having someone who knew how to handle the pyrotechnics was crucial and that's when "Pyro" Pete was hired. Pete Cappadocia excitedly recalled getting the opportunity to work with AC/DC. "I was working for Def Leppard and their production manager was friends with Jake Berry, who was AC/DC's production manager at the time. They wanted to make some changes with the cannons in "For Those About To Rock." So I think Jake was off at the time and he came to one of our shows and I met him and we talked. He said the next time they were ready to go back out on tour, they would call me. So they called, it was about 1983. We made a few changes with the cannons and then we were off and running, every tour since 1983, they've called me, and we've either made changes or built new cannons."

As a true fan of the band's, Pete was one lucky technician. "AC/DC was one of the few bands that I really admired. I really liked them and when I got a chance to work with them, they were one of the few bands that I said, 'Wow! This is going to be cool!' At the time, there were a lot of British bands. I went straight from Todd Rundgren and Steely Dan to The Clash. When the first Clash album came out, I was 15. I had eclectic musical tastes, so I didn't like what was on the radio. I was always looking for weird stuff. So at the time, there was Pink Floyd and Led Zeppelin and then I found punk! And I was like, 'Wow!' Then it was The Dead Boys, The Sex Pistols, Gen X, and all of that. But AC/DC had always been one, that no matter what I was into, I could always listen to because it was just balls-out rock 'n' roll. They kind of transgressed whatever I was into at the time. So I was really intimidated, but they were really cool."

Cappadocia laughingly described what the band thought of him when they first met. "The first time I met them, at the time I had a Mohawk which would either be red, blue, or green, or whatever. Mostly red at that point. I remember going into the dressing room and Jake announced, 'This is going to be the pyro guy.' And I just remember Angus and Malcolm just kind of staring at me with this look like, 'Are you kidding me?' Right away Brian said to me, 'Good to have you aboard!' Cliff was like, 'Yeah, whatever.' And Simon said, 'Hey, good to see you!' Angus and Malcolm were definitely like, 'All right, let's just see.' But then we just hit it off. They explained to me when the cue was and made a few jokes, we did a couple of rehearsals, and they said, 'If you do that all the time, that's fine.'"

People magazine caught up with the band at the Philadelphia Spectrum in November. Describing Angus as, "Dressed in old-school tie, cap, and knickers, the 5'3" musician looks like Tweedledum on acid as he struts, duck-walks, and drops his drawers to the crowd's delight." The article celebrated the band's tenth anniversary tour and worldwide album sales of 25 million.

Circus magazine, reviewing the same concert said, "He's got the audience in his back pocket from the start. For most, Angus Young *is* AC/DC — the man they've all come to see. At 5'4", Young is one of rock's few true originals; the biggest wise ass in the classroom."

The last night of the American tour was December 5, 1983 when they headlined again at Madison Square Garden. The show sold out.

The crowd's reaction to the band that night was as crazy as ever. You could barely hear the music over the din of the audience. All of Angus' classic moves, his strip tease, the mooning, their walk-about, had become solidified staples at an AC/DC concert.

Since Bon's death, Angus had become the real focal point of the band. As *Guitar Player* would state, "Brian Johnson may be AC/DC's leather-throated vocalist, but Angus is the reigning center of attention." Appearing larger than life on stage, Angus once explained how after seeing him perform, that most people expect him to be much taller. "Some of the women that used to come looking for me [after concerts] were like Amazons. I'd open the door and say, 'It's okay, I'm just his butler."

AC/DC ruled the Garden with some of the new album, but most of their set contained tried-and-true scorchers, guaranteed to make a believer out of you...if you weren't one already!

After the holidays, AC/DC went right back into the studio in January 1984 spending several months working on songs for their eleventh album. Ian Jeffery left to work with the band Frankie Goes to Hollywood and AC/DC hired a former Alberts executive, Crisping Dye, as their new manager. By June, the band completed a promotional press tour before meeting back in England to rehearse for their next European tour.

From August 11 through September 7, AC/DC headlined eight Monsters Of Rock festivals across Spain, Sweden, Switzerland, Germany, Italy, and France. On August 18, 1984, they were the first band to return as headliners to the fourth Monsters Of Rock at the Castle Donington. The concert also featured Y & T, Accept, Gary Moore, Motley Crue, Van Halen, and Ozzy Osbourne. As *Circus* pointed out, "even the mighty Van Halen had to settle for guest-star billing."

Angus told *Guitar World* in 1998, "I remember once we were playing the Donington Festival in Britain and I went down the day before the show and they had this gadgetry up there—it looked like Space Station #9! Anyway, I think Van Halen were on the bill too and Eddie Van Halen came up and said, 'Jeez, what's all this!' One of the guys who'd built the thing explained it to him and when he was done I said to Eddie, 'Do you like it?' Eddie went, 'Yeah, it's nice,' so I said, 'Do me a favor mate, take the fuckin' thing with ya! I'm sticking with me Marshalls—simple is better.'"

Angus confirmed the no-frills approach when he was quoted as saying, "I've always liked music because it's simple and direct. You don't have to think about it. It makes you dance and tap your feet. I've never been impressed with someone who can zoom up and down [the guitar neck]. I can do that myself, but I call it practicing."

A mini-album, *'74 Jailbreak,* was unleashed on the U.S., Canada, Japan, Argentina, and Brazil in October. The AC/DC appetizer included Australian-only released songs "Jailbreak," "You Ain't Got A Hold On Me," "Show Business," "Soul Stripper," and "Baby, Please Don't Go." It eventually made it to Number 76 on the *Billboard* charts.

The recording of their next album, *Fly On The Wall,* began at the end of the month at Mountain Studios in Montreux, Switzerland. Wanting to recreate the simplicity of the last album, Angus and Malcolm once again decided to produce it themselves.

For the first time ever, AC/DC had failed to win any category in the 1984 *Kerrang!* Reader's Poll, ending up as fifth top band and considered the eighth biggest disappointment of the year.

Despite the lack of support from *Kerrang!* readers, AC/DC rang in the new year by headlining two days at the Rock In Rio festival at Barra da Tijuca at the Rockdome in Rio De Janeiro, Brazil on January 15 and 19. They performed in front of 400,000 people with The Scorpions, Whitesnake, and Ozzy Osbourne.

That same month, Richard Hogan interviewed Angus and Malcolm for *Circus* magazine. When he asked them how AC/DC had changed over the past 10 years, Malcolm replied, "It's a different group now, but the idea is still the same. The rock 'n' roll's still there." Angus disagreed, "Ah, it's not changed. Malcolm's had on them same jeans for years. Not to mention

Johnson's. I don't think Johnson washes his."

When Hogan asked what they rely on in place of experimentation, Malcolm stated, "We rely on the beat. You name me another brand of music that's been around in the last 30 years as long as rock 'n' roll. Where is punk now? Or disco? Or Rick Wakeman's *Six Wives Of Henry VIII?"* Hogan closed his interview asking Angus if he would still be playing a schoolboy at 50. Angus snapped back, "I hope so!"

Fly On The Wall—with its cover showing, well, a fly on the wall—was released worldwide on June 28 and featured 10 more gems for the archives. The tracks included: "Shake Your Foundations," "First Blood," "Danger," "Sink The Pink," "Playing With Girls," "Stand Up," "Hell Or High Water," "Back In Business," and "Send For The Man." The record peaked at Number 32 in the U.S. and made it to Number Seven on the U.K. charts.

Journalist Jim Farber wrote in *Creem,* "As you've no doubt heard by now, the album sounds like a horde of rabid dogs racing through a hall of razor blades, only catchier. In other words, another utter masterpiece."

Malcolm explained how he felt about the album in *Metal CD,* "We wanted to pick it up a bit more for this album, so we tried our hands at producing ourselves again, but putting some more time and thought into what we were doing instead of just taping ourselves…Our drummer Phil [Rudd] had left and we had Simon Wright playing with us. He knew what he was doing and we just had to guide him in the right direction and leave him to get on with the job. It's a very simple thing, playing drums for AC/DC—but sometimes it can be hard to keep it simple."

Acknowledging MTV's grip on the Eighties, the band took up residence in the World's End Club in New York's Alphabet City to shoot promotional videos for the new album. Not exactly Park Avenue, at least not back then. The video, which was released in July, ran 28 minutes and featured six songs from the album. The concept was based on the band playing a gig in a small New York club filled with shifty characters. A drunken cartoon fly sails through their lives while the band is on stage. Angus quipped that he loved the neighborhood and "was planning on taking his next vacation there."

As soon as the new album was released, AC/DC signed with yet another new manager, their brother, Stewart Young with Part Rock Management. After two days of rehearsal, the band launched a 42-date tour, starting at the Broome County Arena in Binghampton, New York.

On August 31, serial killer Richard Ramirez was caught in California after committing 16 murders. Ramirez claimed the satanic images on the *Highway To Hell* album cover and the song "Night Prowler" incited him to do the killings. The police reported an AC/DC cap was found at one of the crime scenes. The media, particularly in the States, started accusing the band of devil worshipping. To which Angus replied in *Creem,* "We're not black-magic Satanists or whatever you call it. I don't drink blood. I may wear black underwear now and again, but that's about it." Brian echoed the absurdity of the accusations, "I mean the big idea with us isn't Satanic messages. It's to get one line to rhyme with the fucking next." Even Barry Taylor later wrote about the band in his book, mentioning, "the closest they came to Satanic worship is watching *The Addams Family* on television."

Due to all the controversy, officials in Dallas and Springfield, Illinois attempted to ban AC/DC from playing in their cities. Five thousand fans, not the anticipated 8,000 showed up for their concert in Springfield, but the band was refused a place to stay! Can you imagine how many fans would have thrown open their doors if they had only known?! Some live shows were picketed and the band's performance at the Pacific Amphitheater in Costa Mesa, California was cancelled due to narrow-minded pin heads.

Declarations were made on the meaning of AC/DC. Now it stood for Anti-Christ/Devil's Children, or Anti-Christ/Devil's Crusade. Their song titles "Highway To Hell," "C.O.D. (Care Of The Devil)," and "Hell Ain't A Bad Place To Be" were also questioned. Angus stated in the *Los Angeles Times,* "We toured for four years at a stretch with no break. A guy asked how you would best describe our tours. We said, 'A highway to hell.' The phrase stuck with us. All we'd done is describe what it's like to be on the road for four years. When you're sleeping with the singer's socks two inches from your nose, believe me, that's pretty close to hell."

As writer Martin Huxley said, "The only thing AC/DC ever worshipped clearly was rock 'n' roll." In Huxley's book, *AC/DC: World's Heaviest* Rock, *Washington Post* reporter Richard Harrington defended the band, "Heavy metal may be the music that can't get no respect, but in the past six years, it's had no trouble getting attention. Someone once said heavy metal was invented to reassure adolescent boys who have limited experience with women that they're not gay, and there certainly is a blatant misogyny at the root of the music—which may explain why AC/DC fans are overwhelmingly young males. But AC/DC's real force comes from the power chords, shout-along choruses, and a deafening, incapacitating decibel level that millions of adolescents seem to thrive on."

Angus added, "It gives them energy. They can swing their arms, bang their chairs, jump around. It's a form of getting rid of steam. Then they go home happy."

Billboard declared AC/DC as one of the world's bestselling hard-rock acts, with worldwide sales of 25- to 30-million albums. This is despite *Flick Of The Switch* selling short of a million albums and *Fly On The Wall* only sold half a million (being certified Gold in August).

As the band was selling out arenas, many of the venues were taking advantage of them. Mike Andy—who helped manage four world tours—signed on in 1985 as their security director. Andy discovered early on that because of the band's rowdy image, the venues were overcharging for repairs after each show. "The band didn't have the status they do now," said Andy. "Back then, the venues were making their repairs and then charging it back to the band. Promoters loved them because they always sold out, but they were also taking advantage of them. Not so much promoters, but the venue owners. Madison Square Garden used to demand a $25,000 deposit before they played there."

Things do sometimes get crazy at an AC/DC concert, but not to the extent that they were being charged. Andy started doing a walk through a day or two before each concert. Sometimes making notes and taking pictures of existing damage. That way they couldn't charge AC/DC for something that was already damaged before they even got there. He quickly started saving the band thousands of dollars.

Andy also discovered that the band was being charged by the beer vendors for damages, but they weren't getting a cut of the sales. "The band never made any money from the alcohol sales. They didn't want a penny from that. So there was no way they should be paying for their damages on top of everything else! I was one of the first to set up beer gardens at concerts, so people have to stay in one area to drink. That way they can't charge you damages in other parts of the venue. That alone cut way down on the vendors being able to get away with that." After his first tour with the band, AC/DC promoted Andy to tour director.

While the band was out promoting *Fly On The Wall,* horror author and devout AC/DC fan, Stephen King, approached them about using some of their old material for the soundtrack to his new movie, *Maximum Overdrive.* King also suggested they write some new songs to be used exclusively for the film. This would mark AC/DC's first attempt at writing music for a picture. Malcolm commented on *Who Made Who* in *Metal CD* in 1992, "We were asked to provide the soundtrack music for the film, *Maximum Overdrive.* There was some of the old stuff in there, like "Hell's Bells" and, of course, the song "Who Made Who." We had the old team of Vanda and Young back producing the title track and I think that was what we needed. "Who Made Who" was a return to form for the band and it's become one of our most popular live tracks. We even used it as the opening song on our tour that year."

The band returned to Compass Point Studios in the Bahamas, this time putting George and Harry back behind the console. It would be the first time the duo had worked with the band since, *If You Want Blood (You've Got It)*.

AC15DC

WHO MADE WHO

As soon as they wrapped up their American tour in December, AC/DC began recording *Who Made Who*. This album would include six previously released tracks: "You Shook Me All Night Long," "Sink The Pink," "Ride On," "Hells Bells," "Shake Your Foundations," "For Those About To Rock (We Salute You)," and three brand new songs, the title track, "Who Made Who," "D.T.," and "Chase The Ace."

The entire project only took the band two weeks to complete. By mid-January 1986 they were back on the road playing eight dates in the U.K. supported by the band Fastway. The tour continued on through Europe with 17 more dates in Belgium, Holland, Germany, Switzerland, Sweden, Norway, Finland, and Denmark.

On February 27 and 28, the band took over Brixton Academy in South London to film the video for "Who Made Who," with David Mallet directing. Hundreds of AC/DC fans had been summoned from all over the U.K. to act as Angus clones, wearing specially made Angus school uniforms. The concept centered around Angus and his look-a-like minions.

Who Made Who was released in May 1986. The cover of the album featured a picture of Angus with school cap on, head down, standing with his guitar between stone pillars...with rays of light shooting up from behind him. The new record became the band's biggest hit in years reaching Number 11 in Britain. Becoming their first Platinum seller since 1981's *For Those About To Rock*, the album peaked at Number 33 in the States.

To direct a new video for "You Shook Me All Night Long," AC/DC once again called upon Mallet. The filming took place on June 10 and 12 in Jacob Street Studios, with the outdoor scenes being shot in northern England. Any MTV junkie can recall the comical content of the video, with one particular scene showing Brian coming home to find a scantily clad cowgirl riding a mechanical bull in the middle of his living room. Typical teenage fantasy! One of the band's crew fell in love with the girl in the video, eventually marrying her. AC/DC's wedding gift to the couple was, naturally, a mechanical bull.

Once the summer arrived, AC/DC went into the Lakefront Arena in New Orleans to rehearse before their 42-day assault on the U.S. On July 31, the tour opened at the Lakefront Arena in the Big Easy, Queensryche and Loudness supported the show. Tour director Mike Andy claimed that since the band spent several days in the venue before the show, it gave him time to note existing damages. When the band was presented with a bill for $18,000 in damages after playing there, he knew better and the band wound up only paying a third. Although 1986 wasn't the best year for concert sales, AC/DC's entire tour was sold-out, making it one of the most successful of the year.

Aside from the cannons and bell, the Who Made Who tour opened with the title track, which featured local fans dressed as Angus. You would think a one-and-a-half ton bell would pose some problems, but according to "Pyro" Pete, Angus impersonators were much more hazardous. He explained, "When you get the show up and running, it becomes like a machine that just runs. It's like one of those huge printing presses that you can't just turn off or it will rip itself apart...or a locomotive that can't stop on a dime.

"For the Who Made Who tour, there were winners for an Angus look-a-like contest. The show would start and it would be however many they could get, whether it was 10, 20, or even 30...they would be up along the back line of the stage with their cardboard guitars, doing their best Angus impersonation. And then the real Angus would rise up on an elevator in this tube in the center and come up about six or eight feet higher than the fake Angus's. We had a signal where we would grab the first fake Angus, from behind, and they would turn around and come off the stage back down the same way they went up. Well, not always would these guys want to come off the stage!

"So you would get these fake Angus's running around and sometimes it would be like trying to catch a chicken or something. Where everyone else would leave, you would always get this one guy who is still throwing his arm up. And we're back there hitting him with balls of rolled-up tape, or poking him with a yard stick, trying to tell him to get the hell down! We didn't want to ruin the illusion by having somebody on the crew just jump up and grab this guy and wrestle him off the stage!

"The band was always like that, too. [They always said] if a fan got up on the stage, don't run out and tackle him and beat the hell out of him. I never figured out that mentality, either. Some bands are like that. If a fan gets up on the stage and if I'm in a position where I see it happen, I'll run out and put my arm around them and escort them off the stage. If they start to fight, then you have to drag them off. So the band didn't want us pummeling the fake Angus's during the show! But more than once, we had to resort to poking them fairly hard to get their attention.

"I remember one time we grabbed this one guy by his ankles and we were trying to get him off to the side and he fell down. So then he started rolling around on the floor doing Angus's whole solo. The rest of the band didn't even know what was going on! Cliff walks front to back, front to back, and looks down at his feet, and looks at the microphone. Angus runs all around and Brian runs all around. And Malcolm does the same as Cliff, he walks up to the microphone and walks back, he doesn't really look, he looks down at his feet or at the microphone. So Simon was the only one who saw what was going on, and he was really laughing watching us trying to get this guy off the stage. Finally it came to a point where somebody had to go up and grab him and even when we were pulling him off the stage, he's still throwing his arm up into the air! Stage crews always cringe whenever we hear the two words, 'contest winner.'

"For a while, MTV and all the local radio stations and promoters used to hold contests. I remember when they came up with "Roadie For A Day." Which meant that you got some kid who was a fanatical fan who was just insane about it. Another "roadie for a day guy" and he wanted to know what he could do. So you usually give him a cleaning job, like cleaning the bell. And the guy says, 'Oh my God, not the bell!' We told him he didn't really have to clean the whole bell, we just gave him some brass polish and a rag and asked him to just clean around the AC/DC letters. He must have taken a toothpick, a Q-Tip, and a toothbrush and gotten every molecule of dirt off of the bell. When it came down that night and the lights hit it, it looked really good!"

Tickets for their upcoming tour of Australia went on sale in Perth in October, inciting a riot that resulted in the arrest of 63 people. Originally planned to wrap in September, demand for the band extended their tour into November...proving to some of their critics that AC/DC was still at the top of their game.

Angus was happy about *Who Made Who* and told *Guitar World* in March 1986, "We think we've done a good job and we achieved what we wanted. We just wanted to make a tough and exciting rock 'n' roll record. And that's what we made."

After an extensive search for the perfect location, the band chose to record their next album at Miraval Studio in Le Val, France. Pre-production was handled in Sydney by George and Harry from April through July of 1987. This would be their first time in nine years producing a full-length album for AC/DC.

Recording *Blow Up Your Video* officially began in August, with the title reflecting AC/DC's sentiment toward the overall power of MTV. Angus told *Metal Edge* in 1985 regarding the acceptance of their earlier videos, "They said you can't have a guy with a guitar sticking through him and blood gushing out...Why not?...I remember one video we had with me blowing up. And it was done in the best possible taste."

Nineteen songs were recorded, but when the tapes arrived in New York for the final stages of mixing, only 10 made it onto the album: "Heatseeker," "That's The Way I Wanna Rock 'N' Roll," "Meanstreak," "Go Zone," "Kissin' Dynamite," "Nick Of Time," "Some Sin For Nothin'," "Ruff Stuff," "Two's Up," and "This Means War." The cover featured a picture of Angus—guitar in hand—exploding through a television screen.

The first single, "Heatseeker," was released on January 4, 1988, making it to Number 12 on the U.K. charts. [David Mallet directed the video for this single at Cannon Studios in Elstree, England.] *Blow Up Your Video* was released in January and rose to Number 12 on the American charts. The band's thirteenth album made it to Number Two in the U.K., the highest to chart there since *Back In Black*.

AC/DC spent three days rehearsing at the Entertainment Center in Perth before kicking off a "Homecoming Tour" on February 1. They played 17 dates across Australia and New Zealand. These were their first live appearances down under since 1981. Angus was quoted as saying, "There's a whole new excitement about this band these days, and there's a whole new generation of kids to be won over."

The two nights they played in Perth were made even more special by the presence of Bon's parents, Chick and Isa. Acknowledging his popularity, the band's set list was dominated by Bon Scott songs. After shows in Perth, Melbourne, Sydney, Brisbane, and Auckland, AC/DC had rocked 130,000 fans in three weeks. Their return to Australia was extremely successful, except for the 60 people who were arrested in a riot at Melbourne's Myer Music Bowl. *Glad to hear the band didn't disappoint the Parliament.*

Their U.K. tour of six dates began on March 7, covering only two cities, London and Birmingham. While playing the National Exhibition Center in Birmingham, a live video was shot for "That's The Way I Wanna Rock 'N' Roll," under the direction of Brian Grant, Peter Sinclaire, and Jiff Morrison.

AC/DC, supported by Dokken, continued into Europe for 20 more dates. They played shows in Belgium, Germany, Sweden, Norway, Finland, France, and Switzerland before returning to London for one night at the Wembley Arena on April 13, 1988.

For the American leg of their Blow Up Your Video tour, Malcolm claimed exhaustion and chose to stay home and let his nephew, Stevie Young, take his place. Stevie who had been in the successful Australian band Starfighters had been playing AC/DC songs since he was a small child.

At first, the reason given for the change was that Malcolm wanted to take time off to be with his family. Later, the band admitted that he had taken the time off to deal with his alcohol problem. For years when asked why Malcolm didn't play more solos, Angus would always jokingly respond that playing solos would "interfere with his drinking." Eight years after Bon's death, Malcolm's drinking had become no laughing matter.

Angus eventually disclosed that "he [Malcolm] wanted to get rid of his booze problem and clean himself up. I think if you can do that on your own free will, it's great; and having been through that situation with Bon, I don't think I could have gone through it again."

While at home in Australia, Malcolm spent time with his wife Linda and their two kids. He even bought a horse and dabbled in racing. During his recuperation, he never put the guitar down for long and was already working on ideas for their next album. Luckily, nephew Stevie—who was the spitting image of Malcolm—had been so good at nailing his famous uncle's stage moves that most fans didn't notice Malcolm was gone.

Of course, Angus noticed a huge difference being on tour without Malcolm. He remarked to *Hit Parader,* "He's an incredible songwriter and an amazing rhythm guitarist. Playing that kind of guitar takes a special person and Malcolm has just the right feel for it. He's been willing to live a little bit in my shadow over the years, but [touring] without him just reinforced what I already knew—he's a very important member of the band."

Blow Up Your Video became the most successful AC/DC album in the U.S. since *For Those About To Rock.* Writer Jim Farber reviewed the album for *Rolling Stone* in April: "It's time the world stopped thinking of AC/DC as just a heavy-metal band. For 13 albums now, Angus and Malcolm Young have been crafting the kind of guitar riffs any Who-style rock 'n' roll band would kill for. Better yet, the members of AC/DC have allowed no production compromises whatsoever: they've carved every one of those irresistible guitar hooks out of pure stone...aside from that track, the album posits loyalty to one's own style as the ultimate virtue. Fortunately, the Young brothers continue to come up with enough inspired riffs to make the tunnel vision justifiable. In fact, the riffs here add up to the band's catchiest work since its classic album, *Back In Black*. Maybe *Blow Up Your Video* will finally convince those who have doubted the truth about AC/DC: it's the metal band that plays solid-gold rock 'n' roll."

Commenting later on *Blow Up Your Video,* Malcolm said, "We wanted to carry on where *Who Made Who* had left off, although there was a long gap between albums. We'd lost our footing by that time and we needed to get the old feeling back again. So we stuck with Vanda and Young again and went back to our roots. There was more production on the album than there had been on *Fly On The Wall* or *Flick Of The Switch* and we tried to capture that traditional 12-bar rock 'n' roll sound that we'd had in the beginning."

Over the next six months—beginning on May 3, 1988—the band played 113 dates touring throughout the U.S. AC/DC's Blow Up Your Video tour, which closed at the Cow Palace in San Francisco on November 11, ended up being one of the most successful tours of the year.

Once the tour ended, everyone went their separate ways to enjoy the holiday. Deciding to leave Hawaii, Cliff moved near Brian to the Gulf coast of Florida, while Malcolm went back to London and Angus returned home to Holland.

Adding to their rabble-rousing reputation, AC/DC's music helped flush Manuel Noriega out of his refuge at Panama's Vatican Embassy after his country was invaded. Apparently blasting "Hells Bells" and "Highway To Hell," among other rock 'n' roll treats, aided in sabotaging the opera lover's stand-off. This method of metal mental torture worked so well, that it has become a staple used by the American government. *Although I think it's just an excuse for our soldiers to rock out to AC/DC while being all they can be. And for that, we salute you!*

Alternating between each other's homes, Angus and Malcolm started gathering ideas for the new record. Due to the stress of Brian's divorce from his first wife, Carol, he chose not to contribute lyrics this time...leaving the song composition and lyric writing fully to the Young brothers. This caused a flurry of false rumors that Brian had actually left the band.

Aware of the straightforward rock 'n' roll sounds of bands like Guns 'N Roses, which signaled the decline of the Eighties hair bands, Angus and Malcolm prepared to stake their claim on the new decade. Not only would they take on the task of writing the music as well as the lyrics, but they would also change the beat of the band. At first, Simon Wright left on a temporary basis when he was invited to record an album with Dio. But once he was in the band, Dio's offer turned into a permanent position.

That was the official reason given by Wright and AC/DC, but years later Malcolm would admit that during the time he spent off the road, he had the chance to see some of AC/DC's shows from a very different perspective — the audience. The first thing Malcolm decided to do when he returned to the band was to "get rid of the drummer."

AC/DC began rehearsals for their new album in a barn outside of Brighton, England. At the suggestion of their management, drummer Chris Slade was sent in to record with them on a temporary basis. Slade had previously played with Gary Moore, Manfred Mann, The Firm, and with Led Zeppelin's Jimmy Page. Things went so well during the recording that the band asked Slade to join AC/DC.

By early 1990, AC/DC had switched to Windmill Road Studios in Ireland for pre-production work. Although Vanda and Young were originally supposed to produce the album, the band ended up working with Canadian producer Bruce Fairbairn. They all moved to Vancouver for the actual recording, which took place at Little Mountain Studios.

Fairbairn, along with his protege Bob Rock, helped establish Little Mountain as one of the top recording studios in north America. Fairbairn had previously worked with Loverboy, Blue Oyster Cult, Krokus, Aerosmith, and Bon Jovi (whose hit album *Slippery When Wet* sold 12-million copies).

Completing the recording in just six weeks, the band's fourteenth album would feature some of the biggest hits AC/DC had had in 10 years. It was called *The Razors Edge*.

THE RAZORS EDGE

AC/DC, again under the direction of David Mallet, filmed the video for the first single at Brixton Academy in South London on August 17. Close to 1,000 fans showed up to help create a sea of banging heads and waving fists to surround the band while they played "Thunderstuck." During the shoot, Mallet went through over five miles of film. The highlight of the video was seeing Angus duck walk from underneath a Plexiglas stage.

The title of the song had come to Angus while in flight during a thunderstorm. "I was in an airplane over East Germany and the plane got struck by lightning. I thought my number was up. The stewardess said we were struck by lightning and I said, 'No, we were struck by thunder, because it boomed.'"

The Razors Edge was released in September of 1990, featuring a red and silver cover which looked like a cloth slashed open, revealing the album's glistening title. The promotional pictures of the band for the new album were dark and slightly threatening...especially Slade, the new drummer with the bald head and brawny biceps. This was exactly the way the band needed to look, going up against the metal groups of the early Nineties, like Metallica, Faith No More, and Jane's Addiction.

The album was a sharp collection of 12 tracks including, "Thunderstruck," "Fire Your Guns," "Money Talks," "The Razors Edge," "Mistress For Christmas," "Rock Your Heart Out," "Are You Ready," "Got You By The Balls," "Shot Of Love," "Let's Make It," "Goodbye & Good Riddance To Bad Luck," and "If You Dare." In the song "Thunderstruck," Angus plays the intro with all his strings taped up, except the *B* string…a little studio trick George taught him. Soon-to-be hit single "Money Talks" was written with Brian's divorce settlement in mind. And the tongue-in-cheek lyrics to "Mistress For Christmas" proved that Angus and Malcolm had learned well from the School of Scott.

"Thunderstruck," the first single from the album, was released on September 29 and reached Number 13 on the U.K. charts. *The Razors Edge* went all the way to Number Four in Britain and Number Two in the States. Beyond the new album, overall sales were dizzying. On October 4, the RIAA certified Platinum sales for *If You Want Blood (You've Got It), Let There Be Rock,* and *Powerage. Dirty Deeds Done Dirt Cheap* had been certified triple Platinum and by October of 1990. *Back In Black* had sold 10-million copies, pushing AC/DC's total album sales to over 60 million.

Billboard reviewed the new album, claiming, "Aussie headbangers shoot out first release for new label Atco, and it's a doozy. With one of the more distinctive voices on the rock 'n' roll planet, Brian Johnson growls, rasps, screams, and generally peels the paint off the walls through 12 scorchers by the brothers Young…Fairbairn wisely lets the band's true grit shine through and doesn't try to polish the rough edges that make AC/DC one of the most imitated but never duplicated bands in the world."

Mark Putterford wrote in the U.K. publication *Select,* "…Malcolm Young's rhythm guitar still chugs along faithfully, sticking like glue to the relentless thud of the drums, Cliff Williams's bass still rumbles like clockwork thunder, and Angus Young—his lead guitar as mischievous as his spiteful schoolboy stage persona—still buzzes around in the mix like an irate mosquito. And Brian Johnson, the band's singer, still hasn't taken his tonsils back to the parrot house at Whitley Bay Zoo."

AC/DC launched the first leg of their tour with 34 dates through the U.S. and Canada, starting on November 2 at the Worcester Centrum in Massachusetts. Cliff, stricken with a kidney infection, had to be replaced by bassist Paul Greg for several concerts.

On November 6, Mallet shot another video of the band at the Spectrum in Philadelphia for the song "Moneytalks." By the fourteenth of the month, "Moneytalks" would peak at Number 23 on the *Billboard* charts. Two weeks later, the single hit Number 36 in the U.K., making it one of two singles, along with "Are You Ready" to reach Britain's Top 40. As soon as it was released, *The Razors Edge* started flying off the shelves and much of the tour was sold-out. Just as things seemed like it couldn't be better, tragedy struck fans again at AC/DC's concert in New Jersey on November 11.

During their performance at the Brendan Byrne Arena [now Izod Center] in East Rutherford, New Jersey, David Gregory, a 21-year-old fan, was attacked and beaten outside the venue. He died the next day in Hackensack Hospital. A New Jersey state trooper was cleared of any criminal wrongdoing and the family received a settlement in 1992 of $250,000. Unbelievably, this would not be the last time someone would lose their life at an AC/DC concert.

At the time of the album's release, I was working for another music publication and I enjoyed reviewing the album as well. "The whole feel of the album is riveting, reminding one of Back In Black, *and it's more than welcome!* The Razors Edge *should put AC/DC back at the top of the electrifying bands. After all, weren't they the original live wires?"*

The tour promoting the album featured a completely new stage design. Along with the tried-and-true cannons and one very heavy bell, the band included a few more surprises: one being a counterfeit AC/DC dollar with Angus's picture on it. These fake bills rained down on the audience during "Moneytalks."

I finally got my chance to see AC/DC again on December 1 at the Dane County Coliseum in Madison. This time I was reviewing their concert for the local paper, Night Sights and Sounds. *After much wrangling, I had secured an after-show pass to go backstage and see the band. I hadn't seen them live since 1986, and hadn't really talked to them since they played Madison Square Garden in 1983. Plus, the last time I heard from their ex-roadie, Barry, was Christmas of 1981!*

The Coliseum was sold out and the anticipation for the band hung thick in the air. As the lights went down, the darkness was set aglow by red neon tubing outlining the edges of the stage. The effect was accompanied by the sounds of thunder, which led into the opening of "Thunderstruck." As Brian, Malcolm, and Cliff walked out on stage, the amp racks with Chris Slade's drums rose slowly up through the floor. A spotlight revealed Angus in a green velvet suit with his trusty SG, standing on a ramp above Chris's head. As the audience screamed, he looked up and pointed a finger into the air before taking off, abandoning any stationary position for the rest of the show.

Following "Thunderstruck," we were treated to "Shoot To Thrill," "Back In Black," "Fire Your Guns," and "Sin City." The crowd was a sea of flying heads and flailing fists. When "Dirty Deeds Done Dirt Cheap" sent everyone into an energetic sing-a-long, it made me laugh. I couldn't help but wonder if Bon was seeing all of this. "The old man" would have been so proud.

Angus proved during "Jailbreak" that he is the fastest-moving guitarist in the business. I swear he gets more out of one riff than whole bands get in a year. Soaking up every second of it for his striptease, instead of flaunting his "legendary piece of showmanship," that night he gave us stars and strips boxer shorts. Not quite as provocative, but definitely patriotic.

In place of going for his walk-about, Angus appeared toward the back of the Coliseum on a smaller stage which rose up above the soundboard. Further proof that the boys were modifying their behavior a bit. Not surprising, considering they had practically toured non-stop for the past 17 years. While they were playing "Moneytalks," I had to resist the urge to jump off the balcony to catch one of the AC/DC dollars that fluttered down around the audience to the floor. Hey, AC/DC dollars are much cooler than personalized guitar picks!

The band pummeled us for two-and-a-half hours before ending their show with a gigantic balloon of Angus with horns during "Highway To Hell" and cannon blasts in "For Those About To Rock, We Salute You." The title for my review of the show for the paper was, AC/DC Levels Coliseum. No exaggeration there.

When I went backstage to see the band afterwards, I marveled at the true scope of their popularity. Not only did they have a crew of almost 100 people, but the fans who had after-show passes filled up an entire room!

As everyone was ushered into a long line that snaked all the way around one large locker room at the back of the Coliseum, we waited patiently for the band to appear. At the head of the line was a kid who won a radio contest. Standing along side of him were scores of music-business insiders, radio DJs, and limo drivers with good connections. Since I had brought along some gifts for the band, I went all the way to the back of the line.

The first band member to enter the official meet and greet, as they call it today, was Angus. He was accompanied by a very tall tour manager. The first thing Angus did was meet the contest winner and give him a hat. When the kid shook his hand and blurted out how much he loved AC/DC, Angus looked down and thanked him. For the next 30 minutes Angus made his way around the room shaking hands and posing for pictures.

By the time he had gotten to the end of the line, he looked as if he had had enough. When Angus saw me, he gave me a huge smile and said, "Sue!" I smiled back and threw my arms around him, which brought the room to a complete standstill. Even the jocks were gapping at us! Angus hugged me back and we stood there for what seemed like forever catching up on all the news. The best part was being able to congratulate him on the show and the new album.

Angus told me he was still married to Ellen and then asked me if I knew Barry had become the minister. A what? No way! Angus had heard that Barry had become a minister of his own church, which really surprised the whole band. We laughed about how strange it was to think of Barry giving a sermon?—especially if it wasn't in the church of rock 'n' roll!

After we had caught up on the last decade, I pulled out prints of the pictures taken of us at Alpine Valley back in August of 1978. I brought along copies for Angus and Malcolm, plus the original pictures for them to sign. I believe this was the first time I had ever asked them for their autographs. When Angus saw the pictures, the first thing he said was, "Oh, those were taken last week!" Then I'll never forget how he looked at them for a while, getting tears in his eyes. Then he looked up at me and said, "Bon really looked great then, didn't he?" And I said, "Bon was at his peak back then Angus, he looked amazing!" Which made us both smile.

Finally, Malcolm walked in and I got another big hug and lots of laughs. After catching up, I was able to ask them a few questions for my article. Just recently, Guitar Player *had favorably reviewed the new album, claiming that Malcolm's right hand should be declared an Australian national treasure. I asked Malcolm what he thought about that and he quipped, "That review cost me a lot of money!" Then I asked Angus what he thought of being called the God of heavy metal. He just sneered at me and said, "I'm not the God, I'm the monster!"*

Angus and Malcolm were clearly multi-millionaire rock stars, with the entourage to go with it, but their senses of humor hadn't changed at all. Saying goodbye, I wished them the best and told them to stay safe on the road. We promised to keep in touch and they would look for me when the tour came back through Wisconsin the following summer. I went home determined to track Barry down, or should I say, Reverend Taylor.

Before the end of the year, AC/DC would also be awarded a Gold album for *'74 Jailbreak.* It seemed everything they touched turned to precious metal. Taking their holiday break, the band started the second leg of their U.S./Canadian tour of 28 dates on January 9, at the Palace in Auburn Hills, California. Just as the band was proving their brand of rock would rule another decade, AC/DC would again be touched by another tragedy.

On the night of January 18, 1991, AC/DC was appearing at the Salt Palace Arena in Salt Lake City, Utah. The crowd of 13,294 were sold general-admission tickets, meaning you could sit or stand wherever you could find a spot…the closer to the stage, the better.

Before the band came out on stage, three teenagers—Curtis Child, Elizabeth Glausi, and Jimmie Boyd—were crushed to death by the surging crowd pressing toward the front of the stage. Not telling the band, knowing AC/DC would not have performed knowing the circumstances, the promoters decided the show must go on. As soon as the concert ended, the band was told the horrific news.

Making matters worse, press from around the world ran pictures of them on stage, claiming the band went on without regard to the terrible disaster. Angus talked to *Guitar Player* in February 1984 about the risk during his performance of going out into the crowd, "…The biggest thing is that I don't want anyone in the audience hurt. A lot of those kids are all together—they can be crushed and that's a big thing. If there's too much going on, too many people together, then I just won't do it. They [security] are mainly there for the protection of the kids. Every night kids go up and struggle with the security people."

"Pyro" Pete also mentioned their procedure concerning the crowd. "We had a "flying wedge formation" where we made a wedge with one big guy in the middle, with Angus on his shoulders, and a guy on each side. We even made up T-shirts and hats that say, "Angus's Flying Wedge Security." They told us to push gently and not shove anyone out of the way. The band was also very specific not to hurt the fans."

The band would eventually be cleared of any involvement in causing the deaths. On VH-1's *Ultimate Albums,* Brian talked about how devastated they were when they found out what had happened…especially when the press ran pictures of them smiling, inferring that they had gone on and performed anyway. Brian declared that they have never forgiven the British press for such callous treatment. He also added that it was still an extremely sad and painful subject for the band. It's something Malcolm won't discuss to this day.

During this time, two long-form video collections were released. *Who Made Who,* which covered footage from 1980 to 1986, and *Clipped,* a compilation of all the promotional videos from *Blow Up Your Video* and *The Razors Edge.*

Together again with David Mallet, AC/DC filmed a video for "Are You Ready" at Bray Studios in Windsor on March 18. Two day later, the European leg of The Razors Edge tour covered 17 dates through Finland, Sweden, Norway, Germany, and Switzerland. Then AC/DC continued through the U.K. playing nine more dates before coming back to the States. Their album *Highway To Hell* was certified Platinum times four. If the band celebrated, it was somewhere out on the road.

That spring, Angus was asked how AC/DC had maintained their musical consistency over the years. He explained, "The only change that really had a major affect on us is when Bon died. That almost put an end to the group. But when Brian came in, he brought us new vitality and energy that kept everything rolling in the right direction. But my brother Malcolm and Cliff have been here all along, so the core of the band really hasn't changed that much. We do have Chris Slade in the band on this tour, and he's worked out very well. He's just as old and ugly as the rest of us!"

On May 23, the band launched the second leg of their American tour at the Richfield Coliseum in Cleveland, Ohio. Commenting on the new tour, Angus quipped, "We'll play some new songs, but also a lot of the standards—the family favorites…you know, the stuff the local reverends love!"

Laughing at their critics, Brian said, "I'd like to lock them [the critics] up in a cell with the new AC/DC album for a week. They'll be crying to, 'Let me out, let me out!' Then I'll put on a week's worth of disco music and I bet you a pound to a pinch of shit they'll be hung by their own belts. With AC/DC, at least they'll come out singing the choruses!"

One night during a show in Belfast, Angus gave the local reverends more to love, surprising everyone including himself during his striptease. It seems he was wearing two pairs of underwear, not realizing the one underneath was ripped out in the front. When he pulled his shorts down, everyone around him looked quite alarmed, then Malcolm started pointing. Angus said, "And I'm too busy in my own little world. I'm sort of thinking, 'What's he pointing at?' And the police are all sort of looking at me. And I turned around to the audience and they're all sort of stunned. And I sort of look down and there's all my wedding tackle hanging out for all the world to see." Amazing nobody got a picture of that!

Finally on June 28, AC/DC made their way back to Wisconsin playing at Alpine Valley in East Troy. I had still been unable to locate Barry, and I was very curious to see if the band knew where he was. That particular summer day was especially hot, with the temperature in the nineties. The only difference between this show and the one in December was the fact that they had to pause after every song to wipe the sweat off of their guitars. We had great seats under the awning this time and when the band played "Moneytalks," guess who was right underneath one of the bundles of funny money? I swear it opened up and dropped right on my head! Needless to say, we took home plenty of Angus cash that night, plus we gave away dozens of dollars to the fans around us.

Even though we had after-show passes, the immense crowd we were grouped with was left waiting not so patiently in the heat. After close to an hour, it was obvious the band was not coming out of their dressing room, causing me to wonder if they had survived their grueling performance. Just as most of the fans were starting to give up, I grabbed a security guard and told him to go in there and tell Angus that Sue from Madison was waiting to say hello. That request got quite a few comments, not to mention plenty of laughs. Even the photographer I was with looked at me and said, "Yeah, that should do it."

Within 10 minutes, the security guard walked outside and yelled, "Is there a Sue Masino here?"

I, along with several other women, raised my hand and my husband and I were quickly ushered into the back of Alpine Valley into one of the dressing rooms.

As we walked in, I turned around to thank the security guard. When the door shut behind us, we both turned around to realize that we were the only ones in the room, except for all five bands members!

The heat had wiped them out so much, that they had decided to stay in their dressing room. A rare occurrence since the band always loves to meet their fans. I was more than stunned that we were invited in for a visit. I was so astonished, that I complained about the heat. The band just looked at me, until I said, "I'm surprised they didn't have to carry you guys off the stage on stretchers!" That got a laugh and started everyone talking. Malcolm looked over at me and said, "Hey! We saw Barry right after we saw you last December!" Which turned into a long conversation about Barry's chosen profession and the book he wrote which mentions the band.

My husband was wearing a T-shirt from our favorite vacation place in Florida and as soon as Brian saw it, he yelled, "That's where I live!" Then he pointed at his eye and said he had just gotten a shiner down there in a local pub. Apparently no one in the press had gotten a hold of that story. Then he quickly grabbed John and told him that they both needed a drink. Angus and Malcolm were now strictly teetotalers, but Brian traveled with his own bar.

For the next hour, we got to hang out with the band. Angus and I ended up on a couch, comparing how small his hands were to mine. We both have extremely little fingers and he laughed when he told me that's why he plays Gibson SGs. They have the only guitar neck that Angus can get his hands around! After enjoying a great visit, we said our farewells and they vowed to somehow track down Barry's phone number or address for me.

A few days later, I wrote Barry a long letter and mailed it off to the last address I had for him in California. When that letter came back to me, I put it in a new envelope and mailed it off to the last place he lived in England. A few weeks later, that came back undeliverable, as well. It made me sad and I was starting to feel as if I wasn't meant to find Barry after all, so I ripped the letter up and threw it away.

The very same night, I was sitting on the couch flipping through the channels, when I heard someone say the words, "AC/DC." That usually makes me stop and listen, so I flipped back and right in front of me on TV was Barry Taylor! He was on the Christian channel's 700 Club, talking about giving up rock 'n' roll to follow religion. Just to make sure I wasn't hallucinating, I put a videotape in, and recorded the rest of the show. The next day I called the 700 Club and left a detailed message for Barry. Just a few days later, Reverend Taylor called me back directly.

It had been 10 years since we last spoke. I couldn't believe he was really on the other end of the phone! When I told him about seeing AC/DC twice in the last six months, we laughed about how they didn't appreciate his mentioning them in his book.

Barry and his wife Cathy were running their own church in the mountains of California. He hadn't completely turned his back on rock 'n' roll. Barry, a guitarist himself, had formed his own church band, and much of his services were celebrated with music. He had also been traveling the world spreading God's word, particularly in the Soviet Union and Germany during the time the Berlin Wall came down.

Ironically, Barry had just traveled through New Zealand where he saw Phil Rudd. I was flattered when Barry told me that he and Phil had just been talking about me. You know what I said about a small world! Both of us were happy to be able to keep in touch with the band when they were out on tour. We both promised to stay in touch with each other, but wouldn't talk again for another 10 years!

AC/DC played 12 more dates in the U.S. before heading over to Europe. They performed in front of 72,500 fans at the Castle Donington at the first of seven European rock festivals on August 17. Appearing along with Queensryche, The Black Crowes, Motley Crue, and Metallica, the tour covered dates in Hungary, Germany, Switzerland, and Belgium. Headlining the Monsters Of Rock for an unprecedented third time, the Donington stage had required 250 tons of steel, 250 tons of production equipment, and 34 trucks to move it around…Not to mention the 116 crew members it took just to attend to AC/DC.

David Mallet captured the event, using 22 cameras. Comfortable filming with Mallet, Malcolm told *Metal CD,* "We never used to like making videos, but since we met David Mallet, making them has become a lot easier and we actually enjoy watching ourselves at the end of it."

The European tour ended with the biggest concert AC/DC has ever performed. On September 28, 1991, the band was scheduled to play a free show for the youth of Russia at the Tushino Airfield, just outside Moscow. The event was staged as a gift to the younger generation for their resistance against a recent failed military coup. It was called a "Celebration of Democracy and Freedom." Half a million was expected, but an estimated one million showed up. AC/DC was invited due to the high demand for their music, which up until then, could only be purchased on the Russian black market. The concert was also filmed by Wayne Isham for a possible live album.

Even though it was a bright sunny day, the promoters were concerned about the weather. With one million people gathered in one place, the last thing they wanted was to be rained out. That's when the Russian government used the latest in technology. Tour manager, Mike Andy, remembers that he was told by the government that they would make certain there would be no rain. He explained, "Moscow has weather similar to the northwest, very rainy, like Seattle. Well, thank God we don't have hundreds of troops marching around Seattle like they do in Red Square. After telling us it wouldn't rain, the Russian government promptly ordered fighter jets to "seed" the clouds above Tushino Airfield, guaranteeing no rain for at least six to eight hours. Something they commonly did so their troops wouldn't get rained on. That night it didn't pour until less than an hour after the show was over."

With one million Russian rockers let loose to party, things went along peacefully until the band pulled out the cannons in "For Those About To Rock." Angus said, "When the military heard the cannons, they really freaked. You saw their mouths drop. You almost heard them say, 'We've been tricked! It's a dirty imperialist trick!'"

While on stage Brian stated, "Opera and ballet did not cut the ice in the Cold War years. They used to exchange opera and ballet companies and circuses, but it takes rock 'n' roll to make no more Cold War." Unfortunately, the day would not go by without some sadness, when a member of the production crew suffered a fatal heart attack.

Back in the States, *Newsweek* wrote, "Just what are the East Germans who flock across the crumbled Berlin Wall spending their money on? While champagne and fresh fruit were once hot items, recorded music is becoming the purchase of choice. Business in West Berlin record shops is up 300 percent. Wagner and the "Ring" Cycle? Otto Klemperer and Beethoven? No. The top sellers: AC/DC and the *Dirty Dancing* soundtrack."

AC/DC played in France, Luxembourg, and Spain before flying down under for 15 dates...the last two nights in New Zealand. And guess who they ran in to? Since leaving the band in 1983, Phil had retired to New Zealand where he started his own helicopter charter service. When he saw the band again, Phil asked Angus and Malcolm, "Well, are you going to give me another go, or what?" Which set into motion, one more member change for AC/DC.

By December of 1991, AC/DC had played 70 shows in the past year—half of the concerts being sold out—and grossed over 17-million dollars. Another sign that you didn't have to be a metal head to be an AC/DC fan, the Atlanta Falcons officially changed their team uniforms to the original color of black and declared "Back In Black" their new theme song.

Further accolades came with a Grammy nomination for *The Razors Edge* in the hard-rock category. Plus the RIAA certified sales of three million for the album on March 2.

Not to be left out of the sampling craze of the early Nineties, the band filed suit against SBK Records and Vanilla Ice for illegal sampling use of "Rags To Riches" for Ice's *Extremely Live* album.

The first live album since *If You Want Blood (You've Got It)* featuring Brian Johnson, was released on October 29, 1992. Eloquently titled *Live* included songs recorded during their 1990 to 1991 world tour and was produced by Bruce Fairbairn. The album was issued in four different formats including a 14-song single CD, a 23-song single cassette, a specially packaged 23-song double CD, and an 18-song laser disc.

Live included the tracks "Thunderstruck," "Shoot To Thrill," "Back In Black," "Sin City," "Who Made Who," "Heatseeker," "Fire Your Guns," "Jailbreak," "The Jack," "The Razor's Edge," "Dirty Deeds Done Dirt Cheap," "Moneytalks," "Hells Bells," "Are You Ready," "That's The Way I Wanna Rock 'N' Roll," "High Voltage," "You Shook Me All Night Long," "Whole Lotta Rosie," "Let There Be Rock," "Bonny," "Highway To Hell," "T.N.T.," and "For Those About To Rock, We Salute You."

Commenting on *Live,* Angus said, "We wanted to capture it before the hair and teeth drop down. We didn't want to be on life support systems...The album really is more for the AC/DC collector. When you're talking to them at the shows, it's always the first thing — 'When are you guys going to do another live album?' Probably the most-asked question of anyone in the band is, 'When are we going to get another live dose?' But we wanted to wait until Brian had a lot of studio albums under his belt, so he's got a fair shake."

Angus also told *Rolling Stone,* "*Live* is like ordering whiskey. It's gonna go right down the gullet. We're just a good-time rock 'n' roll band — nothing more, nothing less."

"Highway To Hell" from *Live* reached Number 14 in the U.K. a week after the band performed it live on *Top Of The Pops.* The song would also be nominated for a Grammy for Best Hard Rock Performance.

AC/DC was then featured on ABC-TV's *In Concert* "Halloween Jam At Universal Studios" with Ozzy Osbourne, The Black Crowes, En Vogue, and Slaughter. By November, the album had risen to Number Five in the U.K. and Number 15 in the U.S. A limited-release titled *Live: Special Collector's Edition* debuted at Number 34 in the U.S.

Malcolm told *Metal CD* in 1992, "Everyone said right from the start that AC/DC are a live band and that the studio records never matched us live. After *If You Want Blood (You've Got It)* and Bon's death, the question was always there about when we would do another live album. We wanted to wait until we had enough live material with Brian to give him a fair shot, so he wasn't just up there singing old Bon songs. The album has all the best AC/DC songs on it from both eras of the band, and some of the old stuff, like "Whole Lotta Rosie," still has a real kick to it."

The *Live* album, using numbers from 153 shows performed across 21 countries, brilliantly brought their onstage energy home to the fans. As Ian Fletcher wrote in *Classic Rock* Special 2005, "The critical and commercial pull of AC/DC's studio albums may fluctuate these days, but live they've always been unstoppable. And on *Live,* they prove that once again."

At the end of the year, the live footage shot on high quality 35-millimeter film in England at the Monsters Of Rock, was released titled, *AC/DC Live At Donington.* The decade had barely gotten under way and AC/DC had wiped the floor clean with their toughest critics, turning them from future metal dinosaurs into bona fide rock 'n' roll icons. Soon, AC/DC would surpass even that, with a little help from a couple of animated head bangers named Beavis and Butthead.

BALLBREAKER

*B**eavis and Butthead,* an animated television show created by Mike Judge, debuted on MTV in March of 1993. It featured two amusing metal slackers who had a field day critiquing rock videos, most of which always, "Sucked, heh, heh, heh." Beavis, first appeared wearing a Slayer T-shirt, but wound up wearing one that said Metallica. Butthead, Beavis's chemically impaired sidekick, got the honors of wearing a shirt that boasted the hallowed initials, AC/DC. Thanks to pre-teens to twenty-somethings, the cartoon was an instant hit for MTV. Beavis and Butthead's attire made a direct statement on who the real kings of metal were in the early Nineties...rock royalty, who all future bands would bow down to.

That summer, AC/DC was invited to record a new song for the soundtrack to the Arnold Schwarzenegger movie, *Last Action Hero.* The song "Big Gun" was produced by Rick Rubin. The video for the song was shot at the Van Nuys Airport in Los Angeles in Hanger 104 E and was directed by David Mallet. It featured Arnold himself, dressed up as Angus running around the stage while the band plays on. Just the difference in size between Arnold and Angus is hilarious to see. *Now where the hell was this video when the Democrats were running against Arnold for the governorship of Caleefornia?*

The soundtrack to *Last Action Hero*—which included songs by Alice In Chains, Anthrax, Queensryche, Def Leppard, Megadeth, Tesla, Fishbone, and Cypress Hill—was released in July by Atco. The incredibly expensive film flopped at the box office, but the soundtrack album did rather well. AC/DC's single "Big Gun" debuted at Number 23 in the U.K. and made it to Number 65 in the States.

By the fall of 1993, AC/DC's *Live* had reached the two-million mark. *High Voltage* had also sold two million copies and *Who Made Who* had just surpassed three million in sales. In addition, a long-form video titled *For Those About To Rock, We Salute You* was released. It was an 84-minute recording of their momentous appearance in Moscow. The footage featured AC/DC, Metallica, The Black Crowes, Pantera, and E.S.T. Their label also re-released the band's pre-1985 catalog in Europe and the U.S., completely re-mastered.

At the end of The Razor's Edge tour, Phil Rudd had caught their show in Auckland, New Zealand. This was the first time he had seen the band live since his departure. Phil spent several hours visiting with them after the show and in May of the following year, AC/DC invited him back into the studio to record songs for their new album. Having left the music business behind, he seriously had to consider taking up the rock 'n' roll life again. With his wife's encouragement, he decided to go for it. Rumors started to fly that he was back in the band, but his official return wasn't announced until after the album was due to be released.

AC/DC met in New York City in October of 1994 and started recording at Sony Studios with Rick Rubin producing. Rubin had petitioned the band's management many times to work with them, and in light of the success of their single "Big Gun" they chose to go with Rubin and his co-producer, Mike Fraser. After several months in New York, even trying different studios, they were unable to get the sound they were looking for. Once they switched to Ocean Studios in Los Angeles, the band completed the album.

Striving for their original feel, Malcolm and the band went to great lengths to bring back their no-frills sound. This included firing up all the old Marshall amplifiers, complete with vintage tubes. Malcolm even had his guitar tech locate the original Gibson Sonomatics guitar strings that he used to use 20 years earlier. He described the recording of *Ballbreaker* to *Guitar World* in 1995: "We just wanted to get back to the old feel of the rhythm. The feel dominated this time. And really, the best feels are the simplest."

Brian added, "We did all the vocals right in the control room, just sitting around like we're sitting here now. Malcolm was sitting on one side of me with [engineer] Mike Fraser on the other. 'Cause I don't like going into the vocal booth to sing. I like it to be more like when I'm onstage with the others. To have them around me like that."

Having the Rudd backbeat guaranteed AC/DC's ability to capture their original "swing." Cliff was quoted in *Guitar School* in March, 1995, "Yeah, Phil's back! He was the band's original drummer, but needed to step out for a number of years for various reasons. Now he's back with a vengeance and we're working very well with him. It's great to have him back—he's always been the right man for the job."

After all the trouble it took them to finally settle on the right sound, the new album was aptly titled, *Ballbreaker.* It featured 11 gems including, "Hard As A Rock," "Cover You In Oil," "The Furor," "Boogie Man," "The Honey Roll," "Burnin' Alive," "Hail Caesar," "Love Bomb," "Caught With Your Pants Down," "Whiskey On The Rocks," and "Ballbreaker." The Young brothers once again handled the lyrics, which were peppered with sexual innuendo.

To accompany the first single "Hard As A Rock" the band shot another video, their seventh collaboration with David Mallet. Four hundred London-area AC/DC fans were bussed to a soundstage at Bray Studios in Windsor, England on August 22. During the shoot, Angus spent most of his time hanging in mid-air on a giant demolition ball, which he eventually used to crash through a window amidst exploding fireworks and flying shards of sugar glass.

Andrew "Don" Williams was one of the lucky fans to be included in the filming. "I heard about it from the AC/DC fan club, which I don't think is around anymore. The day was boiling hot and inside it was well over 100 degrees. I've even seen the video interviewing Angus and Brian, who said how hot it was in there. They had to keep spraying them with water, but Brian was his usual joking self, and all of them were smoking like troopers. I got to meet all the band, and Phil got great applause from the crowd. It was his first time back, and it was great to see him pounding away on the kit. We were told by the director not to ask the boys for their autographs when they come on stage, because they wouldn't get any work done. They were happy to sign autographs later, and I had to laugh when a guy gave Brian a Led Zeppelin CD to sign, which was all he had with him. Brian said, 'No bloody way!' and pretended to throw it away, but came back with it signed by the whole band."

The only evidence of Williams in the video, is his knee, which he swears is on the upper left side of the screen. "I've got on a pair of red shorts like Angus, but I can't move the same as him." Perhaps the reason why just his knee appears in the video.

The single "Hard As A Rock" was released on September 15 in Australia. The album followed in Europe and Australia on the twenty-second and in the

States on the twenty-sixth. The cover was designed by Marvel Comics and featured Angus, guitar in hand, surrounded by towering skyscrapers amidst shooting rays of light, looking like the superhero he really is.

USA Today reviewed the album on September 27, 1995: "Australia's veteran head bangers haven't matured, but why tinker with a winning formula? Scabrous vocals and jackhammer guitars drive such adolescent fantasies as "Cover You In Oil" and "The Honey Roll." Political stands? Check out the comical slams at Bill Clinton in "Burnin' Alive." This would be one of AC/DC's rare tunes, that touched on subjects other than sex, rock 'n' roll, and lusty women. Yet it refers to Clinton, so maybe not.

Malcolm stated about Ballbreaker, "The title track was the last song we wrote and it came together real quick. We just thought of the hardest and heaviest thing we could, and it came from there and just seemed to sum the whole thing up." Angus added, "I'm really proud of this album. I can honestly say I love every one of the songs—and that's something, coming from a band that started just after the Crucifixion."

Reviewing the new album, I published an article in my music newspaper Rock Central, *that included an old picture of Bon, with memories of my first encounter with the band. As always, I sent off a copy to AC/DC's publicists. A few weeks later, I was astounded to hear back from them, asking for more Bon Scott pictures. They were looking for materials for Marvel Comics, who were designing a comic book for AC/DC. At the time, they were having trouble finding good pictures of Bon.*

I sent them pictures of the band when they played the Stone Hearth, courtesy of the photographer. A representative from Marvel Comics contacted me and explained the concept for the book. The story had Bon playing cards in Hell against Satan and Nixon. Bon wins the right to bring the band down to meet Brian, and play together one more time. When I told the guy I wasn't happy with the concept of Bon being in Hell, he said, "Well, at least we have him running the place!" Thanks to the popularity of video games, the comic-book industry was downsized and the AC/DC comic book never materialized.

On September 13, Angus and Brian performed four songs on the French airwaves for the show, Fun Radio Paris. That same month, Warner Music International honored AC/DC for album sales of 80 million worldwide, excluding Australia and New Zealand.

Ballbreaker, AC/DC's fifteenth album—which quickly went Platinum— debuted at Number Six on the U.K. charts on October 7. It entered the

Billboard charts at Number Four on October 14. At the end of the month, Alberts Music re-issued their post-1985 catalog, completely re-mastered with lyrics. Also released in Australia that month, was the AC/DC tribute album, Fuse Box.

From November 20 through December 20, the band rehearsed for their new world tour in London. During the last week of November, David Mallet joined them to film two more videos for the songs, "Hail Caesar" and "Cover You In Oil."

Right after the holidays, the band continued rehearsals in St. Petersburg, Florida from January 4 to 10. The Ballbreaker tour launched on January 12 in front of a sold-out crowd of 15,899 in Greensboro, North Carolina. The U.S. tour of 49 dates would be supported by the band, The Poor, and for the first time included two performances in Mexico City on February 16 and 17.

Just two weeks into the tour, the band had to cancel four dates so Brian could fly home to England for the funeral of his father, who had been ill for quite some time. He left the tour in San Antonio on January 28 and was back in time for the show in Oakland, California on February 3.

For the first time ever, AC/DC's tour wasn't booked in Madison. The closest they came was a date in Milwaukee at the Bradley Center on March 5. Since I was publishing my own music paper, tickets and aftershow passes were much easier for me to arrange. Since I too had turned 40 the same year as Angus, the big 4-0 motivated me to start writing my first book. It was a memoir of my writing gig in the late Seventies, including all the bands I got to party with along the way. It was something I planned on telling the band about, especially after hearing what they had to say about Barry writing a book!

Each time AC/DC goes out on tour, they make a special effort to keep the stage show new and exciting for the fans. The Ballbreaker stage featured a very large gray, industrial-looking building which ran across the entire stage. Along the top were thin rectangular windows, with several garage doors running along the bottom. The show opened with a video flashing across giant projection screens that hung above the stage. It was a cartoon feature of Beavis and Butthead, backstage looking around for chicks. After knocking on AC/DC's dressing room door, Angus answers and presents them both with one hell of a mighty rock chick who cracks a whip and starts the ball rolling. Or should I say, the wrecking ball—a very large one at that—which lowers down from the ceiling. Accompanied by flashing lights and the sounds of roaring engines and screeching metal, the ball proceeds to swing back and forth, demolishing the building. Among pieces of flying debris, the garage doors open to reveal the band, who immediately break into "Back In Black." The completely new set list included songs original- ly recorded with Bon Scott, like "Dog Eat Dog," "Shot Down In Flames," "Girl's Got Rhythm," and "Down Payment Blues." Plus two songs they hadn't played since 1978, which were "Gone Shootin'," and "Riff Raff."

AC/DC's show that night was amazing, not to mention the wonder of watching the wrecking ball bring down the house! Of course having Phil back on the drums was a dream come true for me. I had always hoped that he would play with them again someday. The one thing that made this show very different, was there being no beer sold at the venue, and no mosh pit thrashing in front of the band. Much of the audience were longtime fans, some with graying hair. Yet, there were plenty of young kids and teenagers singing along in the audience. It was uplifting, entertaining, and after hear- ing the second or third Bon Scott song with the audience singing along to every word, deeply moving for me. That always makes me tear up and I prayed that night that somehow Bon knew how much he was loved.

After almost two solid hours on stage, the band came back out for a three- song encore, which included "Highway To Hell," "Hail Caesar," and a rous- ing rendition of "For Those About To Rock" backed by six blazing cannons.

Once backstage, I had a great time seeing the band again. Especially when I got to give Phil a big hug and congratulate him on his return. When I asked Angus what happened to the beer and the mosh pit, he replied, "Ah, all they do is get drunk and then they don't pay attention to me!" Good point.

Unfortunately, the pass for my photographer didn't make it to the Will Call window, and she was so distraught she left without seeing their show. When I told Angus about this, he insisted I bring her along to see them in Chicago in four days. When I laughed and told him not to sweat it, 'after all, it's not like we're Rolling Stone,*' he shrugged his shoulders and said, "We'll see you in Chicago."*

That night I also gave them each a copy of the audio interview that we did together in Milwaukee back in 1977. Malcolm really laughed when I reminded him how much grief they gave me when I declared back then, that someday they would be huge!

I hadn't yet decided how I was going to close my book, Rock 'N' Roll Fantasy, *which I was working on. It covers AC/DC's rise to stardom between 1977 and 1980. But that night in the dressing room, the ending wrote itself. While we were visiting with the band, we got to meet a fan of theirs from England, named Carl Allen. He often followed the band around while they were on tour, and he knew a lot about them. As they were being hurried out the door to drive to the next city, Carl tried to stop Malcolm and ask him whatever happened to that Marvel comic book that was supposed to come out. When Malcolm stopped, pointed at me and said, "Ask Sue, she knows everything, she goes all the way back!" I knew I had found my closing line.*

Four days later on March 9, my friend and photographer Erin Proctor and I drove to the United Center in Chicago to see AC/DC. Seeing the show right after their performance at the Bradley Center was incredibly enjoyable for me. Hitting the road again to follow the band felt just like the old days! Except for the fact that their tour manager decided I didn't need to say hello to the band again in Chicago, since I had just talked to them in Milwaukee. After hanging out in a locker room after the show with about 100 people who were trying to accomplish the same thing, I realized I would have to take matters into my own hands.

For some reason I knew they were getting ready to leave the building and knowing it might be years before I would see them again, I walked out of the locker room and just started walking past all the security points. I told each security guard that I was going to see the band and if they had a problem with that, they had better call for some help. Obviously I didn't look too threatening, because no one tried to tackle me.

As I was walking towards the dressing rooms, I saw the head of security walking right for me with a stern look on his face. Something you definitely don't want to see anywhere really, especially backstage. As soon as he got close enough, instead of ushering me back to the locker room, he smiled and said, "Have you seen the boys yet?" When I said no, he opened the door I was standing in front of and waved me inside. I walked in and was amazed to see Angus alone, still packing up his bags. He looked over at me and said, "Well there you are!" To which I went off, asking him if he had any idea what kind of circus went on around the band. I guess you could say being trapped in a locker room for over an hour, with still no beer, I was getting slightly bitchy. Sweetly waiting to get a word in edgewise, Angus finally cracked up laughing when I looked at him and said, "Do you think you could get any more famous? I swear the Pope has got to be easier to see than you!"

Luckily he didn't throw me out and he even waved Erin in to meet him and get his autograph. I also got to tell him that I planned to give them a copy of my new book as soon as it was done. I wanted to make sure they didn't have any problems with it.

When the head of security came in to escort him to the bus, Angus introduced me to him and explained what had happened. Then he said, "We go back 23 years, so please make sure this doesn't happen to her again." The guy looked at us and said, "You look old enough to go back 23 years, but she doesn't!" With a laugh and a hug, we said goodbye. I still had a long drive back to Wisconsin, and Angus was headed to Kentucky.

The first leg of the American tour ended in Dallas on April 4 and 16 days later, AC/DC began a 48-date trek through Europe with the British band The Wildhearts opening for them. Through the end of May, AC/DC performed in Norway, Sweden, Germany, Switzerland, Italy, Austria, France, Spain, and Portugal.

When the tickets for Madrid first went on sale, only one show was scheduled for July 4. Two weeks later, no tickets could be found anywhere on the market. This prompted the band to postpone to July 9, with a second show being added on July 10. Several weeks later, a third show was added. The second show at the Plaza de Toros de Las Ventas was filmed for a future video. David Mallet brought in the Manor Mobile studio and used 14 cameras to catch all the action.

At their concert in Portugal, the band brought out the giant inflatable Rosie for the first time since 1991. Rosie has always been the most amusing of their stage props.

"Pyro" Pete always gets a kick out of her, but sometimes things didn't go as planned. "They love their toys, and everyone loves Rosie! Every now and then there wouldn't be enough room. Venues would vary in size, and I've seen Rosie knock over cymbals and stuff. Then roll over on top of the drummer. We would inflate her, and then we would have to pull her back while we were deflating her. If we didn't get her pulled back in time, she would land on the drum kit and pull cymbals over, knocking the drummer off the chair. One time I could still hear the bass drum, but all the cymbals were knocked over, and that's all he could play. Drummers are stuck, they can't run away. If you're the guitar player and you see Rosie deflating on you, you can run! Rosie has definitely caused a fair bit of trouble!"

Unruly balloons weren't the only problems they had to deal with. Pete remembers, "The Ballbreaker tour had these platforms that were *supposed to go up and down*. Supposed to go up and down. I've seen Angus stuck on an elevator, or Brian half way up on a lift. Again, without missing a beat, they would just perform from there. Anytime anything happened with AC/DC, it would always end up being funny. The band would ask what happened and how we could prevent it from happening again."

For one day, the band flew to London to film a private concert for VH1

U.K., which included 14 songs, some never before performed with Brian. They also performed three songs they never played before, "Go Down" and two cover songs: James Brown's "I Feel Good" and Stevie Wonder's "Superstition."

The first 30-minute broadcast of *Take It To The Bridge,* was aired on August 4. Their set included four songs: "Gone Shootin'," "Riff Raff," "Go Down," and "Down Payment Blues," interspersed with interviews with Angus and Malcolm. In September, VH-1 broadcast *AC/DC Uncut,* which included "Riff Raff," "Go Down," "You Shook Me All Night Long," "Shoot To Thrill," "Rock And Roll Ain't Noise Pollution," "Down Payment Blues," "The Jack," and "Whole Lotta Rosie." The show ended with the video clip of "For Those About To Rock, We Salute You."

Their three-month European tour ended on July 13 in Bordeaux, France at a small open-air festival with the French band Silmarils, and the Brazilian metal munchers, Sepultura.

Ballbreaker, with Phil Rudd back in the band, thrilled their old fans and gained them new ones wherever they went. Angus cheerfully told *Hit Parader,* "When we get together and go to work, something special always happens. It doesn't matter how long we may have been apart—once we're all in the same place at the same time, we become AC/DC." *God bless 'em.*

At the time, there were rumors about *Ballbreaker* being the last AC/DC album. When asked about their future, Angus replied, "I never try to look too far into the future. When you do that you can end up tripping over what's right in front of you...I learned a long time ago from Bon Scott that you've just got to make it through that particular day. I hope that at some point in the future, people will look back fondly on AC/DC. That's really all I can ask." *No worries there, Angus.*

AC/DC was filmed live in Bryant Park in New York City on July 27, performing "You Shook Me All Night Long," "The Jack," and "Highway To Hell" for the Howard Stern film, *Private Parts.* Two days later, Brian made an appearance on Stern's radio show. ["You Shook Me All Night Long" was the only song to make it into the movie.]

The second leg of their American tour of 30 dates started on July 29 in Albany, New York, taking them through September.

The single, "Hard As A Rock," made it to Number 33 in the U.K. on September 30. Eleven days later, their South American tour of five dates would include Brazil, and for the first time, Chile and Argentina. The two nights in Brazil they performed in front of 65,000 people in a football stadium in Curitiba and San Paulo. Their appearance in Chile spawned the

Chilean tribute band, Ballbreaker.

Malcolm so eloquently explained their popularity to *Guitar World* in November of 1995 saying, "People can go out and hear R.E.M. if they want deep lyrics. But at the end of the night, they want to go home and get fucked. And that's where AC/DC comes into it. I think that's what's kept us around so long. Because people want more fuckin'." *That works for me.*

The video that had been shot in Spain earlier in July was released world-wide on November 18, titled *No Bull—Live Plaza De Toros De Las Ventas, Madrid*. It featured 20 songs, some including a limited-edition CD single of "Hard As A Rock," "Dog Eat Dog," and "Hail Caesar."

The band traditionally closed the tour in Australia, with 14 dates including two shows in New Zealand. They opened in Perth on November 2 and ended with two open-air shows in Auckland and Christchurch, New Zealand on November 27 and 30.

For many years, the fans had been asking AC/DC to issue any live unreleased recordings of Bon Scott. Owing their record company a boxed set, the band solicited their devoted followers from around the world to contribute materials to be included in it. This would inspire AC/DC, 17 years after his death, to create the ultimate Bon Scott tribute album. The title would even come from Bon himself. He always used to say that one day, "when I'm a fucking big shot, I'm calling my solo album *Bonfire*."

RIDE ON

When the band started gathering materials for the *Bonfire* box set, there were no unreleased tracks with Bon. All they had to work with were demos, which were the recordings right before the final cut was made. Beginning in March of 1997, Angus and Malcolm spent hours in the studio listening to tapes, choosing the ones where Bon sounded his best. With George's help, they remixed songs from the master tapes and had the whole package finished by that summer.

The five-CD box set included Disc One: Live From The Atlantic Studios, recorded live in December 1977 at Atlantic Studios in New York. This recording had only previously been available as a promotional album. The tracks includ-ed were "Live Wire," "Problem Child," "High Voltage," "Hell Ain't A Bad Place To Be," "Dog Eat Dog," "The Jack," "Whole Lotta Rosie," and "Rocker."

Disc Two and Three, Let There Be Rock: The Movie and Live In Paris, included the soundtrack recorded on December 9, 1979. The tracks included were "Live Wire," "Shot Down In Flames," "Hell Ain't A Bad Place To Be," "Sin City," "Walk All Over You," "Bad Boy Boogie," "The Jack," "Highway To Hell," "Girl's Got Rhythm," "High Voltage," "Whole Lotta Rosie," "Rocker," "T.N.T.," and "Let There Be Rock." Some of the special features were the full version of the song "Walk All Over You" and the missing track "T.N.T." which had been dropped from the movie.

Disc Four: Volts featured working and alternative versions of some of their classics: "Dirty Eyes," (which became "Whole Lotta Rosie"), "Touch Too Much," "If You Want Blood (You've Got It)," "Backseat Confidential" (which became "Beating Around The Bush"), "Get It Hot," "Sin City" (live on *The Midnight Special* in September, 1978), "She's Got Balls" (live from a Bondi Lifesaver concert in 1977), "School Days," "It's A Long Way To The Top (If You Wanna Rock 'N' Roll)," "Ride On," and a spoken-word montage from Bon. This CD even includes a guitar solo by Angus that was played at a sound check in Metz, France on December 6, 1979.

Disc Five was a copy of *Back In Black,* released in a double-carton sleeve with all the original components of the vinyl release. This edition of *Back In Black* is exclusive to *Bonfire*. Angus explained why it was part of the package: "It was our tribute to Bon, so we felt it should be included. The whole album was our dedication to him. And also to show how AC/DC carried on afterwards."

Bonfire included a 48-page booklet, a two-sided poster, AC/DC sticker, removable tattoo, guitar pick, and a key chain/bottle opener [*which can come in real handy, let me tell you*]. The booklet, with a brief history of the band, also featured some of Bon's handwritten lyrics and rare photos of the band. The cover of *Bonfire* has a picture of Angus riding on Bon's shoulders, and right inside the cover is the best picture of all: it's a black-and white-shot of Bon as a young boy—in his kilt—beaming with pride, holding up an award. As their promotion said, *Bonfire* was a whole box of goodies "that Bon would have wanted you to have."

That October, the single "Dirty Eyes" was released, but not made available for sale. On Halloween, the world premiere of *Bonfire* was broadcast on the Album Network. To promote the new record, the band added a new facet to their publicity repertoire. For the first time, Angus and Brian sat down for a cyber chat on America Online. The most comical part of the conversation was when someone asked Angus, who was now in his forties, if he was too old to rock 'n' roll. Not hesitating for a second, Angus fired back, "The name's Young, always has been, always will be."

Just before *Bonfire* was unveiled, Bon's friend Bernie from the French band, Trust, appeared on the radio show Zig Mag on November 13. That night, he played the version of "Ride On" that was recorded in London in February of 1980 when Bon popped in on them in the studio just six days before he died. This would be the first time it was heard by the public.

Bonfire was released on November 17, 1997 in Europe and Australia, and in the U.S. the following day. Less than a month later, the box set would be certified Gold by the RIAA. As for waiting 17 years to put *Bonfire* together, Angus told Mick Wall for *Record Collector,* "For us as a band, it's something that we've wanted to do for a long time, but we just didn't know when. There was no way we were gonna do something like this at the time of Bon's death, 'cos it would have been seen as a grave-robbing exercise. And we were very conscious of not letting anything like that happen. For Brian's sake, we had to get space and time between what had happened and allow Brian to give it his best shot. Also, there was too much emotion to handle at the time. For me and Malcolm, the only way we could get through it was by just keeping our heads down and working. If we'd tried to go through loads of tapes of Bon's stuff just after he'd died, I don't think we'd have made it."

Angus also explained to Wall what he missed most about Bon: "His wit and his sense of humor, I think. He was a wild man, but he wasn't stupid. And having him in the band was just a fantastic time in our lives. After he died, it was like we were forced to grow up a bit. It changed things, for sure. Not so much musically, 'cos we've always known what we're doing there, but in our lives, the way we looked at things. But then, nothing stays the same forever, does it?"

Commenting on the loss of Bon, Tony Platt, who worked on *Back In Black* said, "[Bon] was the real spirit of AC/DC, the glue that held the band together. It was such a tragedy because he had everything to live for…but the strange thing was, someone told me he [Bon] had visited a clairvoyant shortly before [his death], and she told him he would die in his thirties. I can't remember where I heard that but…Anyhow, I think the best thing I ever heard about Bon came from Malcolm. He said to me, 'Sometimes Bon would disappear right after a show and we wouldn't see him until just before we were due onstage the next night. But although he wouldn't turn up until the last minute, you knew he'd be there, you knew you could always depend on him. The hardest thing will be getting used to him not being there.'"

Angus added, "We could be somewhere where you would never expect anyone to know him and someone would walk up and say, 'Bon Scott,' and always have a bottle of beer for him. It was uncanny. One time we were broken down in a bus outside this little town in Australia and some guy came along carrying a surfboard and a whole crate of beer. And it was really hot and we were dying for a drink. Anyway, he walked by the bus and looked in and yelled 'Bon Scott!' and came running in and handing out all his beers, and everyone was there having a party while the bus was being fixed. He made a lot of friends everywhere and was always in contact with them, too. Weeks before Christmas he would have piles of cards and things, and he always wrote to everyone he knew, keeping them informed. Even his enemies, I think."

AC/DC kept the RIAA busy re-certifying more of their catalog. *Let There Be Rock* had sold two-million copies and *Dirty Deeds Done Dirt Cheap* had passed the five-million mark. *Back In Black* was certified at 16-million copies sold, making it the second-biggest selling album at that time...just behind Led Zeppelin's IV. Making Malcolm's ambition "to be the next Led Zeppelin" not so far fetched at all!

Bonfire was released in the U.K. on the EMI label. AC/DC had just signed a deal with EMI exclusively covering the United Kingdom. In January of 1998, EMI reissued *Highway To Hell, For Those About To Rock, Flick Of The Switch,* and *Fly On The Wall.* The following month, Angus and Malcolm began pre-production on their next album in London.

Brian and Cliff kept busy jamming at a benefit for the Opera House in Sarasota, Florida on March 28. Together with Billy Leverty on guitar, and Jackyl's Jesse Dupree, they played "You Shook Me All Night Long," "Back In Black," "Long Tall Sally," and "I Saw Her Standing There."

As Angus and Malcolm worked in the studio, once again handling the lyrics, Brian decided to produce Neurotica, a Sarasota band he discovered there in a bar one night. "They're the only band that made me look up from me beer. And it was a good Guinness too," said Brian, who handled production with Mike Fraser mixing. He also co-wrote the opening track "Deadly Sin" and sang back-up vocals for lead singer, Kelly Shaefer.

Shaefer remembers the first time he heard AC/DC. "My dad turned me onto them when I was about eight years old. He is a longtime AC/DC fan, and he had a jeep and I remember cruising around listening to "Let There Be Rock" and I thought that was so cool!"

Having Brian produce Neurotica's first album, *Seed,* was a dream come true for Shaefer. "Brian had lived here for a few years before this and we often said how cool it would be if someday he would come out and see us play. The club that we were playing at the first time he saw us only held about 50 or 60 people and it was called the Monterey Deli. During the day it was a sandwich shop, at night they cleared away the tables and let us play. So we did two sets of original material and invited all our friends out. It was a really low-profile gig and Brian had been in a club right around the corner. The guy behind the bar suggested to Brian and Doug Kaye, a local producer he was with, that they should go next door and check out this band. Doug didn't want to come over because he knew me from when I played in the death-metal band, Atheist. So he reluctantly came over with Brian and we watched them walk in. We were in the balcony looking down on the crowd and when we saw him, we said, 'Oh my God! We gotta throw down!'

So we went down and played and this club was so small that Brian was sitting right in front of our amps. I damn near threw sweat on him, he was that close. So we just gave it all we had and he said, 'Fuckin' hell, buy these lads a round of beer.' So he bought us all a round of Old Speckled Hen. A friend of ours gave Brian our demo on his way out. Two days later I got a call from Doug Kaye, saying Brian was really blown away by our performance and he wanted to hear some more songs." Neurotica's CD, Seed, was released on April 14, 1998 on the independent label, NMG Entertainment.

In commemoration of Australian rock 'n' roll, the Australian Post issued 12 postage stamps featuring various artists. AC/DC was chosen, along with The Easybeats, Billy Thorpe, Skyhooks, and The Masters Apprentices. Angus appears on one of stamps, with the words It's A Long Way To The Top, written across his schoolbag. I guess you could say AC/DC making it onto a postage stamp was a long way from their days of being followed around by the vice squad!

EMI then reissued *High Voltage, Dirty Deeds Done Dirt Cheap, Powerage,* and *If You Want Blood (You've Got It)* in May, followed by *Back In Black, The Razors Edge, Live (Special Collectors Edition),* and *Ballbreaker* in July, and *Let There Be Rock, Who Made Who,* and *Blow Up Your Video* that fall.

Kerrang! magazine honored AC/DC on September 26, 1998 when they presented the band with a Hall of Fame award. Rarely showing up at such events, Angus and Brian actually made an appearance. Receiving their award, Brian took off his hat and Angus took off his pants.

The following spring, reportedly remaining clothed, Brian and Cliff attended an awards presentation at the Roseland Ballroom in New York City on March 16, 1999 to receive the Diamond Award for *Back In Black.* This was given to them by the RIAA to mark sales in the U.S. of over 10-million copies. *Now that's one royalty check I'd like to see!*

Confirming the rumors of who would produce their next album, big brother George—along with Angus and Malcolm—went into Bryan Adams' Warehouse Studios in Vancouver, Canada. George hadn't produced an entire AC/DC album since *Blow Up Your Video* and this would be his first time producing AC/DC without Harry Vanda. Alarming numerologists everywhere, they entered the studio on July 17, 1999 and recorded 17 songs for their seventeenth album, which took them three months to complete.

The band ended up being very proud of *Bonfire* which truly celebrated the time they had spent with Bon. Angus commented to *Guitar World,* "I must admit, though, that while we were digging through the material, a few times, even we were shocked at what was coming back at us off the tapes-blown away. We felt humbled by our own machine."

Malcolm once said, "Bon was the biggest single influence on the band. When he came in, it pulled us all together. He had that real 'stick-it-to-'em' attitude. We all had it in us, but it took Bon to bring it out." Angus was more pointedly said, "I don't think there would have been an AC/DC if it hadn't been for Bon."

No doubt a lot of AC/DC fans regard the years with Bon as pure rock 'n' roll magic. Good friend Vince Lovegrove described Bon's appeal in the DVD, *Life Before Brian,* in November 2005, "What Bon contributed to rock 'n' roll is that he took away all the showbiz. Although he was a showbiz kind of guy, by the very nature of the fact he was on stage, he brought an ordinariness, a slight edge of "amateurness" about rock 'n' roll to the fore. Something that wasn't slick. Bon was certainly not slick, he was a rough diamond and he brought that to AC/DC and he brought that to rock 'n' roll music, and I think that has to be one of the reasons why he's gone on and on and on."

Often described as a "larrikin"—which is Australian slang for a rascal or scallywag—former manager, Michael Browning, told *Classic Rock* in 2005, "He [Bon] brought an enormous presence and character into the group. And I rate Bon as a lyricist up there with the greats, alongside Jim Morrison and the like. Bon was a poet first and a lyricist second. He was a highly intelligent lyricist and poet. He really took the Aussie larrikin archetype to a whole different level. Bon knew exactly why they appealed to the audience so much, when he said, 'Rock 'n' roll is the channel to give us all a vent to those frustrations. Lack of money, lack of alcohol, lack of women, or whatever. Rock 'n' roll is just a damn good outlet for what's hurtin' inside.'"

Rick Brewster of The Angels told me, "Bon was one of the true gentlemen of rock—well spoken, mostly quiet, often kept to himself. And funny—he was full of one-liners that kept the band laughing. There seemed to be a serious side to Bon, too. He was a dedicated musician, proud of the band, committed to performance, and he cared about people. He handled success with grace, dignity, and perspective."

Onetime roadie, Raymond Windlow, said about him, "When I learned of Bon's death in London I was shocked. Whilst he and I were no longer in contact and had not been for so many years, he was still part of me growing up, me in the music industry, and me learning about life. It was a sad day for the man with the unique rock 'n' roll voice that once, a long time ago, I could call a mate."

Angry Anderson, the lead singer of Rose Tattoo, composed a touching memorial for Bon in the February 2005 issue of *Classic Rock*. Anderson wrote, "He [Bon] was the only singer I ever invited to sing with the Tatts whenever he felt like it: we spoke quietly, we laughed loudly, and we drank hard; we were heading in the same direction at different speeds, for a moment we were side by side, then he was gone."

There aren't enough words to describe the impact Bon Scott had on AC/DC, then and now. His spirit fortified the Young brother's heart-and-soul rock 'n' roll and his lyrics moulded their image to this day. Bon was an original character whose over-the-top attitude towards life gave their balls-to-the-wall, no-holds-barred music a rebellious voice that still incites hundreds of thousands to raise a fist in the air.

Angus used to say, "Bon didn't dwell on the meaning of life too much. He lived for the moment." He also enjoyed a lot of those moments, as Angus told *Sounds* in July 1986: "Bon joined us pretty late in life, but that guy had more youth in him than people half his age. That was how he thought and I learned from him. Go out there and be a big kid."

Robin Zander of Cheap Trick quipped, "I liked having breakfast with Bon because he would always order a croissant or something with his glass of whiskey." Kirk Dyer, Cheap Trick's tour manager agreed, "Oh yeah, that's because he [Bon] never gave a shit! His attitude was, 'I don't care if you know me or not; now where's the party?' That's how I remember him the most."

The last photograph taken of him was backstage at the Hammersmith Odeon in London with his friend, bassist Pete Way at UFO's performance in February 1980. In the picture, Bon has a great big smile on his face. Just the way everybody remembers him.

Almost a decade later, *Bonfire* has sold over one-million copies and continues to be a must-have for any AC/DC fan. Everyday you hear Bon's voice on the radio and everyday there is a kid out there whose rock 'n' roll flame is lit because of him. Ride on, Bon.

AC**19**DC

STIFF UPPER LIP

The working title for AC/DC's seventeenth album was *Smokin'*, but the band ended up going with an idea that Angus had come up with. While sitting in traffic one day, he was pondering the early images of rock 'n' roll. When Angus thought of Elvis and his infamous sneer, the phrase "stiff upper lip" came to mind. They recorded 17 songs for *Stiff Upper Lip,* but only 12 made it onto the album. The tracks that didn't make it were "Rave On," "Let It Go," "The Cock Crows," "Whistle Blower," and "Cyberspace."

Stiff Upper Lip was released on February 25, 2000 in Europe, and then worldwide a few days later. It was their first release of new material in five years and only their third studio album since 1990. The cover of the album had a picture of an enormous bronze statue of Angus—looking as he does on stage—possessed. The 12 tracks included were "Stiff Upper Lip," "Meltdown," "House of Jazz," "Hold Me Back," "Safe In New York City," "Can't Stand Still," "Can't Stop Rock 'N' Roll," "Satellite Blues," "Damned," "Come And Get It," "All Screwed Up," and "Give It Up."

AC/DC's new album debuted at Number Seven on the *Billboard* 200, and hit Number One on *Billboard's* Mainstream Rock Tracks chart. Working to get back to their original sound, Angus explained, "We strive for consistency. We spend a lot of time working on it. Rock music is simplicity itself, but [you have to] come up with something that's a little bit different from what you've done before. You don't want to be a clone of what you were before. But you also know you've got to come up with something that sounds like AC/DC. So, you know, there's a lot of searching that we do.

"We have a song on the new album called "Can't Stop Rock 'N' Roll." I don't think anybody is trying to stop it anymore, but when we first released the album, a lot of the media were asking us, 'Yeah, but do you think what you do stands up to what today's youth is looking for?' I think it will always be that way. We know what we do best, which is rock 'n' roll. I think there's always that little bit of hard wall you've got to get through."

Claiming the new album was a joy to make, Brian said, "This one was a 135,000 cigarette album. I can always tell if we're making a good one when the smokes are going before, during, and after a take." That explains the alternative title for the album.

The day before its release, *Stiff Upper Lip* was premiered in the U.S. via a satellite broadcast. The band hosted the two-hour radio show, live from New York's Hard Rock Cafe. To promote the album, the band did several radio and television shows. On MTV they played "Stiff Upper Lip" and "Back In Black" live. On the New York rock station, K-ROCK, Angus, Malcolm, and Brian performed an acoustic version of "You Shook Me All Night Long." Their appearance on *Saturday Night Live* playing "You Shook Me All Night Long" and "Stiff Upper Lip" brought NBC the highest ratings of the season. No doubt about it, AC/DC was back and ready to rock.

Spyder Darling wrote in *New York Rock* in April 2000, "They're baaccckkkk! The Thunder from Down Under, the Wizards of Oz, the foundation-shaking rock 'n' roll station otherwise known to two generations of riff raff and problem children as AC/DC..."

For the title track's video, the band shot footage on May 9, 2000 in the Tribeca area of New York City with director Andy Morehand. Angus was featured in the June issue of *Playboy Germany,* which included an interview and full pictorial spread. *It must have been fairly modest, because if it weren't, we would be seeing naked Angus pictures still floating around the Internet. The only ones I could find are of his arse, and who hasn't seen that already?*

Stiff Upper Lip was certified Gold in the U.S. and Platinum in Europe less than three months after its release. On June 18, VH-1 featured the band in their successful and thoroughly addicting *Behind The Music* series. After its premiere, the *Boston Globe* interviewed Brian, where he openly slammed VH-1's sensationalizing the darker part of the band's history. Due to his complaints the show was re-edited, including interviews with Cliff this time, and aired on August 12, 2000. *Now somebody tell me how Cliff could have been left out? That alone is reason to edit!*

...lcolm, Simon Wright, Brian, Angus, and Cliff in Providence, Rhode Island (November 22, 1985). © Ebet Roberts

...ian having fun with his clangor, at the Nassau Coliseum in Uniondale, New York (November 21, 1985). © Ebet Roberts

Angus sweating off pounds during a show at the Festival Hall in Frankfurt, Germany (May 1996). © Anna Meuer/S.I.N./Corbis

The first glossy of the band after Phil Rudd rejoined, promoting the new album *Ballbreaker*. © Michael Halsban

rian on the stage screen next to the 38-foot bronze likeness of Angus as the band performs at the Thomas & Mack Center in Las Vegas.
September 14, 2000) © Ethan Miller/Reuters/Corbis

Angus going for a "flat on his back solo." © LFI

Angus and me outside the Kohl Center in Madison, WI (May 11 2001). © Photo by John Masino

Brian and Angus at the Roseland Ballroom in New York City (March 11, 2003). © Frank White

Brian keeping a stiff upper lip at the N.E.C. Arena in Birmingham on November 28, 2000. © Simon Meaker/LFI

Brian and Angus—you would never know by looking at them (1992).
© Tony Mott/S.I.N./Corbis

Brian, always happy to sign autographs at the Roseland Ballroom in New York City (March 11, 2003). © Frank White

Angus giving us an idea of where all the trouble may have started (March 11, 2003). © Frank White

Brian communing with half a million at the Molson Canadian Rocks For Toronto show (July 30, 2003). © Kevin Mazur/WireImage

/DC "abducted" into the Rock and Roll Hall of Fame (March 2003). © Kevin Mazur/WireImage

rian and Angus at the Thomas & Mack Center in Las Vegas
September 14, 2000). © Ethan Miller/Corbis

Cliff Williams belting it out at the Roseland Ballroom in New York
City (March 11, 2003). © Frank White

AC/DC live on the Black Ice Tour, Nashville, Tennessee (January 31, 2009). Photo by Veronica Handeland

Malcolm Young, James Masino, Angus Young and author, backstage in Chicago, Illinois (November 1, 2008).
Photo from Susan Masino Collection.

To celebrate the twentieth anniversary of Bon Scott's death, original singer Dave Evans was invited to appear at a special memorial performance with the tribute band Thunderstruck at the Edwards Tavern in Prahran, Melbourne. The CD from the event, *A Hell Of A Night,* featured covers of eight AC/DC songs, including a version of "Can I Sit Next To You Girl."

Commenting on what Bon would think of the band now, Angus and Brian talked to *Request* magazine in June. Angus said, "I think he would've been proud, just knowing how he was as a person. Bon's biggest idol was actually George, going back to when he was in The Easybeats. And when he came to see us for the first time, he said, 'Well, I get to work with these two guys, and I get to work with their brother.' So I always think he would look well on what we've done, and I believe he does know, in a way."

At the end of July, AC/DC went into River City Studios in Grand Rapids, Michigan to rehearse for their upcoming tour. They moved to the DeltaPlex for production rehearsals, which involved 68 crew members and 13 trucks.

The stage design for the new tour featured a 38-foot bronze statue of Angus, complete with billowing smoke and glowing red horns. Or as Angus said, "There's lots of surprises. It's a big show. I know, because I'm paying the bills!" Adding another visual treat—along with the cannons and bell— was not without its challenges. "Pyro" Pete explained how the tours have changed over the years: "When I first started, we had two cannons, which we used for a couple of tours. And then they went to a different stage set and they built cannons into the stage set that had big deck guns that looked like they were off a battle ship. They came up and telescoped out. That was one of the first real departures from the original cannons. And then we did the Monsters Of Rock in 1991, where we had 21 cannons. We had seven up each side for an outdoor stadium show, and seven across the middle, for a total of 21 guns. We actually had a whole truck just for these fiber-glass cannons, but they had to be made a little bit shorter and a little bit squatti- er so we could fit them all in the truck.

"The bell went through as many variations as the cannons. Every tour was like, 'What can we do to the bell this time, how can we make the bell's appearance look different.' One tour, Brian used to like the bell to come down, and he would grab a big clangor. It was an actual bell clangor that should have been on the inside of a bell, but we had a wooden handle put on it, something the size of a sledgehammer. But it was made specifically for hitting a bell, so it wouldn't break. So Brian would hit the bell with this thing, and that's what he really enjoyed, he really liked that.

"But one year we decided to build a mechanism that would swing the bell, so it looks like the bell is swinging like in a bell tower. Brian had a button at the end of the rope that would actually activate the clangor. So they would lower down this big black metal structure, that was like a frame, and you really couldn't see the frame around it, because it was painted flat black. So one of the carpenters would turn on the mechanism to swing the bell, as Brian would pull on the rope.

"Brian had a bit of a bungee cord at the top so he could look like he was pulling on this thing. Which he was, so the bell would start swinging back and forth, and when he pressed the button, the bell would clang. So fine, we've got everything going, and he gets out and the bells swinging, and he's having fun with it, and he's deciding he likes it, and he jumps up really high and grabs the rope, and comes down on it with all his weight! The bungee cord snaps, and Brian lands on his back! And the whole rope, all 40 feet of it, landed on his chest. He immediately got up and started prancing around on stage, and all he said was, 'Cheap fucking rope!' He never missed a beat!

"One time we had the cannons on these electric lifts that would lift them up and one night only one side would rise, because the other side had gotten unplugged or blown a fuse, or any of the million things that go wrong at a show. We're trying to lift this thing manually, and Brian is singing away, looking at the one that wasn't working and right in time with the music, he sings, 'Come on, you bastards!' It's so much fun when things go wrong, it's not like someone is stamping their feet, or there's a meeting where heads are going to roll…which is so unusual. Any other rock star, where the bungee cord broke, would have wanted to know who was responsible.

"Pyro" went on to explain the difficulties of firing off cannons every night. "Outside the United States, I've set up the cannons and left for the next city. Sometimes we weren't exactly cleared to use them, and I was the only one who knew how to set them up. Shooting the cannons involves a trigger or a pickle, as it's known in the demolition business. A button in a hand-held device that goes through a firing system. Once you press the button, it would shoot a concussion mortar from the backstage area and simultaneously it would shoot a flash device in the cannon. So the cannon would do the puff of smoke, and a big flash, but the loud bang comes from a device next to the cannon.

That's one of the great things about the band. They know they're a rock band, and they know they could go out with no stage set, no nothing and just play, and the people would be happy. But they want to do a different look without being overly theatrical. They at least wanted to make it so each time they went out, their stage set mimicked the album cover or the art. Although they didn't need any of these things. Unlike a lot of groups that need the production because the band isn't that good, or the music isn't that good. Some acts need the production to hide the flaws. These guys don't need the production, but they think the fans enjoy it. You get a double bonus: you get an excellent band and a good stage production to watch, as well.

"When we used the statue for Stiff Upper Lip, it didn't quite come apart like it was intended to. It was supposed to fall apart during the show and there were guidelines to keep it falling in the right places. I remember during one of the rehearsals, the head almost coming down and barely missing Phil. It landed right next to the drum kit with a huge thud. And everybody just stood there and said, 'Wow! Now that's not good!' Then we had to slow down the falling apart of it. We added pyrotechnics to it, so it looked like it was blowing apart. It used to blow smoke out of its mouth, the horns would light up, and then it would fall apart. We added all the pyro to the joints, so when the arm fell off, it would blow a bunch of sparks. It would also throw sparks, and flash and smoke. That way, we could use the ropes to pull the arm in a little slower. There were actually air bags for these pieces to land on. The real reason for the ropes was in case you had to, you could stop a piece. Even though they had something to land on, these pieces were 200 pounds each of Styrofoam, fiberglass, and fire coating. It took quite a bit to make it work right. The real fun about that was backstage when the statue fell apart. Now that was the place to be!"

The first leg of the American Stiff Upper Lip tour of 34 dates started on August 1, 2000 in Grand Rapids, Michigan at the Van Andel Arena. A month later they landed at the Bradley Center in Milwaukee on August 30. Their set list for this tour included "You Shook Me All Night Long," "Stiff Upper Lip," "Shot Down In Flames," "Thunderstruck," "Hell Ain't A Bad Place To Be," "Hard As A Rock," "Shoot To Thrill," "Rock And Roll Ain't Noise Pollution," "Sin City," (or "Safe In New York City"), "Bad Boy Boogie," "Hells Bells," "Meltdown" (or "Get It Hot"), "The Jack," "Dirty Deeds Done Dirt Cheap," "Back In Black," "Highway To Hell," "Whole Lotta Rosie," "Let There Be Rock," "T.N.T.," and "For Those About To Rock."

The Milwaukee show was sold-out and the audience couldn't have been happier to see the band. Once again, by the second or third Bon song, my eyes filled with tears. His memory was so tangible, that at times you could almost hear him singing along with Brian. And I'm not the only one who notices that. Brian once said, "I feel him around us when I sing the old stuff. Some nights you feel it more than others, especially if you're having a good time singing it."

Everyone enjoyed the regular toys: the cannons, the bell, Rosie larger than life, and the menacing Tower of Angus, as I like to call it...which explains why Angus is so small in real life. If his size matched his energy level, he wouldn't fit into the building! Watching the statue "deconstruct" was an amazing sight.

After the show, the band hosted a meet and greet, which my husband and I were lucky enough to get in on. There were about 20 to 30 people all waiting in a backstage locker room, with the assurance of the whole band doing a walk through. Disposable cameras and black Sharpies were at the ready. I always like to bring something with me for the band and this time I brought along black and white photos of them when they played at the Stone Hearth in 1977.

All of a sudden the band started filing in the door and I got a huge treat when Phil walked in. He looked through all the people across the room and as soon as he saw me, he shot me a quick excited wave. I was so proud and happy for him for getting back in the band.

On this rare occasion, I got to say hello and visit with all five band members. When I gave Angus a copy of the pictures I had brought for them, he moaned when he saw one of my favorites. It's a close-up of his face, grimacing in the spotlight mimicking the scream coming out of his guitar. We both sighed, and I said, "Oh, look how young you were in this picture! You were a baby!" Angus laughed and said, "Oh, me wife is going to be jealous!"

I asked him what he thought of the manuscript for my book, Rock 'N' Roll Fantasy. He smiled and said, "You've got to get more dirt! You don't have enough dirt!" We laughed about that and I mentioned to him that I hadn't found a publisher yet. I had gotten a couple of rejections, which made me put it back on the shelf. Angus encouraged me, "Put it out yourself, like Stephen King. You can do it!" So I have to thank Angus for his advice. Without his prompting, I wouldn't have published my book Rock 'N' Roll Fantasy as an eBook myself. After we took pictures together, it was time for the band to take off. We knew they would be back the following spring, so we said our goodbyes until then.

A week later their performance at the Compaq Center in Houston was reviewed by Greg Barr, "This is a band that has, over the past 25 years, barely varied from a formula of beefy chords, bombastic bass lines, meat-and-potatoes drumming, tongue-in-cheek lyrics, and song titles that are an adolescent boy's wet dream...The 47-year-old [Malcolm] Young and his

44-year-old brother Angus—the pasty skinned, elfin chain smokers who are the brains behind AC/DC—are part of a cock rock tour de force that can still kick some serious ass."

Around this time, AC/DC always seemed to be in the news for one reason or another. Unearthing a rock 'n' roll rarity, Cheap Trick's drummer Bun E. Carlos released a video of one of the infamous jams actually caught oncamera between AC/DC and Cheap Trick. It took place at the Sioux Falls Arena in Sioux Falls, South Dakota on July 7, 1979 and features a rendition of "Johnny B. Goode."

Placing their hands in concrete on September 16, AC/DC was immortalized in the Rock Walk in Los Angeles in front of Guitar Center on Hollywood Boulevard. At the end of the month, the SFX Radio Network broadcasted a two-hour AC/DC concert over 175 stations across the country. The show had been recorded in Phoenix, Arizona on September 13.

The European leg of the Stiff Upper Lip tour started on October 14, 2000, with the band playing at the Flanders Expo in Ghent, Belgium. During AC/DC's encore, a fan in the balcony stood on his chair and fell over the railing. Thirty-eight-year-old Isidoor Thennissen died the next day in the hospital. It was very sad news for the band that genuinely cares for their fans.

Appearing on the French television program *Nulle Part Ailleurs on Canal* on October 30, AC/DC played "Stiff Upper Lip," "Back In Black," "Highway To Hell," "Satellite Blues," and "T.N.T." On Halloween, the band released a boxed set of their entire CD catalog featuring 17 albums. The set was minus *Stiff Upper Lip,* but included *Live From The Atlantic Studios.*

Covering 39 dates total, AC/DC traveled through Belgium, France, Germany, Norway, Sweden, Finland, Holland, Switzerland, Austria, the U.K., and Spain. The closing date of the tour was December 14, 2000 in Barcelona, Spain. (Coincidently, this was also Cliff's birthday.)

Proving George's theory of the basic construction of AC/DC's song, bluegrass band, Hayseed Dixie released an entire album of AC/DC covers called *A Hillbilly Tribute To AC/DC.* The band members included "Einus Younger" and "Barley Scotch." The CD was quite successful, impressing Cliff Williams so much that he hired the Hayseeds to play a housewarming party for one of his houses in the Appalachian mountains.

More evidence that AC/DC's appeal crosses over many genres, multi-Platinum band Green Day's *Dookie* album featured a picture of Angus on its cover. Just look for the guitarist on the roof of the building in the bottom right-hand corner: there's Angus, shorts and all.

The band was also featured in a Budweiser beer commercial that included two lizards and a ferret. The ferret is singing and one of the lizards holds up a lighter, while "Back In Black" is playing in the background. This put a new spin on calling some of their fans, "animals."

The Australian leg of the Stiff Upper Lip tour started on January 19, 2001 in Perth. One of the nights in Adelaide had to be postponed due to Phil suffering from a minor kidney infection. AC/DC played 15 days in Australia, breaking the record for the number of consecutive performances at Sydney's Entertainment Center. From February 19 to 22, the band appeared in Japan for three dates before flying back to play the postponed Adelaide date on February 24, 2001.

Earlier that month, on February 7, the RIAA announced that 14 of AC/DC's albums totaled sales of over 70 million, tying the band for ninth place on the RIAA's Top-Grossing Artist list. This now made them the fifth highest certified band in United State's music history, coming in behind The Beatles, Led Zeppelin, Pink Floyd, and The Eagles. RIAA CEO Hilary Rosen said, "AC/DC is one of rock 'n' roll's greatest assets and has truly earned the right to be called legendary."

By the middle of March, AC/DC was back in the States for the second leg of the American tour that started on March 18 at the National Car Rental Center in Ft. Lauderdale, Florida. The band was due to play Madison, Wisconsin on May 1, but the show was postponed due to Brian's sore throat.

"Pyro" mentioned how they will only postpone a show if they absolutely have to. "I've seen Brian sick, go out and sing, come back and sit down and take his cough medicine. He would have a cup of tea with honey in it, and go right back out on stage and give it 110% intensity. And no one would ever know that right after the show he would be in bed for two days. They're working men. They are clocking in, it's their jobs. If they sold tickets in your town, it's their job to come and play your town. If they got sick and they had to come back, they would get it in as soon as they could fit in another date."

AC/DC was back in town on May 11 and the first thing Brian did when he stepped on stage that night was to apologize for postponing the show. You couldn't tell he had been sick at all by the way he was performing. For nearly two solid hours, the band never let up.

After only a couple of weeks off, AC/DC resumed the second leg of the European tour with 15 "open air" stadium dates on June 8 starting at the National Bowl in Milton Keynes, U.K. Supporting bands included Offspring, Queens Of The Stone Age, Rammstein, Buddy Guy, and Megadeth. Offspring had included a cover of "Sin City" on their latest album, *Million Miles*. Other bands appearing with AC/DC while in Europe were George Thorogood, The Black Crowes, and Krokus.

Not to be outdone by his sibling's enormous fame, George Young and The Easybeats were honored when their hit "Friday On My Mind" was voted the Number One song of all time in Australia on May 29, 2001. Little brothers Angus and Malcolm made the list with "It's A Long Way To The Top," coming in at Number Nine.

At their concert in Paris on June 22, AC/DC included a special encore of "Ride On," complete with blue French football T-shirts. The song was in honor of John Lee Hooker, who had passed away the day before. If you really listen to John Lee Hooker, you can hear how much his music influenced AC/DC.

After the Stiff Upper Lip tour ended on July 8 in Koln, Germany, AC/DC gave away "the world's greatest lawn ornament." Some lucky fan won a life-size replica of one of their cannons. The remaining cannons, along with the bell, rest between tours in a warehouse somewhere in England.

In time for the anniversary of his birthday on July 9, Bon Scott was honored at the Kirriemuir Gateway to the Glens Museum in Scotland. On display celebrating Bon's life were old photographs and a copy of his birth certificate.

Angus reached a milestone in celebrity himself, when McFarlane Toys released an Angus Young doll in October of 2001. It was timed perfectly to compliment the giant statue of Angus that had dominated the stage on the Stiff Upper Lip tour. The doll was 16 inches tall, inspiring some to cheekily describe it as "almost life size."

For the first time in 21 years, Brian reunited with his old mates and did a brief tour with his former band Geordie. They played at the Newcastle Opera House and also recorded two songs, "Biker Hill" and "Wor Geordie's Lost His Liggy."

After his tour with Geordie, Brian appeared at the Sammy Johnson Memorial Concert at City Hall in Newcastle. He played with the house band that included Jimmy Nail and Tim Healey.

A new DVD of the Stiff Upper Lip tour was released featuring the band playing live in Munich, Germany on June 14, 2001. The video included 21 songs, backstage footage, and exclusive interviews.

Possibly topping Hayseed Dixie for pure shock value, Sixties singing sensation Lesley Gore—known for "It's My Party"—covered "Dirty Deeds Done Dirt Cheap" for the CD, *When Pigs Fly—Songs You Never Thought You'd Hear*. It should have been called *Songs You Never Want To Listen To*.

While on tour with Elton John, Billy Joel went into a rant onstage in Tampa in March of 2002 about AC/DC not being inducted into the Rock and Roll Hall of Fame. At the end of his tirade, he surprised the audience by bringing Brian Johnson and Cliff Williams out on stage where they launched into "Highway To Hell." The next night Joel had to cancel due to laryngitis. *See Billy, Brian just makes it look easy.*

In April, it was announced on MTV News that Brian was working with British composer Brendan Healy and Sarasota Ballet Artistic Director Robert de Warren on a musical called, *Helen Of Troy*...an action-filled love story based on Greek Mythology. He wrote 14 songs for the show, which was originally scheduled to open at the Van Wezel Performing Arts Hall in Sarasota, Florida in March 2003. The show featured five singing roles, a chorus of 15, a dance troupe of 15, acrobats, jugglers, and fire eaters and cost 1.2 million dollars to produce. Brian's friend, actor Malcolm McDowell (*A Clockwork Orange*) was chosen to play Zeus. He also served as the narrator.

Robert de Warren was quoted in the MTV News in April 2002 regarding Brian's creativity, "It's not all based on rock. It's rather like Gilbert and Sullivan. It's very British, actually. There's a lot of very beautiful melodies and it's amazing how literate [Brian] is, which is quite unusual for a rock star."

While not on tour with AC/DC, Brian and Cliff both enjoyed working on outside projects. Again teaming up with Jesse Dupree, Brian co-wrote the song "Kill The Sunshine" for Jackyl's new album, *Relentless*. Cliff made a guest appearance on Bosnian-American musician Emir Bukovica and his band Frozen Camel's album, *San*. He also played four dates with them in Bosnia, Croatia, and Slovenia.

When the Scorpions played in Tampa, Florida, Brian surprised the audience by joining them onstage for their encore. Scorpion's drummer, James Kottack recalled, "About two years ago, we were doing a show in Florida and Brian Johnson showed up in the dressing room just before the show! Of course we asked if he wanted to sing one, so he came up for "Rock You Like A Hurricane." Not only did he and Klaus rip the song a new one, at some point Klaus jumped on the drum riser. Brian then got in front of the riser and Klaus climbed on Brian's shoulders. As if that wasn't enough, Brian took off down the stairs like a tank on a mission with Klaus on his shoulders and he proceeded to run a couple of laps around the arena for the next 10 minutes while we continued playing the longest version of "Hurricane" ever! Brian did finally bring Klaus back for the end. We laughed 'til we were crying. Then we had a couple of thousand beers back in the dressing room!"

Angus and Malcolm showed up on stage when The Rolling Stones appeared in Sydney at the Enmore Theater, playing B. B. King's "Rock Me Baby." Always huge fans of the Stones, these performances were still taken in stride by the Young brothers. "Pyro" explained, "I remember when we were doing the European Stones 2003 Licks tour and Angus and Malcolm came out and played a few songs with them. And everyone came out to watch, but Angus and Malcolm were the only ones who were going to play. They were standing on the side of the stage, and they were acting just like any of the stagehand's friends, except that they were going to go out and play! I was talking to Malcolm, and his guitar tech came over and told him he was going to go out right after the next song. And Malcolm just said, 'All right, nice talking to you, Pyro,' and that was it. Like it was an everyday occurrence. Then afterwards, you would see them with the crew in catering, and they would just be sitting there. Which is one of the coolest things about them."

Always willing to help a good cause, AC/DC and Elektra Records raised over $43,000 for the VH-1 Save The Music and the Nordoff Robins Foundation by auctioning off several AC/DC items, including one of Angus' school caps, one of Brian's trademark flat caps, and a personal guitar jam with Angus. The one-hour jam went to the highest bidder for $28,100!

After some controversy, it was finally announced that AC/DC would be inducted into the Rock and Roll Hall of Fame, along with The Clash, The Police, and Elvis Costello And The Attractions. At first it was stated that original bassist Mark Evans would be inducted, as well. With no explanation, that decision was quickly rescinded. Right after the announcement, AC/DC signed a multi-album deal with Epic/Sony Music after spending 26 years with WEA (Warner/Elektra/Atlantic). The new deal reunited the band with Dave Glew, who worked with them at Atlantic, and Steve Barnett, who was once their manager. Epic made plans to re-release 15 of their 17 album catalog.

Beating Black Sabbath and The Sex Pistols by two years, their induction into Rock and Roll's Hall of Fame was fitting for the band that toured nonstop for years. Or as Malcolm put it, "It was more like an abduction!" The ceremony was held at New York's Waldorf Astoria on March 10, 2003 and their award was presented to them by Steven Tyler of Aerosmith. Representing Bon, were his nephews Daniel and Paul Scott, who joined the band on stage.

Tyler's induction speech declared "AC/DC became the litmus test of what rock does. Does it make you clench your fist when you sing along? Does it scare your parents to hell and piss off the neighbors? Does it make you dance so close to the fire that you burn your feet—and still don't give a rat's ass? Does it make you want to stand up and scream for something that you're not even sure of yet? Does it make you want to boil your sneakers and make soup outta your girlfriend's panties? If it doesn't, then it ain't AC/DC!"

The band briefly thanked the fans for their support and Brian said, "In the beginning, back in 1955, man didn't know about the rock 'n' roll show and all that jive. The white man had the schmaltz, the black man had the blues, but no one knew what they was gonna do, but Tchaikovsky had the news, he said, 'Let there be rock!' Bon Scott wrote that. And it's a real privilege to accept these awards tonight."

Never ones to conform to a black tie event, Malcolm commented, "When we got there it was like playing in front of a bunch of fucking penguins in a restaurant. The guys from The Clash were up before us, and The Edge of U2 got up to introduce them. Fuck, he made this 40-minute speech [about late Clash guitarist Joe Strummer]. He was the most boring bloke I've ever had the misfortune to witness. We were at the side [of the stage], waiting and getting madder and madder, even though we had sympathy [for the rest of The Clash]. So when they said to go, we fuckin' took off. It was an anger-fueled performance. We ripped the place apart. They were dancing up in the balconies in their tuxes. It was quite a moment for us. The rest of the bands were pretty mild in comparison."

The band played "Highway To Hell" and "You Shook Me All Night Long" accompanied by Steven Tyler who was doing his best to keep up with Brian. The latter tune has the stature of being the most popular song played in strip clubs…Something truly to be proud of.

Soon after their appearance at the Rock 'n' Roll Hall of Fame, Angus, Malcolm, and Brian played an acoustic version of "The Jack" and "You Shook Me All Night Long" on the Howard Stern radio show. On the night of March 11, the band treated a select number of fans to a free show at the Roseland Ballroom, supported by Vendetta Red. It would be their only American concert in 2003.

Angus and Malcolm received the Ted Albert Music Achievement Award from Albert Music at the 2003 APRA Music Awards in Sydney on March 26. Malcolm sent a taped message from London saying, "On behalf of AC/DC and Bon Scott, especially Bon because he's a big part of this, we're proud of the honor of receiving this award." [Ted Albert, the man who started it all by signing The Easybeats, had died of heart failure in 1990 and this award was named in his honor.]

Songstress Celine Dion covered "You Shook Me All Night Long" for the VH-1 television special, *Divas Las Vegas*. Malcolm told *Guitar World* in April 2003, "Somebody sent me a video of that. I was impressed-not necessarily with the vocals, but with the fact that she was able to do Angus' duck walk with the fucking shoes she had on! Fucking hell, she's got some balls to do that!

VH-1, the only cable music channel with real taste, featured AC/DC on *Ultimate Albums,* a one-hour special spotlighting their milestone creation, Back In Black. The show included rare footage and interviews with the band.

During the summer, AC/DC played five dates in Germany: two headlining shows and three supporting The Rolling Stones. Also appearing with them were The Pretenders. There were rumors that the tickets for the Stones weren't selling that well in Europe until they added AC/DC. It would be the first time since 1980 that AC/DC was billed as a supporting act.

Both AC/DC and the Stones made Canadian history when they played in front of 490,000 people in Downsview Park in Toronto on July 30, 2003. "Molson Canadian Rocks For Toronto," a benefit for SARS, was hosted by Dan Akroyd and Jim Belushi. Also appearing were Rush, The Guess Who, The Isley Brothers, Sass Jordan, and Justin Timberlake.

AC/DC whipped the crowd into a frenzy, ending their set with "Let There Be Rock" and "Highway To Hell." Later, Angus and Malcolm joined The Rolling Stones on stage to jam on the song "Rock Me Baby." There were lots of pictures of Justin Timberlake singing with them, as well. Brian had been asked to come out and sing too, but decided against it. Something about singing alongside a Backstreet Boy. You've got to draw the line somewhere.

Martin Popoff wrote in *Metal Hammer* Special 2005, "A definite highlight of the band's touring history occurred on July 30, 2003 when AC/DC put in a blistering 70-minute set second to a show-closing Rolling Stones at the Toronto Rocks festival, before a crowd of 450,000. It is widely believed that the band stole the show that night. Later, Angus would jam with the Stones during their set, capping off the all-day event and resulting in AC/DC being raved about for months afterward. It was a fitting finale as now, we all wait for the new record and the rabble-roused performances to come…"

Five days later, while I was on my annual vacation in Florida, I ran into

Brian right after he got home from Canada. I made a point to give him a copy of my book, which had been published in paperback. He got a laugh out of looking at all the pictures. When he got to the one of me dressed as Dorothy from the Wizard of Oz, to promote the newspaper I worked for called the Emerald City Chronicle, *he looked at me and said, "Oh, look what they made you do!"*

Brian invited us to meet him for a drink that afternoon at a local pub. Pulling up in his Aston Martin, Brian walked in, ordered a Guinness, and regaled us with stories about the Stones, among others for over an hour. Not realizing how big the crowd was that they had just played in front of in Toronto, Brian remarked how loud they were. I was floored when I got home and read reports of how big the audience actually was! He acted so nonchalant about it, like it was an everyday event. Throughout our visit, Brian had us in stitches with impersonations of The Rolling Stones, his southern racing buddies, and anyone else who came to mind. He told us that Keith Richards traveled with a big road case with four drawers that were labeled, "Guns, Ammunition, Drugs, and Guitar Strings." I told Brian, 'at least Keith has his priorities straight!'

Brian is so funny he could easily be a stand up comedian. That is, if you could understand what the hell he was saying. Perry Cooper, who became one of his close friends, laughed about him, "Number one, he tells the worst jokes! He's hilarious; he's just so funny. He has no pretension, he's not a star. He doesn't act like one. He's written some of the greater lyrics for the band, and he just slid into that place, like he was made to be there. It was unbelievable, just brilliant! If you had to find a replacement and wanted the band to continue, Brian was perfect."

Angus and Malcolm jammed one more time with The Rolling Stones on stage at their Twickenham Stadium show in London on September 20. They again played "Rock Me Baby." Ronnie Wood even managed to get Malcolm to solo during the song.

On October 21, 2003, for one night only, AC/DC played at the Hammersmith Odeon in London. The 4,000 available tickets sold out in just under four minutes. Released the same month, the movie *School Of Rock*—starring Jack Black—confirmed the band's place as rock 'n' roll icons. Especially when Black appears on stage in a mail carrier's uniform altered to look like a schoolboy's outfit. The comedy hit Number One at the box office and featured the AC/DC song, "It's A Long Way To The Top (If You Wanna Rock 'N' Roll)."

Filming then began down under for the movie *Thunderstruck*. The plot centered around a group of diehard AC/DC fans who make a pact that if any one of them dies before they turn 40, the rest will bury him next to their hero, Bon Scott. It was the first movie released by Mel Gibson's production company, Icon Films. The soundtrack included covers of three AC/DC songs: "Thunderstruck," "T.N.T.," "It's A Long Way To The Top," and "Jupiter's Landscape." A song Bon recorded with the band Fraternity.

Playing 139 shows across 17 countries, performing with the Stones and being inducted into the Rock and Roll Hall of Fame, AC/DC continues to conquer new territory. Angus told Gene Stout in the *Wisconsin State Journal* on April 26, 2001, "There's an old saying that the quickest way to get from point A to point B is to go in a direct line. And that's how we've always approached our music. We've always felt our music should be for people who really want to rock 'n' roll. So we came in on the deep end and we just went go-for-broke. We've always had this do-or-die attitude."

Cheap Trick's ex-tour manager, Kirk Dyer, was always impressed with how they handled themselves. "They always had the goal, no matter what the goal was, in mind. They never lost sight of what they were trying to accomplish; that's the part that I think struck me the most. In just talking to the guys, they always said they wanted to be big, they always wanted to be the best. There is no tighter five-piece band around. The rhythm section is the best in the world, in my opinion. They just blew me away. They don't sit on their laurels or sit around and rehash old stuff. Sure, everyone puts out a greatest-hits album now and then, when they don't have their songs together, but those guys have always managed to come up [with something new]. They take three chords and twist them so many different ways it never gets boring. That's what I love about them, they just rock! I never ever, ever get tired of them."

Or as Spyder Darling in *New York Star* so expressively said, "These guys wouldn't lose their granite-solid $\frac{4}{4}$ groove if the recording studio were on fire during an earthquake, while atomic bombs were dropping from a sky full of alien invaders." That's because at the volume they play at, who the hell would notice?

AC**20**DC

CAN'T STOP ROCK 'N' ROLL

Toronto Rocks, the DVD capturing the largest concert in Canadian history, was released in June 2004. Now you can see why Brian talked about the audience being incredibly loud. A half a million people tend to get a little noisy! Especially when Angus and Malcolm share the stage with The Rolling Stones.

Twenty-four years after the release of *Back In Black,* the RIAA awarded the album with a double Diamond, signifying over 20-million copies sold in the U.S. alone. *Back In Black,* has now sold more than 42-million copies worldwide, putting it in fifth place on the list of Top 10 biggest-selling albums of all time. It also qualified to be included in the *Guinness Book Of World Records.* In addition, the song "Back In Black" was voted the eighth-best guitar riff in a poll of the 100 Greatest Riffs Ever in *Total Guitar* magazine,

Bon Scott was honored as well, when *Classic Rock* voted him Number One in the 100 Greatest Front Men of all time...nudging out Queen's Freddie Mercury and Led Zeppelin's Robert Plant for first place. Bon's leather jacket, along with Angus' guitars, now reside in an Australian museum and Bon's hand-written lyrics can fetch thousands at auction.

While still in England on July 3, Brian made a guest appearance in Penrich Derbyshire. He joined Twisted Sister during their set for a version of "Whole Lotta Rosie" at the Rock And Blues Custom Show. Lending their star power to various benefits around the state of Florida, Brian joined Velvet Revolver on September 6 at the Hard Rock Cafe in Orlando, helping raise money for the victims of Hurricane Katrina. They jammed on a rendition of Led Zeppelin's

"Rock And Roll." Two days later, both Brian and Cliff appeared at the Germain Arena in Estero, Florida benefiting the American Red Cross Hurricane Charley Disaster Relief.

Famous fellow Floridian, guitarist Rick Derringer, organized Musicians 4 Disaster Relief which was held in Orlando on February 5, 2005. The event was in association with the John Entwistle Foundation, the American Red Cross, and the Florida Hurricane Relief Fund. Brian and Cliff performed, along with Michael Bolton, Dickey Betts from The Allman Brothers, Chuck Negron from Three Dog Night, Loverboy, Robin Zander, Eddie Money, Mark Farner from Grand Funk Railroad, and Dee Snider and Twisted Sister. The concert was recorded by DiscLive on CD and was available for sale immediately after the show.

Donating a specially signed guitar to the "Designer Gibson Guitar Auction," Brian also helped raise money for the Expedition Inspiration Fund, which benefits breast cancer research. The event was held at the Hard Rock Cafe in Los Angeles.

When asked to lend his voice to the Play Station 2 game, *Call Of Duty: Finest Hour,* Brian was inspired by his late father. The elder Johnson once served in the British Army's Durham Light Infantry, and his experiences motivated Brian's authentic portrayal of a "desert rat."

AC/DC was honored in Spain when a street right outside Madrid was named after them. Malcolm and Angus, clad in his schoolboy suit, were present at the christening of Calle de AC/DC. Australian fans also successfully petitioned to get a street named after them in Melbourne. Formerly Corporation Lane, on October 1, 2004 it was renamed AC/DC Lane. The street runs parallel to Swanston Street, where the video for "It's A Long Way To The Top" was filmed in 1976.

When the city wouldn't allow a lightning bolt to separate the letters, local artist "Knifeyard," crafted a lightning bolt out of the same metal as the street sign is made of and bolted it above and below the sign with a hammer drill. To say AC/DC fans are passionate, doesn't quite cover it.

Nearly 1,000 fans commemorated the twenty-fifth anniversary of Bon's death at a memorial service in Fremantle, Australia. Re-enacting their infamous ride through Melbourne, the tribute band Riff Raff traveled through the streets on a flat-bed truck playing "It's A Long Way To The Top." Bag pipers, dressed in black, marched into the cemetery playing songs that Bon learned to play as a child. Later that night, Riff Raff held a concert at the Leopold Hotel. On February 22, Bon Scott's achievements and contributions to rock 'n' roll were recognized by The Western Australian Music Industry (WAMI) when they inducted him into the West Australian Music Hall of Fame.

Just in time to celebrate, AC/DC released a double DVD called *Family Jewels*. The new video featured 40 performances — 20 with Bon and 20 with Brian — spanning the years 1975 to 1993. This most-worthy AC/DC item debuted at Number One on the Music Video sales charts. For the price, it is the AC/DC bargain of the century. The funniest part of the earlier videos is that it shows as their income got bigger, their teeth got better.

Some of the highlights of the Bon years: "Baby, Please Don't Go" where Bon appears on live television in a dress, wig, and make-up. This was the show where they didn't know what Bon was planning ahead of time and the best part is how hard Phil Rudd is laughing at him.

I also love "Jailbreak" which was the song Bon thought was his best. His death scene, which is ironic in itself, shows his potential as an actor. He really does put a lot into rolling around on the ground!

Another favorite is "Dog Eat Dog" which has the most brilliant lyrics. Bon succinctly sums up the simple lessons of life in that song. The best shot of him is when he crinkles up his nose at the camera. It's the perfect image of Bon's elfin magic and how fans like to remember him best.

"Let There Be Rock" comically features Bon dressed as a preacher, Angus as an angel, and the rest of the band clad as choir boys. You can bet for their first and last time. Although I do believe this song was heaven sent.

The first four songs of the second DVD with Brian are from *Back In Black* and are a little hard for some fans to watch. Those songs were filmed barely five months after Bon's death and even though the band is performing spot on, they look devastated. Bon's gone and you can see it in their faces. That's not to take away from how hard Brian is working it. He stepped into some very big shoes and never once let the boys down.

The entire DVD vividly shows the evolution of AC/DC. If you've never had the pleasure to see them live [and let's hope that's not the case], you can put this in your DVD player, crank up the volume, push back the furniture and go nuts. Within six months of its release, *Classic Rock* voted *Family Jewels* DVD Of The Year.

Malcolm was voted the "Most Underrated Guitarist" in the June issue of *Guitar World,* and Angus won the top position for "Who You Would Like To Have A Drink With." That'll work if you're drinkin' tea!

Keeping his chops up, Brian performed with two bands at the Khrome Club in Sarasota, Florida. He sang "Dirty Deeds Done Dirt Cheap" and "Back In Black" with Big Machine and "Rock And Roll Ain't Noise

Pollution" with The Greg Billings Band.

Big Machine is the band Brian put together to perform songs he and producer Doug Kaye had written together. After Neurotica broke up, Brian hired vocalist Kelly Shaefer to handle the vocals. Shaefer explained why Brian choose him to sing his lyrics, "Brian once told me, 'At one point, your voice always reminded me of Bon. You've got a timbre in your voice like Bon, and it reminds me of him.' That was the coolest moment ever for me, in my experiences with Brian. I just always wondered why he took the time to produce our record. He felt he saw a fire and he pursued it, and I'll love him to death for that, forever."

While we were on vacation in Florida in 2005, my husband and I visited with Big Machine. They were working at Southern Sound Studios that was once owned by The Allman Brothers. Kelly and the band generously invited us to sit in on their rehearsal as they were getting ready to fly up to New York to play a showcase at the legendary CBGB's. After getting the hair blown off of my head, I could see why Brian was so happy with the band!

An unauthorized DVD—*And Then There Was Rock, Life Before Brian*—was released in September by Chrome Dreams. It featured lots of interviews with friends and former bandmates.

Brian made his acting debut in the movie *Goal*. He appears in two scenes as a Newcastle United fan, sitting in a pub, watching the game. Luckily he didn't have to stretch much for the part. Angus also made a rare public appearance, introducing Ozzy Osbourne's solo band's performance at the ceremony for the United Kingdom Music Hall of Fame awards. Receiving his own accolades, Angus was voted Number One out of "25 Greatest Short Dudes of All Time." Officially standing at five-feet-two inches tall, he came in only five spots ahead of Yoda.

Again helping out their home state, Brian and Cliff appeared at the 96 K-Rock For Relief II benefiting Hurricane Wilma victims. The concert took place at the Germain Arena in Estero, Florida on December 15, 2005. Also performing were Robin Zander of Cheap Trick [another of Brian's neighbors], Joe Lynn Turner of Deep Purple, Eddie Money, Loverboy, Mark Farner of Grand Funk Railroad, and Buck Dharma of Blue Oyster Cult. Dharma being the only guitarist in rock who can stand eye to eye with Angus.

Marking the twenty-sixth anniversary of Bon's death, Max TV (an Australian cable channel) ran eight hours of continuous AC/DC videos to commemorate Bon's passing and the 30-year anniversary of the release of the album *T.N.T. Arena TV* re-ran the *Saturday Night Live* episode the band played on and Gavin Miller at 96 FM took care of the radio airwaves by playing the entire *T.N.T.* album over his three-hour shift.

Also in February, the National Trust of Australia decreed Bon's Fremantle gravesite to be included on the list of classified heritage places. The listing is usually reserved for buildings, but due to the amount of fans who visit the cemetery every year, his resting place was recognized.

Doug Thorncroft, who started his own Western Australia (WA) Bon Scott fan club, has petitioned the city to erect a bronze statue of Bon in time for the anniversary of his sixtieth birthday in July of 2006. To celebrate his passing, AC/DC tribute band Thunderstruck played at Melbourne's Hi Fi Bar. Joining them onstage was former bassist, Mark Evans. Bon's ex-wife, Irene, was also in attendance.

Thorncroft is now working on something similar to a Hollywood Walk of Fame and he is trying to get nearby Short Street renamed Bon Scott Place. Also announced in February, Irene made arrangements with an auction house in Melbourne to sell Bon's love letters and postcards, upsetting some of his fans. His words to her are touching examples of how loving and thoughtful he was. The auction was held in April, and Bon's letters and personal photos were not sold failing to bring in the desired amount. But a personalized shaving mirror—given to him by his mum—sold for $12,540, and a test pressing of *High Voltage* with it's original wrapping went for $8,655.

At Bon's birthplace in Kirriemuir, a permanent memorial was placed in Cumberland Close on May 6. It is a plaque that reads, Ronald Belford 'Bon' Scott, Born Kirriemuir 9th July 1946, Died 19th February 1980, Let There Be Rock, Song Writer and Singer with AC/DC, World's Greatest Rock 'N' Roll Legend.

Rocking into their third decade, AC/DC's presence is felt everywhere. Still a fan long after he stopped working with them, the late Perry Cooper said in an interview shortly before his death, "Who would ever think the band would have made it eight or nine years, and here it is 30 years later. Every time I get in my car, I can't drive anywhere without hearing two or three AC/DC songs on the radio. Angus and Malcolm come up with such classic riffs. They [the songs] are anthems, absolute anthems. Now, when you watch a football game or a baseball game, you always hear "Hells Bells" or "For Those About To Rock" or any of those. They're anthems! They put together songs that are anthems, that are easy to identify with, and people love them. AC/DC are the anthem kings! Now that is success and they absolutely deserve it!"

You can also find ads in your Sunday newspaper for Shopko, Sears, and JC Penney's, all offering AC/DC T-shirts, sweatshirts, and hoodies. Right before the 2005 Christmas season, AC/DC struck a deal with the telephone company, Cingular, making their song, "Back In Black" available for the ringtone on the new paper-thin black cell phone, the Razor.

Every year fans also gather from all over the world to attend AC/DC conventions. The largest, called The Big Ball, featured Hayseed Dixie and Simon Wright playing in the tribute band, Dirty/DC in 2005. Some of the funniest AC/DC tribute band names are Seedy DC, Fat Angus Band, Hells Balls, and (*my personal favorite*) the all-female band from San Francisco called, AC/DSHE. Band members include Agnes and Mallory Young, Riff Williams, Phyllis Rudd, and Bonny Scott. You can just bet that Bon would have had a field day with that bunch!

According to Mat Croft in *Metal Hammer* Special 2005, two of the best AC/DC covers are Quiet Riot's "Highway To Hell" on the album *Thunderbolt* and Motorhead covering, "It's A Long Way To The Top" with Lemmy "sounding so hoarse you expect a bloody lung to come flying out of your speakers."

Just as The Beatles did in the Sixties and Led Zeppelin in the Seventies, AC/DC defined the Eighties, influencing hundreds of bands around the world such as Australia's Rose Tattoo, Silvertide, Jet, Midnight Oil, and The Angels; in Europe: Switzerland's Krokus, Spain's Baron Rojo, France's Trust, and Germany's TNT; in America and the U.K. the list includes Guns N' Roses, Motley Crue, Def Leppard, Quiet Riot, Twisted Sister, Kix, Danger Danger, The Cult, Buckcherry, and The Darkness. Not forgetting the most blatant AC/DC clone of them all, Rhino Bucket...who for a while had ex-AC/DC drummer Simon Wright behind the kit.

There are also a slew of country artists whose music has a touch of AC/DC in it. Just listen to Garth Brooks, Montgomery Gentry, and Big and Rich. *You can't tell me anyone who wrote, "I feel like Tonto, driving a Pinto, trying to chase the Lone Ranger down," hadn't listened to Bon Scott at some point!*

Shania Twain warms up on AC/DC, as does Chuck Garrick, the bassist for The Alice Cooper Band. The drummer for Gretchen Wilson sported an AC/DC T-shirt while on stage. And, supposedly, when Metallica's tour manager gave drummer Lars Ulrich an AC/DC tour jacket, he wore it for years.

Reportedly starting on the new album in London in early 2006, Angus and Malcolm alternate working at each other's homes. They may have recently purchased new recording equipment, but you won't see them playing anything different in the studio or onstage. Malcolm prefers his original 1963 Gretsch Jet Firebird and Angus favors his vintage 1968 Gibson SG. All this is run through Marshall stacks, with the only gadgets being their wireless systems. No wah-wah pedals for these guys.

The only song Malcolm recorded playing something other than his Gretsch Jet Firebird is "High Voltage." Because his guitar was broken, Malcolm had to use a Gibson L-5 on that song, which still bothers him every time he hears it. Angus had to do the same on "Live Wire," playing a Les Paul. But you won't hear it, because as soon as his Gibson SG was fixed, he re-recorded the song!

Malcolm recently commissioned another bell to be made by the John Taylor Bell Founders. It was a copy of the original "Hells Bells" but this one says "Home Bell" and hangs in place of a candelabra at the top of a sweeping staircase at his Hertfordshire home. Proof that there is no rivalry among band members, *Guitar Player* once asked Malcolm if it bothered him that Angus gets more attention. He said, "No, because we all get the same money. If he was getting more money, then it would bother us." Spoken like a true professional.

When he's not breaking land-speed records, Angus likes to spend his time painting. Perry Cooper raved about his talents on canvas. "Angus is a brilliant painter. I was in shock, because I've seen some of it, and he is absolutely brilliant! He does watercolors and things, and he is just a great painter! Once, Angus drew a bunch of caricatures of us on a note with little devils on it and sent it to me at Atlantic."

The brothers also enjoy the distinction of having a pair of fossils named after them. In November 1998, the Australian Museum reported that the fossils were two species of a "strange joint-legged" animal which was believed to be related to millipedes or the horseshoe crab. I think it's more than appropriate that AC/DC should be linked to a prehistoric chunk of rock, er fossil, well you know what I mean.

Brian, said to have tonsils of leather, is a serious gourmand and an avid racecar driver. He owns several cars and placed in the Daytona 500 in 2003. His wife, Brenda, shares his passion and gets behind the wheel herself. When at home, they enjoy an exact replica of a Newcastle pub Brian used to go to, called the Queen's Head, which he had built to scale right inside his house. Never one to slow down, Brian was also the executive producer of the movie, Half Baked, where he wrote three songs for the soundtrack.

Living just a few miles south of Brian Johnson's place, Cliff fills in occasionally with the rhythm and blues band, The Juice. Cliff's contribution to the sound of AC/DC cannot be underestimated. He is known as the master of the eighth note, attacking each note, as *Guitar School* wrote, "with the vengeance of a teen in heat." Cliff explained, "I never get bored playing eighth notes. In this band, I play what's best for the song. I play what needs to be played—and I feel good about it. Know what I mean?"

Cliff's favorite AC/DC songs are "Let There Be Rock," "Live Wire," "Gimme A Bullet," "Gone Shootin'," and "Down Payment Blues." When he plays live, he wears a leather brace strapped onto his right arm, which keeps him from wearing away the skin.

Phil, "the Charlie Watts of heavy metal," as Martin Popoff called him in *Metal Hammer,* continues to live in New Zealand. In January of 2005, Phil sponsored New Zealand's race car driver, Jared Carlyle, who drove a Ford Falcon owned by Phil's Mountain Recording team. He started out playing Ludwig drums, but for years has preferred his Sonor kit. As Cliff told *Guitar School* when Phil came back into the band, "Phil always had a natural feel for what this band does...it just fits like a glove with Phil. You can't really put your finger on it—it's just a feel."

Describing AC/DC's longevity, John Doran wrote in the 2005 Special issue of *Metal Hammer,* "...They [Angus and Malcolm] took a clinical look at what was wrong with rock and stripped it all away, leaving a primitive riff-based caveman rock, that was so simple and effective it would become an instantly recognizable and much-copied trademark over the next three decades."

Rick Brewster from The Angels said, "There is no better example of a band who began with a strong vision and refused to divert from it. AC/DC took the "circus element" of rock 'n' roll performance to new extremes. They took the antics of Jerry Lee Lewis, Chuck Berry, Jimi Hendrix...and exploded into a giant spectacle whose true strength has always been in the music—the songs and the musical ability."

One of their biggest fans and producer of *Ballbreaker,* Rick Rubin told *Classic Rock,* "I'll go on record as saying they're the greatest rock 'n' roll band of all time. They didn't write emotional lyrics. They didn't play emotional songs. The emotion is all in that groove. And that groove is timeless."

Cooper agreed, "Nobody can copy Angus, no one can copy Malcolm, or Cliff. They have got that very basic stage act that is brilliant, and they make brilliant music. And it all comes down to the music."

Aside from being amazing musicians, many of their fans don't know how incredibly grounded the band members really are. "Pyro" Pete didn't have any dirt to dish. "They turned out to be like what I'd hoped they would be like. Because when you look at them from the album covers, it's just guys. Like you would come across these guys in a bar, drinking, or at a soccer game, or you would see them anywhere and they were just like a group of guys. And that's exactly what they were! Aside from Angus's schoolboy outfit, the rest of them were like whatever they turned up in, was what they were going to walk onstage with. It was really cool, because during rehearsals, you would see them walking around, and if you didn't know who they were, you would think they were truck loaders, or lighting guys or something. Just kind of hanging around.

"I have met other 'rock stars,' that were all in spandex and leather, but these guys were just *guys!* Even if you talked to them about the band, they would say they started this band, then they played in bars, if you heard them talk about it, they were so nonchalant, it would seem like they just formed a band a week ago, they played in a bar yesterday, and today they're playing in an arena!

"I've met their wives and family, and they're real nice people. If we were in the same hotel and Brian or Angus or anyone was in the bar or restaurant, you couldn't walk through without one of them saying hello and asking how your day was going. They would always ask you what you were doing, or what you were doing later, and would often socialize with us.

"You could talk to anybody who has ever worked on an AC/DC road crew, and I don't think you could find a person to say a bad thing about an AC/DC tour. It was always a fun tour. You knew you were going to have fun. It was never like you feared the band. Like during rehearsals when the band comes in, you usually say, 'Oh no! The band's coming in!' I've been on some tours when the band comes in for rehearsals, you have to put the caution tape up, and get all the workers back. Only the people who need to be in the area should be there. I could never see AC/DC be like that. They would not allow something like that to happen."

"Pyro" went on to explain how other rock stars felt about the band. "You could be anybody. You could be Eddie Van Halen, or the guy who played in the opening band that went on at 2 pm that afternoon. And now you are everybody, who has been stripped of everything, and are on the same level. And that level is, standing on the side of the stage trying to watch Angus play. I remember asking Eddie Van Halen and Valerie Bertinelli to stand by me. There used to be so many people on the side of the stage, that we would have to rope off areas to work in. No matter who was the opening act, even the guys in Metallica wanted to be able to get a good spot to be able to watch Angus. Lots of times you would hear some rock star was out at the front of the house at the mixing console, having a drink, watching the show and wanting to be seen. When people come to an AC/DC show, they would want to be on the side of the stage. The guys from The Scorpions, ZZ Top, name a band, and I've seen them standing on the side of the stage with a wide-eyed look, watching Angus."

As Scorpion's drummer James Kottak declared, "AC/DC is the Ford, the baseball and the apple pie of rock 'n' roll!" Legendary guitarist in his own right, Rudolf Schenker added, "[Their staying power comes from] sticking to their unique style and being great musicians!"

When asked who his favorite member of the band was, "Pyro" couldn't decide. "That one I have to actually think on. I've spent time with all of them, and their families, and have gotten Christmas cards and postcards. It's kind of like a family vibe. If you asked me that about a lot of other bands, I'd have an answer for you right away. It would be easier if someone was an asshole, but there isn't one in this band."

Ex-tour director, Mike Andy, agreed. "I've worked with Motley Crue, Bon Jovi, U-2, The Bee Gees, ELP, Bruce Springsteen...I've worked with everybody but Elvis Presley! And there is no harder-working band than AC/DC. There is no one better. They are the nicest guys in the world. They are very well-educated, family oriented, and they're just great people!"

In the summer of 2007, Brian and Cliff once again lent a hand at raising money for the John Entwistle Foundation by joining the Classic Rock Cares Tour. The concerts helped raise money to provide free music education and instruments through the public library system for kids in need. The Foundation also donated instruments for the kids at the Sarasota Memorial Hospital, where they christened a room The Brian Johnson Music Therapy Room, in appreciation to all Brian has done for their city.

The Classic Rock Cares band also featured drummer Steve Luongo, guitarist Mark Hitt, vocalists Mark Farner of Grand Funk Railroad, Joe Lynn Turner of Deep Purple and Rainbow, Cheap Trick's Robin Zander, and Eddie Money. The band played nine dates in Florida, Las Vegas, Chicago, Atlantic City, and New York. Brian and Cliff even wrote a couple of original songs to perform along with many of their AC/DC hits.

As destiny would have it, my annual Florida vacation just happened to coincide with their show in Clearwater, Florida on July 3, 2007. After enjoying performances by Joe Lynn Turner, Eddie Money and Robin Zander, the sold-out crowd of 2,000 patiently waited through an intermission before Brian and Cliff took the stage. Judging from how many members of the audience sported AC/DC t-shirts, it was clear who everyone came to see. When they both walked out onto the stage, the audience exploded with cheers.

For the next hour, Brian and Cliff treated everyone to such AC/DC classics as "Hell's Bell's," "Sin City," "Dirty Deeds Done Dirt Cheap," and "Given' The Dog A Bone." Closing the show with "Highway To Hell," Turner, Money, and Zander returned to the stage to share vocals with Brian. Considering the band hadn't toured since 2001, this was truly a rare occasion for any AC/DC fan.

After the show I was able to talk with Brian and Cliff about AC/DC's future plans. Although it was rumored that Angus and Malcolm were working on new songs, they were both reluctant to promise anything. After all, a new album had been talked about for several years, and there was no indication that they would ever tour again. It was definitely not the news I was hoping to hear. Luckily by the spring of the following year, this was all about to change.

AC 21 DC

ROCK 'N' ROLL TRAIN

Managing to keep their return to the studio under wraps, AC/DC quietly convened at the Warehouse Studio in Vancouver in March of 2008 to work on the new album with producer Brendan O'Brien and engineer Mike Fraser. O'Brien's credits included Pearl Jam, Soundgarden, Bruce Springsteen and Rage Against The Machine. Fraser had previously worked with the band on *Back In Black*, *Razor's Edge*, *Ballbreaker,* and *Stiff Upper Lip*.

During their hiatus, AC/DC left their longtime label, Atlantic Records, and signed a new deal with Sony Music. To whet the fan's appetites, they released a double and triple DVD titled *Plug Me In* in October of 2007. The set included five and seven hours of rare concert footage, including AC/DC performing "School Days," "T.N.T.," "She's Got Balls," and "It's A Long Way To The Top (If You Wanna Rock 'n' Roll)" at St. Alban's High School in Australia in March of 1976.

The band also announced their debut into video games on Rock Band 2, with "Let There Be Rock," as a playable track. This was followed by AC/DC Live: Rock Band Track Pack, which included their entire set list from the *Live At Donington* album. The game featured 18 tracks and was specially remixed by Mike Fraser.

To celebrate the upcoming release of the new album, Sirius and XM Satellite Radio launched AC/DC Radio, a channel that will air AC/DC music 24/7, from September of 2008 to January of 2009. Featured will be classics like "You Shook Me All Night Long," and "Back In Black," along with songs from the new album.

Laying down fifteen tracks in just six weeks, *Black Ice*, AC/DC's eighteenth studio album, was released in Australia on October 18, and in the United States on October 20. Included on this musical monument heralding AC/DC's return to the forefront of rock were "Rock N Roll Train," "Skies On Fire," "Big Jack," "Anything Goes," "War Machine," "Smash N Grab," "Spoilin' For A Fight," "Wheels," "Decibel," "Stormy May Day," "She Likes Rock N Roll," "Money Made," "Rock N Roll Dream," "Rocking All The Way," and "Black Ice."

The video for their first single, "Rock N Roll Train," was shot in London on August 15, in front of several hundred fans who were lucky enough to win a chance to be part of the audience. On August 28, the song was released to radio and three months later, "Rock N Roll Train" garnered a Grammy nomination for Best Rock Performance By A Duo Or Group With Vocals.

Being one of the few bands on the planet who refuse to offer their songs through download, AC/DC's new album was mysteriously leaked on the Internet before its official debut. Surprising some, the band signed a deal in the United States with Walmart and Sam's Club to sell *Black Ice* exclusively. The new album would also be available for sale on AC/DC's official website. Shedding light on the logic behind this decision, Malcolm revealed that not only did Walmart pre-order 2.5 million copies, but the exclusive deal eliminated all of their distribution costs.

Fulfilling the wishes of millions of loyal fans, AC/DC followed the release of their new single by announcing a worldwide tour that would keep them on the road until the end of 2009. Opening on October 28, 2008 in Wilkes-Barre, Pennsylvania, the tour would include 42 dates in North America, with the first leg ending in Nashville, Tennessee on January 31. Taking a short break, AC/DC would continue their global assault through Europe, South America, Asia and Australia.

To coincide with the US release of *Black Ice*, Columbia Records (Sony Music) and Walmart created "Rock Again AC/DC Stores," making it the first time in the history of Walmart that such a large area of floor space would be dedicated to celebrate the release of a new album. Of course according to any faithful AC/DC fan, this royal treatment was long overdue for the kings of rock and roll. Columbia Records also teamed up with MTV to create "AC/DC Rock Band Stores" in Times Square in New York and Los Angeles. To herald the event, *Black Ice* trucks rolled through both cities loudly playing AC/DC music, stopping at various places to sell merchandise.

When the album finally made its long awaited debut, *Black Ice* charted at Number One in 29 countries, becoming platinum within days. Selling more than 780,000 copies in the US in the first week alone, it also marked the band's first-ever debut at Number One on the album charts here in the United States. Not bad for a band that many thought would never record another album.

Also breaking records were the ticket sales for the new tour. Seats sold out in minutes for their appearance at the Allstate Arena in Chicago, forcing them to add a second show. Both nights at Madison Square Garden in New York City were snapped up within minutes and their concert at Vancouver's General Motors Place broke a record in itself by selling out in just four minutes.

As the band took to the road, their first tour in seven years brought an avalanche of rave reviews from the press. The Boston Globe declared, "AC/DC is the greatest band ever," the Chicago Tribune stated, "AC/DC: Rock 'n' roll that outlasts time," and the Associated Press confirmed, "Critical acclaim escaped them...until now."

Not one to be complimentary of the legendary band, Rolling Stone finally put AC/DC on the cover of their November 13, 2008 issue. Barely covering the band for the past thirty years, executive editor Jason Fine was quoted as saying, "It's their best record since *Back In Black*, since 1980. Unlike some of the records they made over the last 20 years, this one really sounds alive."

Brian Johnson told the Associated Press, "The critics have always been a little flippant with AC/DC about Angus and the school suit, and it's always easy to have a quick little joke or a dig at the expense of it, the easy riffs, and such and such, and they're all dead wrong. The easiest riffs in the world are the hardest ones to write, because they are very few."

After being off the road for seven years, the protocol for this tour would be very different. Not only were they not giving many interviews, but there would be no meet and greets after each show. Of course that didn't stop me from requesting an interview with Angus, and asking for the chance to say hello to the boys when they rolled through Chicago on November 1, 2008.

Gracing me with one of the best rock and roll surprises of my life, AC/DC's tour manager called me the day before the tour started, to tell me that not only would Angus be happy to give me an interview, but I also had tickets and aftershow passes waiting for me in Chicago. Even though they were limiting the interviews, when Angus heard that I wanted to talk to him, he said, "If Sue wants an interview, Sue gets an interview." I guess you could say that there are some perks to having known the band since 1977!

After waiting seven years to see AC/DC perform again, the anticipation of my trip to Chicago was completely overwhelming. When they hit the stage at the Allstate Arena, there were no doubts that one of the most successful bands in the world hadn't lost their rock and roll Midas touch. In front of 17,000 screaming fans, AC/DC's show opened with an animated cartoon of the band traveling on what else, but a rock and roll train, surrounded by devilish girls trying to seduce them. Just as the boys in the band manage to overcome temptation, Angus narrowly escapes the train before it comes crashing off the tracks.

As the cartoon ended, a life-size black locomotive comes barreling out over the stage halting just above the drum riser amid flying sparks and a thunderous roar from the audience. Suddenly Phil appeared behind the drum kit, and Brian, Malcolm, Cliff and Angus strode out onto the stage. Like a dream unfolding in front of our eyes, the band launched into "Rock N Roll Train," heralding the return of the greatest rock and roll band in the world.

For the next hour and forty-five minutes, AC/DC played five songs from their new album, *Black Ice*, which included the title track, along with "Big Jack," "War Machine," "Anything Goes," and "Rock and Roll Train." The rest of their show was dedicated to hammering out an amazing string of rock anthems, including "Hell Ain't A Bad Place To Be," "Dirty Deeds," "Thunderstruck," "The Jack," "Hells Bells," "Shoot To Thrill," "You Shook Me," "TNT," "Whole Lotta Rosie," and "Let There Be Rock." Their performances were incredible, and I can't say I have ever heard them sound better.

As they closed their show with "Let There Be Rock," Angus careened out onto a walkway that led to a circular stage that rose up above the crowd. From this perch, he tore through a scorching solo while spinning around on his back. Generating enough energy to power an entire city, after thirty-four years, Angus proved that he could still bring it. The whole crowd, many of them sporting glowing red devil horns, went completely wild for the diminutive school boy, who barely stands five foot two. That's Angus Young; the real live Guitar Hero.

Only minutes after leaving the stage, AC/DC returned for a two-song encore which included "Highway To Hell," and "For Those About To Rock." During "Highway To Hell," pictures flashed above the stage of days gone by with singer Bon Scott at the helm. It never fails to bring tears to my eyes when the audience is singing along to Bon's lyrics, honoring the legendary front man. Bon had such an impact on their music and definitely helped forge their salty image. Always a prankster and a man who truly loved life, Bon's memory is never far from the band.

After the show, my 14-year-old son Jamey and I had the privilege of visiting with Angus and Malcolm in their dressing room in the basement of the Allstate Arena. Sitting together sipping tea and smoking cigarettes, it was amazing to see how relaxed and down-to-earth they both were, considering they had just gotten done tearing up the stage in front of thousands of people.

Once again acting like we had seen each other just last week, we joked about their ability to make it through the show, since I was tired and sweaty from just watching them! I asked Malcolm if he starts counting how many songs are left, by the time they get to the middle of their set. He laughed and said, "Yeah, I do!" When we talked about the fans fearing that they would never tour again, Malcolm assured me that they always intended on going back out on tour. Then he looked over at Angus and said, "Well this has been the first real break we've had since 1974, right?" I also asked Angus if he would ever consider having an art show to display his paintings, and he immediately told me no. Then Malcolm laughed and said, "He's saving that for his old age!"

Over the course of our visit, we talked about how devoted their fans are, and how well the new album was being received. Of course I had to bring up the night I first met AC/DC in 1977, when I predicted that someday they would be as big as the Rolling Stones. At the time the band laughed their heads off at me, but when I reminded Malcolm of that comment, he grinned and claimed, "Well, we did blow them off the stage at the Sars Benefit in Toronto, I know that much!"

Angus and Malcolm were both especially kind to my son, asking him all about school and what his interests were. When Angus mentioned how tall he was for a 14-year-old, he quickly added, "Well then, everyone's taller than me."

As we said our goodbyes, Jamey got some posters signed, and our pictures taken. If that wasn't enough to give my son memories of a lifetime, Angus reached into his pocket (at his wife Ellen's suggestion), and gave Jamey the guitar pick he had used that night. Talk about the "pick of destiny!"

A few days later, Angus was generous enough to call me to talk about *Black Ice* and the incredible longevity of AC/DC.

It's been a long time in-between albums, how long did it take you to put together the songs for the new album?

It starts with the last tour, you get some ideas then. It might be a song title or something, or a riff that you would get at a sound check, or backstage, and you keep a log of it. And that kind of becomes the basis of when you start to write. And also you do a lot of writing at home, when you take a break off the tour and have a rest.

After writing songs for over 30 years, does it get any easier?

Does it get any easier? Sometimes you rely on a lot of things through experience. But I think writing songs is something you learn, but it's a kind of learning through a kind of experience. Then after a while, you hope you get better at it.

Well, I don't think you have to worry about it. I think you have that down!

Yeah, but sometimes you wish you could write like I did when I was really young. You always want to write something that strikes a chord with a lot of people. I think that's the magic.

Well, I think you did that with the new album. I think you have some classics on here.

All right, good! (Laughs)

I heard that you wanted to come up with a title for the new album that would be tough, something that sounded hard. Who came up with the title, Black Ice?

Well, it was me that came up with it. But we had already had a song called "Black Ice," and at the end of the day, we thought it would make a good album title.

Do you have a favorite song on the album?

I like a lot of them. But when you're writing and playing them, they all become your babies. Usually you do a lot of demos of the songs, and try to pick the ones that capture the spirit of the band.

Everything was written by you and Malcolm. Do you write the lyrics togeth-er or do you write one song and then Malcolm writes another?

Well, you kind of bounce off each other. I might come up with a line or he might come up with a chorus.

Who decides on the design of the album and the staging for the tour?

We come up with the album title, and then the artists bring you their ideas for it. They come up with things trying to see what matches your ideas best.

Well, I love the way the stage looks with the big locomotive; it all looked so cool!

Yeah! Well, a lot of it, again, we had enough time, and sometimes you get very rushed. A lot of things fall into place, and sometimes you have to sac-rifice some things because of the time factor. This time we were very lucky because we already had all the songs that would definitely be on the album. Again, they (the artists) took the songs and came back with different ideas.

I realize you've only done about four shows so far, but what part of the show is your favorite, and why?

Favorite part? I think probably for me, it would be the anticipation. You get ready, and then you think, 'I wish I was on now. I'm ready to go now!' I guess it would be for me, waiting to go out there and get wild.

Were you surprised by the fans and how much they wanted the band to come back out on tour?

I suppose, you hear a lot of it. People around the band tell us what's going on. There's always a lot of people talking, but no one takes the time to check with the band. So sometimes we're the last to hear about something. Even when we went up to Vancouver to record, it was several weeks before anyone knew about it.

Back when we first met, some of the band talked about being rich and famous. Do you miss those days when you could go out and not be stopped by people everywhere you go?

I don't think I ever thought about being rich and famous. I think when you're young, and at that age, everything is an adventure. When you're living it at the time, you don't think that far ahead. Even today, I try to take things day to day. When someone asks me about something six months from now, I don't think that far ahead. I think at the time, I was happy to be doing what I was doing. It was an education, in a way.

Of course when I watched the show the other night, you can't help but think about Bon and how much he contributed to the band. What do you think Bon would have to say about how successful AC/DC is today?

He would love it! He would be living it to the hilt. It was just the nature of his character. He always used to say to me, 'Whatever I do, don't do!'

When you're on stage playing some of the older songs, do you feel his presence around you?

Yeah, of course. Even sometimes when I'm just walking around, I think, Am I walking like him? The way Bon walked, with kind of a swagger. (Laughs)

It's amazing how well Brian was able to fit into the band.

Brian is his own character. He has such a good time. He was a fan of the music and brings something to it which is totally different from Bon. He's definitely his own character.

He is so funny, always cracking jokes.

That's right. For us, he keeps us highly entertained. And he brings a lot of things down to earth.

I know when I interviewed the late Perry Cooper, who was with Atlantic Records, and very close to Bon, he didn't think it was possible for you to replace him. Then he went out on the road with you after Back In Black *came out, and he was floored by how funny Brian was. I can't imagine during the recording of the album, being in so much pain, that you knew at the time that it would become one of the top-ten biggest-selling albums in history!*

Yeah, I think at the time, you really don't know. But we had some strong songs, and we wanted to finish them. In a way, the recording was very therapeutic for us, because after a while you can start wallowing in it. It's always harder for the people left behind. The hardest part when you lose someone very close to you, is how do you do this? How do you go on?

To Brian's credit, look how great he did, and how loving and respectful he's been toward Bon's memory.

That's right! He's also a fan of those songs, and every time we get together to tour, he always wants to do one of the old tracks, 'Let's try this one!' And he always does it in his own way.

It's funny to be talking about him like the new guy, considering he's been in the band now for 28 years.

Yeah, well I'll always be the youngest! And I always say, don't have birthdays!

After seeing the band close to twenty times over the years, I don't think I have ever heard you sound better! It was so perfect, it was like listening to the album!

Good to know. Then the sound system was worth the money! (Laughing)

How do you feel about how the band is playing? Have they surprised you at all?

Yes, they have. I was in shock that they had done the album! (Laughing) From that point on, how everyone sounded, and that we did it in a very short time. It was a good experience also working with Mike Fraser again. It was also very good to work with Brendan O'Brien, who has a musician's background, and communicating with someone like that is also very good, because he knows exactly what you need. He knows what you're talking about. He is very, very sharp.

You didn't take that long to record the new album. How long were you actually in Vancouver?

About six weeks. You've got to do your homework first. Get all of that done before you go in. Then once you go in, it's all about getting the right sound. And then it's all about capturing the moment.

If there was one thing you are most proud of AC/DC, what would that be?

I think it's just the band being able to keep going. It's probably surviving this long. And playing what we've always played. From the moment I joined the band, Malcolm asked me to come along and play second guitar. And I asked him what we were going to play, and he said, "That's obvious. We're just going to play rock and roll!"

Some describe AC/DC as a metal band, but I love the fact that you always claim to be a rock and roll band.

That's what we are (a rock and roll band), and that's what we do best!

Selling over 200 million albums and counting, AC/DC remains one of the purest and most successful bands in rock 'n' roll. They stuck to their guns and definitely did what they do best, which is rock! I knew the day I met them that AC/DC would someday become one of the greatest rock 'n' roll bands in the world. At the time, did I really grasp the ultimate impact that they would one day have on the world? Probably not. But Bon did...

> *...And it came to pass that rock 'n' roll was born, all across the land every rockin' band, was blowin' up a storm. And the guitar man got famous, The business man got rich, And in every bar there was a superstar, with a seven-year itch. There were 50 million fingers learnin' how to play, and you could hear the fingers pickin' and this is what they had to say, Let there be light... sound... drums... guitar... let there be rock!*

—Let There Be Rock

DISCOGRAPHY

It's A Long Way To The Top (If You Wanna Rock 'N' Roll) / High Voltage
November 1976 / Atco Records

Problem Child / Let There Be Rock
September 1977 / Atco Records

Rock 'N' Roll Damnation / Kicked In The Teeth
July 1978 / Atlantic Records

Whole Lotta Rosie / Hell Ain't A Bad Place To Be (Live)
January 1979 / Atlantic Records

Highway To Hell / Night Prowler
September 1979 / Atlantic Records

Touch Too Much / Walk All Over You
December 1979 / Atlantic Records

You Shook Me All Night Long / Have A Drink On Me
August 1980 / Atlantic Records

Back In Black / What Do You Do For Money Honey
December 1980 / Atlantic Records

Let's Get It Up / Snowballed
December 1981 / Atlantic Records

For Those About To Rock (We Salute You) / T.N.T. (Live)
March 1982 / Atlantic Records

For Those About To Rock (We Salute You) / Let There Be Rock (Live)
May 1982 / Atlantic Records

Guns For Hire / Landslide
September 1983 / Atlantic Records

Flick Of The Switch / Badlands
November 1983 / Atlantic Records

Jailbreak / Show Business
October 1984 / Atlantic Records

Danger / Back In Business
July 1985 / Atlantic Records

Shake Your Foundations / Send For The Man
October 1985 / Atlantic Records

Who Made Who / Guns For Hire (Live)
May 1986 / Atlantic Records

You Shook Me All Night / She's Got Balls (Live)
July 1986 / Atlantic Records

That's The Way I Wanna Rock 'N' Roll / Kissin' Dynamite
May 1988 / Atlantic Records

Moneytalks / Borrowed Time
November 1990 / Atlantic Records

Highway To Hell (Live) / Hells Bells (Live)
December 1992 / Atlantic Records

Dirty Deeds Done Dirt Cheap (Live)
December 1992 / Atlantic Records

Big Gun / Back In Black (Live)
May 1993 / Atlantic Records

Cover You In Oil (Not Available For Retail)
November 1995 / EastWest Records

Dirty Eyes (Not Available For Retail)
October 1997 / EastWest Records

Rock N Roll Train
August 2008 / Columbia Records

Australian Singles:

Can I Sit Next To You Girl / Rockin' In The Parlour
July 1974 / Albert/EMI Records
July 1974 / Polydor Records (New Zealand)

Love Story (Oh Jene) / Baby, Please Don't Go
March 1975 / Albert/EMI Records

High Voltage / Soul Stripper
June 1975 / Albert/EMI Records

It's A Long Way To The Top (If You Wanna Rock 'N' Roll) / Can I Sit
Next To You Girl
December 1975 / Albert/EMI Records

T.N.T. / Rocker
March 1976 / Albert/EMI Records

Jailbreak / Fling Thing (B-Side not on any album)
July 1976 / Albert/EMI Records

Dirty Deeds Done Dirt Cheap / R.I.P.
October 1976 / Albert/EMI Records

Love At First Feel / Problem Child
January 1977 / Albert/EMI Records

Dog Eat Dog / Carry Me Home (B-Side not on any album)
March 1977 / Albert/EMI Records

Let There Be Rock (Part 1) / Let There Be Rock (Part 2)
October 1977 / Albert/EMI Records

Rock 'N' Roll Damnation / Cold Hearted Man
June 1978 / Albert/EMI Records

Whole Lotta Rosie (Live) / Dog Eat Dog (Live)
November 1978 / Albert/EMI Records

Highway To Hell / If You Want Blood
August 1979 / Albert/EMI Records

You Shook Me All Night Long / What Do You Do For Money Honey
August 1980 / Albert/EMI Records

Rock And Roll Ain't Noise Pollution / Hells Bells
January 1981 / Albert/EMI Records

Let's Get It Up / Snowballed
February 1982 / Albert/EMI Records

For Those About To Rock (We Salute You) / Let There Be Rock (Live)
August 1982 / Albert/EMI Records

Nervous Shakedown / Brain Shake
October 1983 / Albert/EMI Records

Flick Of The Switch / Badlands
November 1983 / Albert/EMI Records

Danger / Hell Or High Water
August 1985 / Albert/EMI Records

Sink The Pink / Back In Business
September 1985 / Albert/EMI Records

Shake Your Foundations / Stand Up
February 1986 / Albert/EMI Records

Who Made Who / Guns For Hire (Live)
May 1986 / Albert/EMI Records

You Shook Me All Night Long / She's Got Balls (Live)
October 1986 / Albert/EMI Records

Heatseeker / Go Zone
January 1988 / Albert/EMI Records

That's The Way I Wanna Rock 'N' Roll / Kissin' Dynamite
April 1988 / Albert/EMI Records

Thunderstruck / Fire Your Guns
September 1990 / Albert/EMI Records

Moneytalks / Down On The Borderline
December 1990 / Albert/EMI Records

Are You Ready / Got You By The Balls / DT / Chase The Ace
April 1991 / Albert/EMI Records

Rock Your Heart Out / Shot Of Love
July 1991 / Albert/EMI Records

Highway To Hell (Live) / High Voltage (Live) / Hell Ain't A Bad Place
To Be (Live)
October 1992 / Albert/EMI Records

Dirty Deeds Done Dirt Cheap (Live) / Shoot To Thrill (Live)
February 1993 / Albert/EMI Records

Big Gun / Back In Black (Live) / For Those About To Rock (We Salute You) (Live)
July 1993 / Albert/EMI Records

Hard As A Rock / Caught With Your Pants Down
September 1995 / Albert/EMI Records

Hail Caesar / Whiskey On The Rocks / Whole Lotta Rosie (Live)
February 1996 / Albert/EMI Records

Ballbreaker / You Shook Me All Night Long / Back In Black / Thunderstruck (Live)
August 1996 / Albert/EMI Records

Stiff Upper Lip / Hard As A Rock (Live) / Ballbreaker (Live)
April 2000 / Albert/EMI Records

Safe In New York City / Cyberspace / Back In Black (Live)
July 2000 / Albert/EMI Records

Satellite Blues / Let There Be Rock (Live)
January 2001 / Albert/EMI Records

Rock N Roll Train
August 2008 / Columbia Records

U.K. Singles:

It's A Long Way To The Top (If You Wanna Rock 'N' Roll) / Can I Sit Next To You Girl
April 1976 / Atlantic Records

Jailbreak / Fling Thing
July 1976 / Atlantic Records

High Voltage / Live Wire
October 1976 / Atlantic Records

Dirty Deeds Done Dirt Cheap / Big Balls / The Jack
February 1977 / Atlantic Records

Let There Be Rock / Problem Child
September 1977 / Atlantic Records

Rock 'N' Roll Damnation / Sin City
May 1978 / Atlantic Records

Whole Lotta Rosie (Live) / Hell Ain't A Bad Place To Be (Live)
October 1978 / Atlantic Records

Highway To Hell / If You Want Blood
August 1979 / Atlantic Records

Girl's Got Rhythm / Get It Hot
November 1979 / Atlantic Records

Girl's Got Rhythm / If You Want Blood You've Got It / Hell Ain't A Bad
Place To Be (Live) / Rock 'N' Roll Damnation (Live)
November 1979 / Atlantic Records

Touch Too Much / Live Wire (Live) / Shot Down In Flames (Live)
January 1980 / Atlantic Records

You Shook Me All Night Long / Have A Drink On Me
August 1980 / Atlantic Records

Rock And Roll Ain't Noise Pollution / Hells Bells
November 1981 / Atlantic Records

Let's Get It Up / Back In Black (Live)
January 1982 / Atlantic Records

For Those About To Rock (We Salute You) / Let There Be Rock (Live)
April 1982 / Atlantic Records

Guns For Hire / Landslide
September 1983 / Atlantic Records

Nervous Shakedown / Rock And Roll Ain't Noise Pollution (Live)
July 1984 / Atlantic Records

Danger / Back In Business
June 1985 / Atlantic Records

Shake Your Foundations / Stand Up
January 1986 / Atlantic Records

Who Made Who / Guns For Hire (Live)
May 1986 / Atlantic Records

You Shook Me All Night Long / She's Got Balls (Live)
August 1986 / Atlantic Records

Heatseeker / Go Zone
January 1988 / Atlantic Records

That's The Way I Wanna Rock 'N' Roll / Kissin' Dynamite
March 1988 / Atlantic Records

Thunderstruck / Fire Your Guns
September 1990 / Atco Records

Moneytalks / Mistress For Christmas
November 1990 / Atco Records

Are You Ready / Got You By The Balls
April 1991 / Atco Records

Highway To Hell (Live) / Hells Bells (Live)
October 1992 / Atlantic Records

Big Guns / Back In Black (Live)
June 1993 / Atco Records

Hard As A Rock / Caught With Your Pants Down
September 1995 / EastWest Records

Cover You In Oil / Love Bomb / Ballbreaker
March 1996 / EastWest Records

Stiff Upper Lip / Hard As A Rock (Live) / Ballbreaker (Live)
March 2000 / EastWest Records

Satellite Blues / Whole Lotta Rosie (Live) / Let There Be Rock (Live)
October 2000 / EastWest Records

Rock N Roll Train
August 2008 / Columbia Records

AC/DC Albums:

High Voltage
Baby, Please Don't Go - She's Got Balls - Little Lover - Stick Around
- Soul Stripper - You Ain't Got A Hold On Me - Love Song - Show
Business
February 17, 1975 / Albert/EMI Records (Australia/New Zealand only)

T.N.T.
It's A Long Way To The Top (If You Wanna Rock 'N' Roll) - Rock 'N'
Roll Singer - The Jack - Live Wire - T.N.T. - Rocker - Can I Sit Next To
You Girl - High Voltage - School Days
December 1975 / Albert/EMI Records (Australia/New Zealand only)

High Voltage
It's A Long Way To The Top (If You Wanna Rock 'N' Roll) - Rock 'N'
Roll Singer - The Jack - Live Wire - T.N.T. - Can I Sit Next To You Girl
- Little Lover - She's Got Balls - High Voltage
May 14, 1976 / Atlantic Records (U.K.)
September 28, 1976 / Atlantic Records (U.S.)

Dirty Deeds Done Dirt Cheap
Dirty Deeds Done Dirt Cheap - Ain't No Fun (Waiting Around To Be A Millionaire) - There's Gonna Be Some Rockin'- Problem Child - Squealer - Big Balls - Rock In Peace - Ride On - Jailbreak
September 20, 1976 / Albert/EMI Records (Australia/U.K.)
March 23, 1981 / Atlantic Records (U.S.)

Let There Be Rock
Go Down - Dog Eat Dog - Let There Be Rock - Bad Boy Boogie - Problem Child - Overdose - Hell Ain't A Bad Place To Be - Whole Lotta Rosie (Original Australian and European releases include "Crabsody In Blue" instead of "Problem Child.")
March 21, 1977 / Albert/EMI Records (Australia)
June 23, 1977 / Atlantic Records (U.S.)
October 14, 1977 / Atlantic Records (U.K.)

Powerage
Rock 'N' Roll Damnation - Down Payment Blues - Gimme A Bullet - Riff Raff - Sin City - What's Next To The Moon - Gone Shootin' - Up To My Neck In You - Kicked In The Teeth ("Cold Hearted Man" included on European vinyl release only).
May 5, 1978 / Atlantic Records (U.K.)
May 25, 1978 / Atlantic Records (U.S.)
June 19, 1978 / Atlantic Records (Australia)

If You Want Blood You've Got It
Riff Raff - Hell Ain't A Bad Place To Be - Bad Boy Boogie - The Jack - Problem Child - Whole Lotta Rosie - Rock 'N' Roll Damnation - High Voltage - Let There Be Rock - Rocker
October 6, 1978 / Atlantic Records (U.K.)
November 21, 1978 / Atlantic Records (U.S.)
November 28, 1978 / Atlantic Records (Australia)

Highway To Hell
Highway To Hell - Girls Got Rhythm - Walk All Over You - Touch Too Much - Beating Around The Bush - Shot Down In Flames - Get It Hot - If You Want Blood (You've Got It) - Love Hungry Man - Night Prowler
July 27, 1979 / Atlantic Records (U.K.)
July 30, 1979 / Atlantic Records (U.S.)

Back In Black
Hells Bells - Shoot To Thrill - What Do You Do For Money Honey -
Given The Dog A Bone - Let Me Put My Love Into You - Back In Black
- You Shook Me All Night Long - Have A Drink On Me - Shake A Leg
- Rock And Roll Ain't Noise Pollution
July 21, 1980 / Atco Records (U.S.)
July 31, 1980 / Atlantic Records (U.K.)
August 11, 1980 / Atlantic Records (Australia)

For Those About To Rock
For Those About To Rock (We Salute You) - Put The Finger On You -
Let's Get It Up - Inject The Venom - Snowballed - Evil Walks - C.O.D.
- Breaking The Rules - Night Of The Long Knives - Spellbound
November 23, 1981 / Atlantic Records (Worldwide)
December 7, 1981 / Atlantic Records (Australia)

Flick Of The Switch
Rising Power -This House Is On Fire - Flick Of The Switch - Nervous
Shakedown - Landslide - Guns For Hire - Deep In The Hole - Bedlam
In Belgium - Badlands - Brain Shake
August 15, 1983 / Atlantic Records

'74 Jailbreak
Jailbreak - You Ain't Got A Hold On Me - Show Business - Soul
Stripper - Baby, Please Don't Go
October 15, 1984 / Atlantic Records

Fly On The Wall
Fly On The Wall - Shake Your Foundations - First Blood - Danger -
Sink The Pink - Playing With Girls - Stand Up - Hell Or High Water -
Back In Business - Send For The Man
June 28, 1985 / Atlantic Records

Who Made Who
Who Made Who - You Shook Me All Night Long - D. T. - Sink The Pink
- Ride On - Hells Bells - Shake Your Foundations - Chase The Ace -
For Those About To Rock (We Salute You)
May 20, 1986 / Atlantic Records

Blow Up Your Video
Heatseeker - That's The Way I Wanna Rock 'N' Roll - Meanstreak - Go
Zone - Kissin' Dynamite - Nick Of Time - Some Sin For Nothin' - Ruff
Stuff - Two's Up - This Means War
February 1, 1988 / Atlantic Records

The Razors Edge
Thunderstruck - Fire Your Guns - Moneytalks - The Razors Edge -
Mistress For Christmas - Rock Your Heart Out - Are You Ready - Got
You By The Balls - Shot Of Love - Let's Make It - Goodbye & Good
Riddance To Bad Luck - If You Dare
September 21, 1990 / Atco Records

AC/DC Live (Complete Version)
Thunderstruck - Shoot To Thrill - Back In Black - Sin City - Who Made
Who - Heatseeker - Fire Your Guns - Jailbreak - The Jack - The Razors
Edge - Dirty Deeds Done Dirt Cheap - Moneytalks - Hells Bells - Are
You Ready - That's The Way I Wanna Rock 'N' Roll - High Voltage -
You Shook Me All Night Long - Whole Lotta Rosie - Let There Be
Rock - Bonny - Highway To Hell - T.N.T. - For Those About To Rock
(We Salute You)
October 27, 1992 / Atco Records

AC/DC Live (Abridged Version)
Thunderstruck - Shoot To Thrill - Back In Black - Who Made Who -
Heatseeker - The Jack - Moneytalks - Hells Bells - Dirty Deeds Done
Dirt Cheap - Whole Lotta Rosie - You Shook Me All Night Long -
Highway To Hell - T.N.T. - For Those About To Rock (We Salute You)
October 27, 1992 / Atco Records

Ballbreaker
Hard As A Rock - Cover You In Oil - The Furor - Boogie Man - The
Honey Roll - Burnin' Alive - Hail Caesar - Love Bomb - Caught With
Your Pants Down - Whiskey On The Rocks -Ballbreaker
September 26, 1995 / East/West Records

Bonfire Boxset
Live From Atlantic Studios
Live Wire - Problem Child - High Voltage - Hell Ain't A Bad Place To
Be - Dog Eat Dog - The Jack - Whole Lotta Rosie - Rocker

Let There Be Rock—The Movie - Live In Paris (Disc One)
Live Wire - Shot Down In Flames - Hell Ain't A Bad Place To Be - Sin
City - Walk All Over You - Bad Boy Boogie (Disc Two) - The Jack -
Highway To Hell - Girls Got Rhythm - High Voltage - Whole Lotta
Rosie - Rocker - T.N.T.- Let There Be Rock

Volts
Dirty Eyes - Touch Too Much - If You Want Blood (You've Got It) -
Back Seat Confidential - Get It Hot - Sin City - She's Got Balls - School
Days - It's A Long Way To The Top (If You Wanna Rock 'N' Roll) -
Ride On

Back In Black
Hells Bells - Shoot To Thrill - What Do You Do For Money Honey -
Given The Dog A Bone - Let Me Put My Love Into You - Back In Black
- You Shook Me All Night Long - Have A Drink On Me - Shake A Leg
- Rock And Roll Ain't Noise Pollution
November 11, 1997 / EastWest Records

Stiff Upper Lip
Stiff Upper Lip - Meltdown - House Of Jazz - Hold Me Back - Safe In
New York City - Can't Stand Still - Can't Stop Rock 'N' Roll - Satellite
Blues - Damned - Come And Get It - All Screwed Up - Give It Up
February 28, 2000 / EastWest Records

Black Ice
Rock N Roll Train - Skies On Fire - Big Jack - Anything Goes - War
Machine - Smash N Grab - Spoilin' For A Fight - Wheels - Decibel -
Stormy May Day - She Likes Rock N Roll - Money Made - Rock N Roll
Dream - Rocking All The Way - Black Ice
October 20, 2008 / Columbia Records

Music Videos/DVDs:

AC/DC
High Voltage - Jailbreak - Let There Be Rock - Riff Raff - Dog Eat Dog - Highway To Hell - Shot Down In Flames - Touch Too Much - If You Want Blood You've Got It
1987 / Albert Productions (Australia Only)

Let There Be Rock
Live Wire - Shot Down In Flames - Hell Ain't A Bad Place To Be - Sin City - Walk All Over You - Bad Boy Boogie - The Jack - Highway To Hell - Girls Got Rhythm - High Voltage - Whole Lotta Rosie - Rocker - Let There Be Rock
1980 / Warner Home Video

Fly On The Wall
Fly On The Wall - Danger - Sink The Pink - Stand Up - Shake Your Foundations
1985 / Atlantic Video

Who Made Who
Who Made Who - You Shook Me All Night Long - Shake Your Foundations - Hells Bells - For Those About To Rock (We Salute You)
1986 / Atlantic Video

Clipped
Thunderstruck - Moneytalks - Are You Ready - Heatseeker - That's The Way I Want To Rock 'N' Roll
1990 / Vision Entertainment

The Interview Sessions
1990 / Secret Squirrel

The Razors Edge
Thunderstruck - Moneytalks - Are You Ready
1991 / SMV

Live At Donington
Thunderstruck - Shoot To Thrill - Back In Black - Hell Ain't A Bad Place To Be - Heatseeker - Fire Your Guns - Jailbreak - The Jack - Dirty Deeds Done Dirt Cheap - Moneytalks - Hells Bells - High Voltage - Whole Lotta Rosie - You Shook Me All Night Long - T.N.T. - Let There Be Rock - Highway To Hell - For Those About To Rock (We Salute You)
1992 / Vision Entertainment

For Those About To Rock (We Salute You)
Back In Black - Highway To Hell - Whole Lotta Rosie - For Those About To Rock (We Salute You)
1992 / Warner Home Video

Ballbreaker
Hard As A Rock - Cover You In Oil - Hail Caesar
1996 / Albert Productions

No Bull Live - Plaza De Toros, Madrid
Back In Black - Shot Down In Flames - Thunderstruck - Girls Got Rhythm - Hard As A Rock - Shoot To Thrill - Boogie Man - Hail Caesar - Hells Bells - Dog Eat Dog - The Jack - Ballbreaker - Rock And Roll Ain't Noise Pollution - Dirty Deeds Done Dirt Cheap - You Shook Me All Night Long - Whole Lotta Rosie - T.N.T. - Let There Be Rock - Highway To Hell - For Those About To Rock (We Salute You)
1996 / Warner Music Vision

Thunder Rock
1999 / Frantic Films

Long Way To The Top
2001 / ABC Video

Stiff Upper Lip Live
Stiff Upper Lip - You Shook Me All Night Long - Problem Child - Thunderstruck - Hell Ain't A Bad Place To Be - Hard As A Rock - Shoot To Thrill - Rock And Roll Ain't Noise Pollution - What Do You Do For Money Honey - Bad Boy Boogie - Hells Bells - Up To My Neck In You - The Jack - Back In Black - Dirty Deeds Done Dirt Cheap - Highway

To Hell - Whole Lotta Rosie - Let There Be Rock - T.N.T. - For Those About To Rock (We Salute You) - Shot Down In Flames
2001 / Warner Music Vision

Live '77
Let There Be Rock - Problem Child - Hell Ain't A Bad Place To Be - Whole Lotta Rosie - Bad Boy Boogie - Rocker - T.N.T.
January 2003 / Image Entertainment (Available only in Japan)

Family Jewels
Disc One
Baby, Please Don't Go - Show Business - High Voltage - It's A Long Way To The Top (If You Wanna Rock 'N' Roll) - T.N.T - Jailbreak - Dirty Deeds Done Dirt Cheap - Dog Eat Dog - Let There Be Rock - Rock 'N' Roll Damnation - Sin City - Riff Raff - Fling Thing / Rocker - Whole Lotta Rosie - Shot Down In Flames - Walk All Over You - Touch Too Much - If You Want Blood (You've Got It) - Girls Got Rhythm - Highway To Hell
Disc Two
Hells Bells - Back In Black - What Do You Do For Money Honey - Rock And Roll Ain't Noise Pollution - Let's Get It Up - For Those About To Rock (We Salute You) - Flick Of The Switch - Nervous Shakedown - Fly On The Wall - Danger - Sink The Pink - Stand Up - Shake Your Foundations - Who Made Who - You Shook Me All Night Long - Heatseeker - That's The Way I Wanna Rock 'N' Roll - Thunderstruck - Moneytalks - Are You Ready
2005 / Epic Music Video

And Then There Was Rock
2005 / Chrome Dreams

Plug Me In
Disc One
High Voltage - It's A Long Way To The Top (If You Wanna Rock 'n' Roll) - School Days - T.N.T. - Live Wire - Can I Sit Next To You Girl - Baby Please Don't Go - Hell Ain't A Bad Place To Be - Rocker - Rock 'n' Roll Damnation - Dog Eat Dog - Let There Be Rock - Problem Child - Sin City - Bad Boy Boogie - Highway To Hell - The Jack - Whole Lotta Rosie

Disc Two

Shot Down In Flames - What Do You Do For Money Honey - You Shook Me All Night Long - T.N.T./Let There Be Rock - Back In Black - T.N.T. - Shoot To Thrill - Guns For Hire - Dirty Deeds Done Dirt Cheap - Flick of The Switch - Bedlam In Belgium - Back In Black - Highway To Hell - Whole Lotta Rosie - For Those About To Rock (We Salute You) - Gone Shootin' - Hail Caesar - Ballbreaker - Rock And Roll Ain't Noise Pollution - Hard As A Rock - Hells Bells - Ride On - Stiff Upper Lip - Thunderstruck - If You Want Blood (You've Got It) - The Jack - You Shook Me All Night Long

Disc Three

She's Got Balls - It's A Long Way To The Top (If You Wanna Rock 'n' Roll) - Let There Be Rock - Bad Boy Boogie - Girls Got Rhythm - Guns For Hire - This House Is On Fire - Highway To Hell - Girls Got Rhythm - Let There Be Rock

No Bull Live—Plaza De Toros, Madrid (Director's Cut)

Back In Black - Shot Down In Flames - Thunderstruck - Girl's Got Rhythm - Hard As A Rock - Shoot To Thrill - Boogie Man - Hail Caesar - Hells Bells - Dog Eat Dog - The Jack - Ballbreaker - Rock And Roll Ain't Noise Pollution - Dirty Deeds Done Dirt Cheap - You Shook Me (All Night Long) - Whole Lotta Rosie - T.N.T. - Let There Be Rock - Highway To Hell
September 2008

BIBLIOGRAPHY

Books

Engleheart, Murray. *Bonfire: AC/DC Boxed Set Band Biography.* East West, 1997.

Huxley, Martin. *AC/DC: The World's Heaviest Rock.* St. Martins Press, 1996.

Masino, Susan. *Rock 'N' Roll Fantasy: My Life and Times with AC/DC, Van Halen, Kiss....* Badger Books, 2003.

Putterford, Mark. *Shock To The System.* Omnibus Press, 1992.

Rees, Dafydd, Crampton, Luke. *Encyclopedia Of Rock Stars.* DK Publishing, 1996.

Taylor, Barry, Wooding, Dan. *Singing In The Dark.* Kingsway Publications, 1990.

Walker, Clinton. *Highway To Hell: The Life and Times of AC/DC Legend Bon Scott.* Verse Chorus Press, 2001.

Wilmoth, Pete. *Glad All Over: The Countdown Years 1974–1987.* McPhee Gribble, 1993.

First-Hand Interviews

Mike Andy

Jack Ballas, Jr.

Rick Brewster

Pete "Pyro" Cappadocia

Peter Cliff

Perry Cooper

Keith Dabbs

Kirk Dyer

Keith Emerson

Dave Evans

Julius Grafton

James Kottak

Tommy Redd

Kelly Shaefer

Doug Thorncroft

Andrew (Don) Williams

Raymond Windlow

Angus Young

Robin Zander

Magazine Articles

Balfour, Brad. "AC/DC's Short Circuit The Angus and The Ecstasy: You Can't Tie These Kangaroos "Down, Sport!" *Creem* Magazine September 28, 1978.

Barr, Greg. "The Riff Factory." Houston, Texas newspaper.

Barton, Geoff. "A Touch Too Much." *Classic Rock,* February 2005.

Barton, Geoff. "A Touch Too Much." *Metal Hammer* & *Classic Rock,* Special 2005.

Barton, Geoff, Rasmussen, Jens Jam. "For Whom The Bell Tolls." *Classic Rock,* August 2005.

Barton, Geoff. "Brother's Got Rhythm." *Metal Hammer* & *Classic Rock,* Special 2005.

Barton, Geoff. "What Really Happened To Bon Scott?" *Metal Hammer* & *Classic Rock,* Special 2005.

Bienstock, Richard. "Dirty Deeds Re-Done." *Guitar World,* Guitar Legends Special Collector's Issue February 7, 2005.

Billboard Spotlight. September 22, 1990.

Beaujour, Tom. "Bon Voyage." *Guitar World,* Guitar Legends Special

Collector's Issue February 7, 2005.

Blake, Mark. "Stage-Struck!" *Metal CD,* 1992.

Boddy, Selma. "Roadshows." *Record Mirror,* October 22, 1977.

Bowcott, Nick. "Let There Be Rock." *Guitar World,* Guitar Legends Special Collector's Issue February 7, 2005.

Bowcott, Nick. "Let There Be Rock If It Ain't Broke, Don't Fix It!" *Guitar World,* July 1998.

Cashmere, Paul. *Undercover Media Circus*, May–June 1981.

Coles, Brian. *Electric Basement,* September 2000.

Creem Magazine, "Close-Up Metal." May 1984.

Creem Magazine, "Rock 'N' Roll News," May 1980.

Croft, Mat. "Whole Lotta Tributes." *Metal Hammer & Classic Rock.*

Cummings, Winston. "AC/DC End of The Line?" *Hit Parader,* 1995.

Cummings, Winston. "AC/DC Lightning Strikes Angus and the Boys Sell Out Arenas From Coast To Coast As Razor's Edge Reaches The Top." *Hit Parader.*

Darling, Spyder. "AC/DC: Still Stiff After All These Years." *New York Rock,* April 2000.

DiPerna, Alan. "Hard As A Rock." *Guitar World,* Guitar Legends Special Collector's Issue February 7, 2005.

DiPerna, Alan. "Young Lust." *Guitar World,* Guitar Legends Special Collector's Issue February 7, 2005.

DiPerna, Alan. "Working Stiffs." *Guitar World,* Guitar Legends Special Collector's Issue February 7, 2005.

Doran, John. "It's Electric." *Metal Hammer & Classic Rock,* Special 2005.

Doran, John. "Down and Dirty." *Metal Hammer & Classic Rock,* Special 2005.

Dorland, Jodi. Summers *Hit Parader,* Winter 1985.

Ducat, Alan. "Rock Legend Remembered." *The Dispatch Herald,* February 2, 2006.

Duclos, Michael. "Cliff Notes: Interview with Cliff Williams." *Guitar School,* March 1995.

Elliot, Paul. "Angus Beefed Up! Or: dirty deeds redone rather expensively!" *Kerrang!*

Ewing, Jerry. "Hell On Two Legs." *Metal Hammer & Classic Rock,* Special 2005.

Farber, Jim. "AC/DC The Big Crunch." *Metal Edge,* Fall 1985.

Farber, Jim. "Blow Up Your Video." *Rolling Stone,* April 7, 1988.

Finley, John. *Louisville, Kentucky Courier Journal,* December 13, 1977.

Flavin, Ian. "Front Row Reviews." *National RockStar,* March 5, 1977.

Fricke, David. "AC/DC: Wired For Success There's No Keeping A Live Band Down" *Circus,* January 16, 1979.

Fricke, David. "AC/DC only stops for tea on the 'Highway to Hell,' thank you kindly." *Circus,* November 1979.

Fricke, David. "AC/DC And the Gospel of Rock & Roll, *Rolling Stone,* November 13, 2008

Fyfe, Steven Scott. "Interview with Phil Rudd." *Cyber Drum,* August 15, 2000.

Garbarini, Vic. "60 Minutes with Angus Young." *Guitar World,* August 1996.

Godschalk, Johan. *Rock-E-Zine,* September 2000.

Hedges, Dan. "Stage Pass AC/DC flick the switch at Philadelphia's Spectrum." *Circus,* January 31, 1984.

Hit Parader Legends of Metal AC/DC Angus Young and the Boys Take Us All On The Highway To Hell, Winter 1989.

Hogan, Richard. "AC/DC Salutes The Stadium Circuit." *Circus,* 1982.

Hogan, Richard. "Photo Journal." *Circus,* December 31, 1982.

Hogan, Richard. "With A Flick Of The Switch, AC/DC Stays Current And Powers Into A 10th-Anniversary Tour." *People,* December 1983.

Hoggard, Stuart. "Front Row Reviews." *National RockStar,* February 26, 1977.

Howe, John. "Boy Wonder Canes 'em!" *Record Mirror,* October 22, 1977.

Hoysted, Peter. "High Voltage History," *Axs,* October 1998.

Jinman, Richard. "25 years on, AC/DC fans recall how wild rocker met his end." *The Guardian,* February 19, 2005.

"Thunder From Down Under." *Kerrang!* No. 11 March 11–24, 1982.

Lalaina, Joe. "Live Wire." *Guitar World,* Guitar Legends Special Collector's Issue March 1986.

Masino, Susan Severson. "AC/DC Spreading Sparks." *Emerald City Chronicle,* January 1978.

Matera, Joe. "Hometown Heroes." *Metal Hammer & Classic Rock.*

Mayco, Marc. "AC/DC: Young-Fast." *Trouser Press,* November 1977.

Metal CD Double Decade of Dirty Deeds, Vol. 1 No. 1 1992.

Obrecht, Jas. "Angus Young: Seriously." *Guitar Player,* February 1984.

Obrect, Jas. "Malcolm Young: Heavy Metal Rhythm Specialist." *Guitar Player,* February 1984.

Popoff, Martin. "Duck-Walkin' All Over You." *Metal Hammer & Classic Rock,* Special 2005.

Popoff, Martin. "Who Made Who?" *Metal Hammer & Classic Rock,* Special 2005.

Popoff, Martin. "AC/DC For Those About To Rock We Salute You." *Metal Hammer & Classic Rock,* Special 2005.

Putterford, Mark. "High Vaultage: A delirious delve into the AC/DC album archives." *Kerrang!* Summer 1984.

Putterford, Mark. "Select Review of Razor's Edge." October 1990.

Q Magazine Blackened Sabbath—The Official Account of Events from the insert inside the AC/DC bootleg called Swedish Neurotica

Rabow, Steve. "Jerry & Brian: Two Rocks On A Sarasota Roll." Sarasota Downtown, Summer 1998.

Reesman, Bryan. "AC/DC Certified Legends." *Metal Edge,* 2000.

Request "Speak For Yourself: AC/DC." June 2000.

Rockford Register Star "Cheap Trick Rocks Filled Fairgrounds." July 5, 1979.

Rolling Stone Random Notes Review of Live October 1, 1992.

Rosen, Steve. "Young At Heart." *Guitar World,* Guitar Legends Special Collector's Issue March 1984.

Rudis, Al. "A New Era In Rock-It's Brutal." *Chicago Tribune,* November 1977.

Simmons, Sylvie. "Satan's Pigeons." *Creem,* 1984.

"Body Music from Wagga Wagga" *Sounds,* October 22, 1977.

Stout, Gene. "AC/DC plugs into it's roots." *Wisconsin State Journal,* April 26, 2001.

Super Polly "High Voltage (& AC/DC!) makes 'gig of the year'!" October 1977.

Sutcliffe, Phil. "Sounds Sex, Snot, Sweat and Schoolkids (Or: AC/DC are back in town)." October 29, 1977.

Wall, Mick. Bonfire! "The Genesis of AC/DC." *Record Collector,* February 1998.

Wishart, Eric. "AC/DC Glasgow University." *Record Mirror,* February 26, 1977.

Movies

And Then There Was Rock—Life Before Brian Chrome Dreams,
November 2005

Let There Be Rock (Warner Home Video, 1980)

Live At Donington (Atco Video, 1992)

No Bull AC/DC Live—Plaza De Toros (Madrid Atco, 1996)

Websites

Bedlam in Belgium, www.ac-dc.cc, accessed February 2, 8, 2006.

Crabsody In Blue, www.crabsodyinblue.com, accessed November 21, 2005, December 28, 2005, January 8, 2006.

Electric Shock, www.ac-dc.net, accessed August 26, 2004, February 10, 2005, June 22, 2005, August 17, 2005, August 29, 2005, November 16, 2005, December 28, 2005, January 15, 2006, February 8, 2006.

No Nonsense, www.kolumbus.fi/nononsense, accessed November 17, 2005.

Rising Power, acdcpower.net, accessed November 17, 2005, February 6, 2006

Western Australian Bon Scott Fan Club www.bonscott.com.au, accessed November 17, 2005

ACKNOWLEDGMENTS

First and foremost, I want to thank my editor, Andrea Rotondo, for believing in me. Andrea's humor, spirituality, and love of rock 'n' roll has made working with her a pure joy. And to everyone with Omnibus Press, I am very honored to be part of the Music Sales Group family.

I would also like to thank all my family and friends for their love and support. Especially my husband John, for his patience, proofreading, and computer wizardry. My son Jamey for the use of his dictionary, and daughter Teal, for all the encouragement. My sisters Kathy and Lori, who both make me feel loved and admired. My best friend Jennifer, who freely administered thousands of Tarot card readings, which inspired and guided me along the way. Marv Balousek, Mary Lou Santovec, and everyone at Badger Books for asking me to write *Famous Wisconsin Musicians* and believing in *Rock 'N' Roll Fantasy*. God bless you! And to all the bands and fans who make working in the music business so much fun!

I have always believed in things happening for a reason and writing this book has been a whole new lesson in synchronicity. Things got so spooky at times, that I would often comment that I needed to write a book about the writ-ing of the book. Once the news got out that I was working on *Let There Be Rock,* people from around the world sent encouragement, prayers, and extreme-ly helpful information.

This book was blessed with so many great stories and fond memories. I can't thank you all enough: Mike Andy, Rick Brewster, Charlie "Cosmo" Wilson, "Pyro" Pete Cappadocia, Perry Cooper, Kirk Dyer, Keith Emerson, Dave Evans, Julius Grafton, Mike Huberty, Bobby Ingram, Gary Karnes, James Kottack, Karl Kuenning,

Tommy Redd, Glenn Robertson, The Scorpions, Kelly Shaefer, Raymond Windlow, Ken Adamany, Ida Langsam, Anne Leighton, Connie Ward, and Robin Zander. Extra blessings to Perry Cooper, who unexpectedly passed away on May 28, 2005. Not only did he promote the hell out of AC/DC when they first came over to the States, but he probably loved them more than all of us put together.

Special thanks to some key AC/DC fans scattered around the globe: Jack Ballas, Jr. for his discography, countless pictures and articles, and his love of AC/DC. Keith Dabbs for his geography lessons on Perth and the secret gift waiting for me down under. Andrew "Don" Williams for the *Classic Rock* magazines, right when I needed them! Peter Cliff for the best presents from Liverpool, including a hard-to-find English printing of Barry Taylor's book, *Singing In The Dark*. Doug Thorncroft, for his work on petitioning for the bronze statue that's being made of Bon for his sixtieth birthday and the improvements to Bon's gravesite, the twenty-fifth anniversary T-shirt, and most of all, for helping keep Bon Scott's flame burning brightly.

To Cody Jessup, a musician and AC/DC fan that I met in December of 2005. He was terminally ill with cancer and Thursday's Child contacted me in regard to helping make his wish come true. Cody loved AC/DC so much, that his last wish was to meet Angus Young. I did what I could and thanks to Dorothy Ferguson of Thursday's Child, just as I promised Cody, Angus tried to reach him. Unfortunately Cody was too ill to speak with him, but he did know Angus called him. Less than a day later, on the afternoon of New Years Eve, Cody passed away at the age of 15. It was such an honor to meet him, and his grace in fighting his illness was a lesson in humility. Cody was a brave soul and I hope he's jammin' with Bon right now.

To Barry Taylor, for being such a sweet and sincere friend, and for all the postcards, letters and phone calls that were a true highlight of my life.

And most of all, to the sweetest guys a girl could ever hope to meet, Angus and Malcolm Young, Bon Scott, Phil Rudd, Cliff Williams, and Brian Johnson. The divine source of some of the greatest rock 'n' roll music ever made. Somebody pinch me! No, I mean that...

INDEX